IMAGES
of America

DE SMET

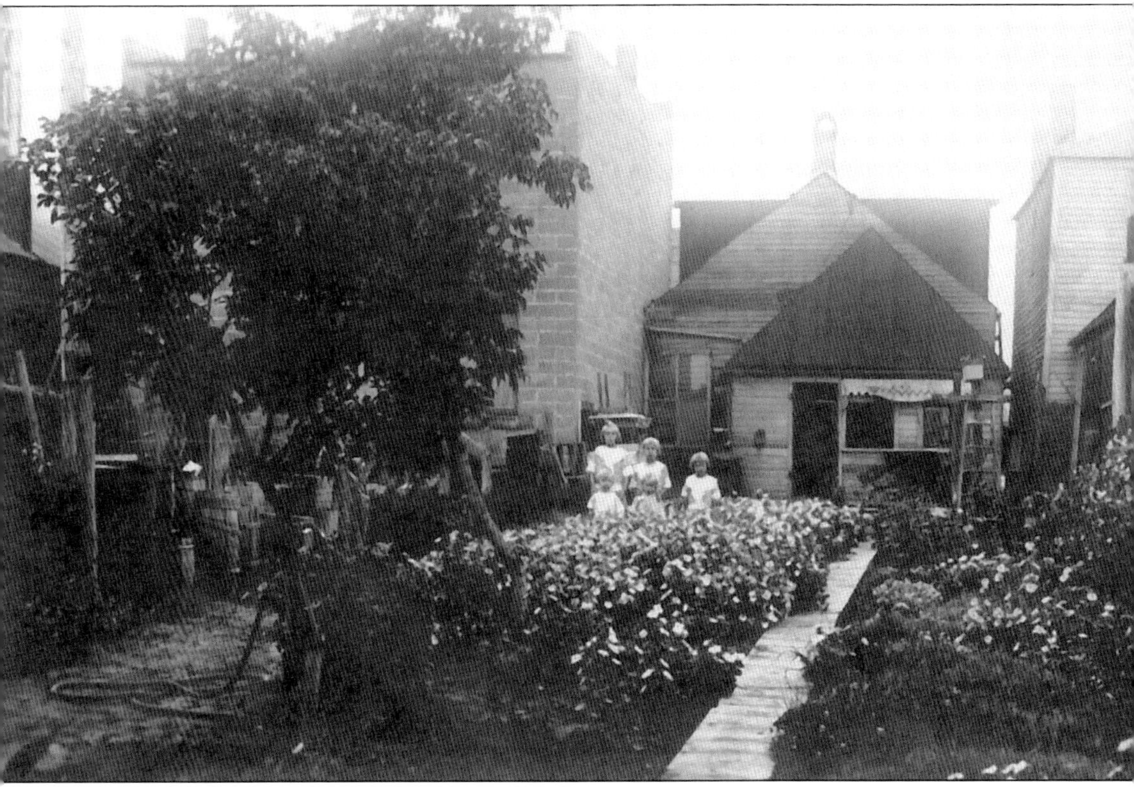

These young Dakota children stand in a garden of flowers behind the café that faced Calumet Avenue. The café, operated by Carrie Ely, was moving into a new era, along with Munger's Café, owned by Howard and Flossie Munger, and Lorane's Café, owned by Lorane Washburn. (Courtesy of an anonymous collector.)

ON THE COVER: The Pony Brigade rides down Calumet Avenue. (Courtesy of the Laura Ingalls Wilder Memorial Society.)

IMAGES of America

DE SMET

Laura Ingalls Wilder Memorial Society

ARCADIA PUBLISHING

ISBN 978-1-4671-1355-7

Published by Arcadia Publishing
Charleston, South Carolina

Printed in the United States of America

Library of Congress Control Number: 2014958861

For all general information, please contact Arcadia Publishing:
Telephone 843-853-2070
Fax 843-853-0044
E-mail sales@arcadiapublishing.com
For customer service and orders:
Toll-Free 1-888-313-2665

Visit us on the Internet at www.arcadiapublishing.com

This book is dedicated to the early settlers of De Smet and to the future residents who will maintain its history.

Contents

ACKNOWLEDGMENTS

With some gentle prodding by Dennis Goreham and through their love of De Smet's history, the authors, Cheryl Palmlund and Sharon Peterson, set about to bring you the history of De Smet through the use of postcards and pictures.

Appreciation is extended to the people of the community who gave of their time and knowledge to assist the authors in putting this book together.

The authors are grateful to Dennis Goreham for loaning his extensive collection of De Smet postcards, as well as to the Laura Ingalls Wilder Memorial Society and an anonymous collector. They are thankful to those who loaned their family pictures and organization pictures, including the following: De Smet Fire Department, Caryn Hojer, James Brandt, Bob and Nancy Montross, Greg and Kay (O'Keefe) Wolkow, Fred Peschl family, Denise (Pratt) Larson, Dollie Purintun, Margaret Schultz, Gordon Skyberg, Patti Ward-Slater, Dennis and Sheila Smith, and Dr. Richard Tschetter. Unless otherwise indicated, all images are from the Laura Ingalls Wilder Memorial Society.

It is hoped this book will instill in others how important it is to be a caretaker of the past, so that our future can always be guided by what has been achieved.

INTRODUCTION

What caused the pull of the prairie? Did it beckon with the promise of great fortunes or the promise of free land? What brought the early settlers to De Smet? To hear the actual truth, one would need to visit face-to-face with a settler. Since that is not possible, it can be surmised that the free land brought most of the early settlers because of the hope of improving their status in life.

The original Dakota Territory consisted of parts of Idaho, Wyoming, Montana and the two Dakotas. In 1873, only the two Dakotas made up the territory. In that same year, Kingsbury County was created, but it was rearranged in 1879 and organized by Governor Howard. Kingsbury County was named for George W. Kingsbury, an editor, historian, and legislator.

As settlers arrived and railroads were built, towns began to spring up all over the countryside. De Smet was platted by the Chicago and North Western Railway on March 28, 1880. Even though Father Pierre De Smet, a Jesuit Catholic missionary to the Indians, was never in the vicinity of De Smet, the railroad deemed to call this early settlement De Smet, Dakota Territory. A railroad construction camp was located on the shores of Silver Lake, just on the northeast edge of De Smet. The first construction train went through De Smet around May 1, 1880, and the first passenger train's whistle was heard on May 10 of the same year.

The small town of De Smet was incorporated September 22, 1883, and was known as "Cream City" in the late 1800s and through the turn of the century. Settlers came from the eastern United States, Canada, Germany, Ireland, Norway, Sweden, England, and Denmark, to name a few.

There was no guarantee that towns would survive, but survive De Smet did. In fact, it became the county seat of Kingsbury County in 1888.

Laura Ingalls Wilder's book exploded on the market in 1932, and De Smet became the setting for the bygone days of yesteryear. De Smet is the setting for five of her books and is a history lesson for all who read them. The "Little Town on the Prairie" is privileged to receive thousands of visitors each year as people seek to walk the prairie that Wilder writes of in her books.

Harvey Dunn, illustrator, teacher, and painter of the prairie, was born approximately eight miles from De Smet and adopted the small town when he became friends with Aubrey and Laura Sherwood. The community shares a rich heritage of Dunn's paintings on display at the Hazel L. Meyer Memorial Library. The citizens of De Smet recognize Dunn's efforts when they hold a yearly Plein Aire Event art show during the summer.

Old Settlers Day is commemorated each year by the City of De Smet. From its inception until the early 1960s, the celebration was always held on June 10, unless it fell on a Sunday. At the present time, the celebration is held on the weekend closest to June 10. The event is believed to be the oldest continuous celebration in eastern South Dakota, dating back to 1890.

The lakes have long shared a prominent place in the history of De Smet. Fred Dow, homesteader of De Smet, claimed in 1879 that he had never seen anything like Silver Lake, which lies just southeast of De Smet. Caroline Ingalls named the lake because of its shimmering water. Unfortunately, today it can only be see through the many rushes that have made their home within its waters.

Lake Henry has been a favorite for fishing, skating when frozen, and duck and goose hunting. In 1910, when it was a resort-type area, picnics and ball games took place on its shores. For many years, the lake had little water, and activities on it became almost nonexistent.

Lake Thompson, the twin to Lake Henry, had a rebirth in 1988. In 1975, it was named a National Natural Landmark by the National Park Service because the lake illustrated the succession of reverting from open water to emergent vegetation (having most of the vegetation growth above water). From 1984 to 1986, weather conditions caused the ground to become supersaturated, and 110,000 acres of existing cropland and pastureland were flooded. In 1987, Lake Thompson became the largest natural lake in South Dakota, with surface acreage of 17,856 acres and water depth of 1,690 feet. The enormity of the rebirth has restored fishing and waterfowl hunting in the De Smet area even though the water has receded in many places.

Today, as one visits the city of De Smet, he or she will find a city with a good quality of life. The community offers a shopping district, medical facilities, development park, accredited educational system, mainstream churches, swimming pool, golf course, motels, bed-and-breakfast accommodations, and restaurants.

With every generation, there is additional history in De Smet, whether it is on a grand scale or a small pinch. There are so many sweet memories to talk about, that it is difficult to know which are the "good old days?" Is this the best, or is it yet to come?

One

In the Beginning

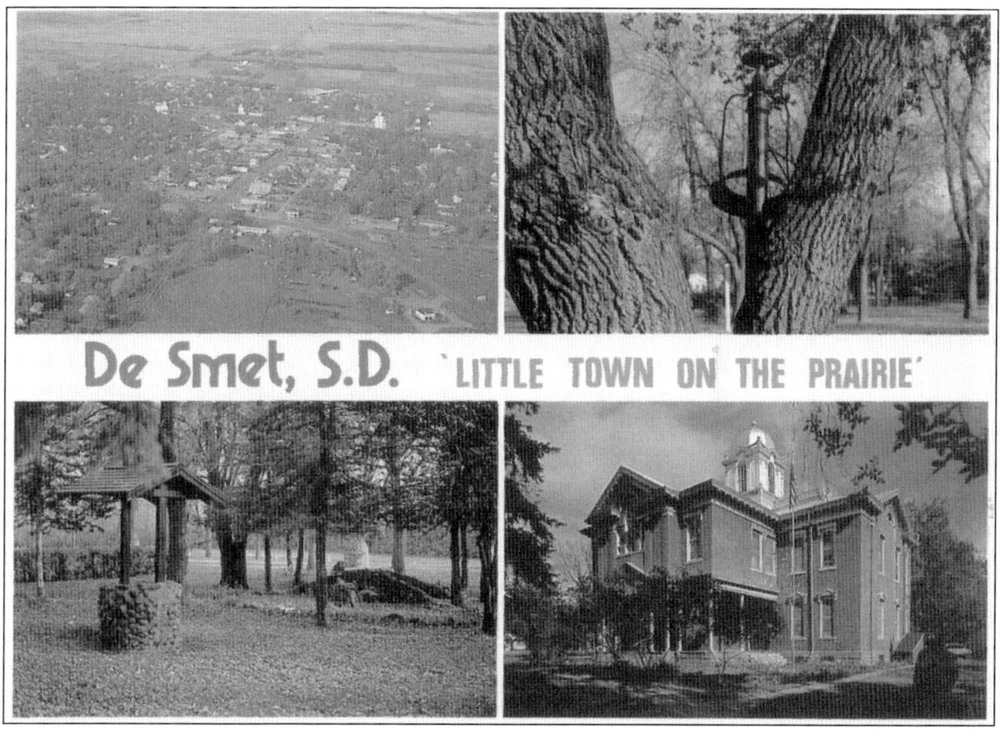

Families in covered wagons rolled into Dakota Territory as the West expanded. Railroads were being built, and it was not long before they steamed and whistled into De Smet. De Smet, the "Little Town on the Prairie," has stretched its borders in all directions and has seen people arrive from all over the world.

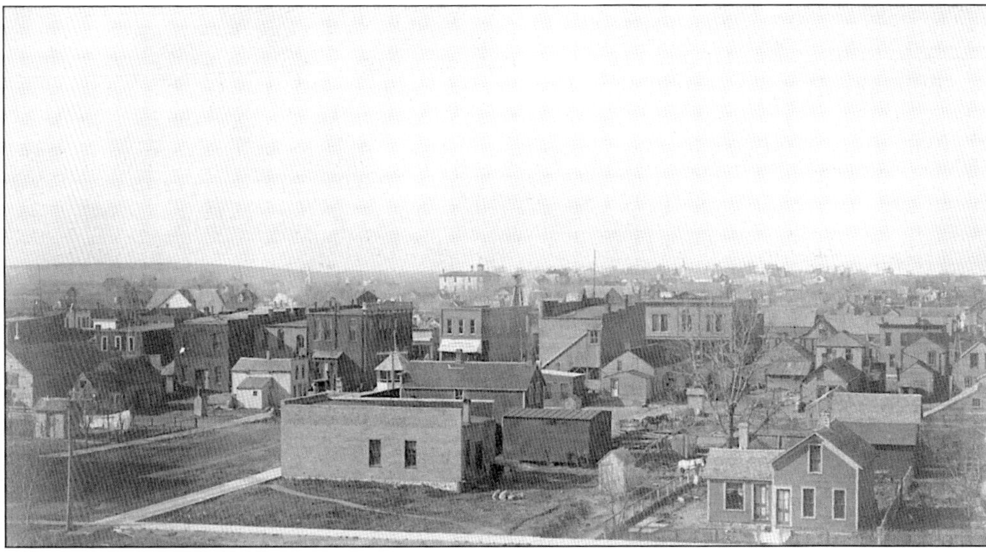
Only stakes in the prairie grass indicated the site for the town of De Smet in early 1880. As the Chicago and North Western Railway extended its Dakota Central branch from Tracy, Minnesota, to Pierre, South Dakota, on the Missouri River, it established small towns along the way, including De Smet. The stakes in the ground soon became a bustling little community.

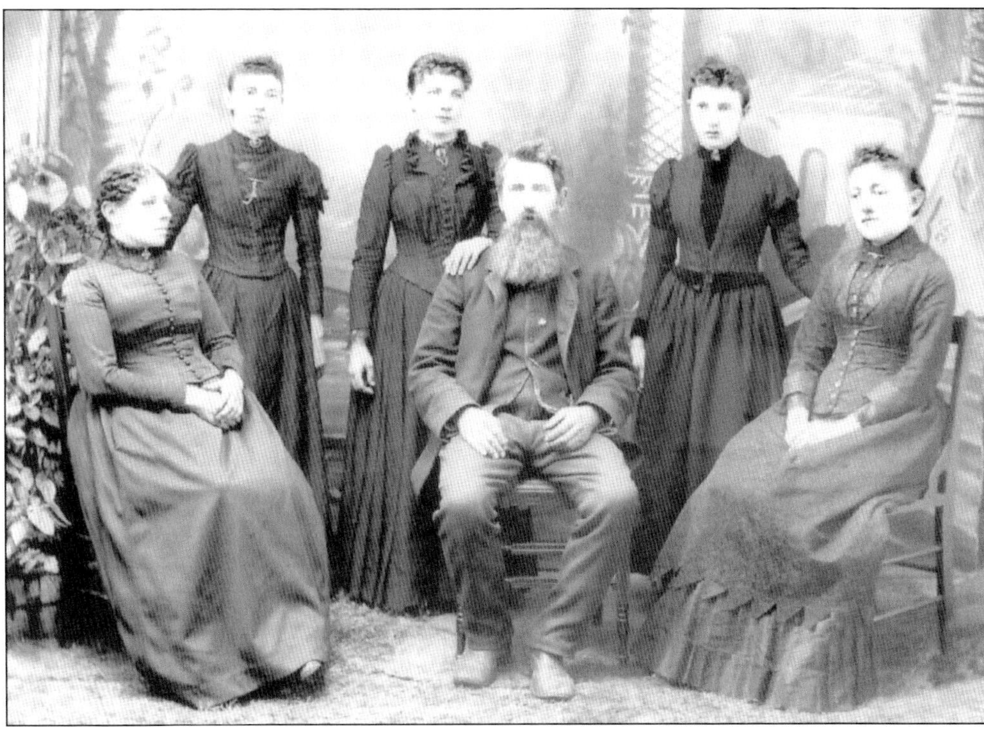
The family of Charles Ingalls became the first family of De Smet when they followed the Chicago and North Western Railway to Dakota Territory. The family includes, from left to right, Caroline, Carrie, Laura, Charles, Grace, and Mary. Charles worked as the timekeeper and paymaster for the railroad. He played an active part in the development of De Smet and had the distinction of being the first justice of the peace and the first town clerk.

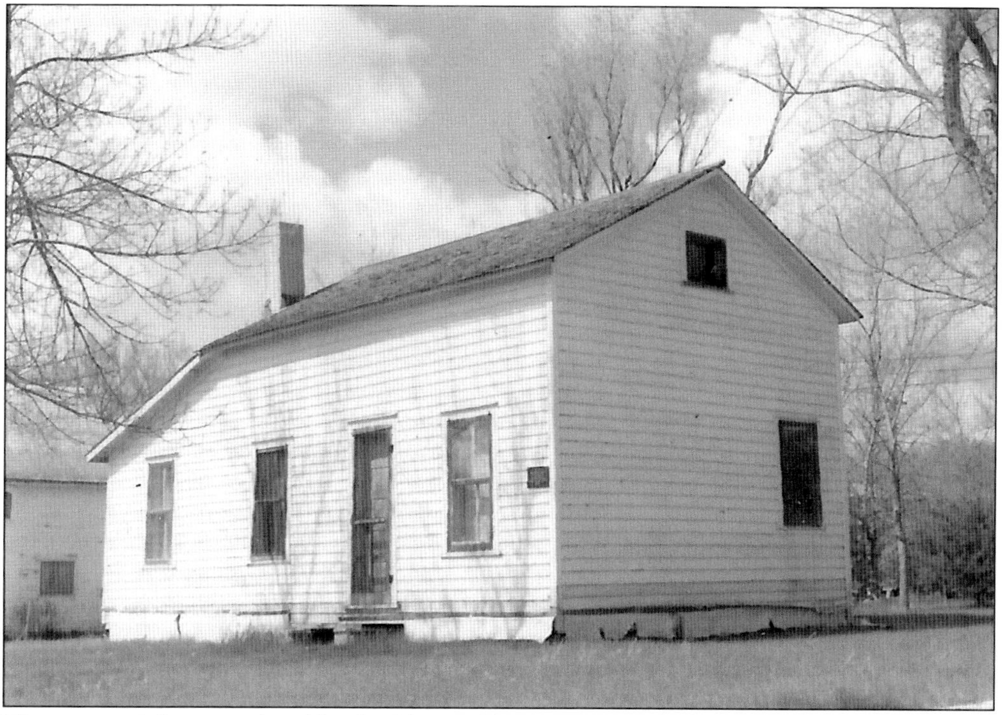

The surveyor's house is the oldest building in De Smet; it was built in 1879, a year before there was even a town. Built by the Dakota Central Railroad (a branch of the Chicago and North Western), it was located on the north shore of Silver Lake. The Charles Ingalls family lived here during the winter of 1879–1880. In 1884, the house was moved near the east end of the railroad switch in De Smet.

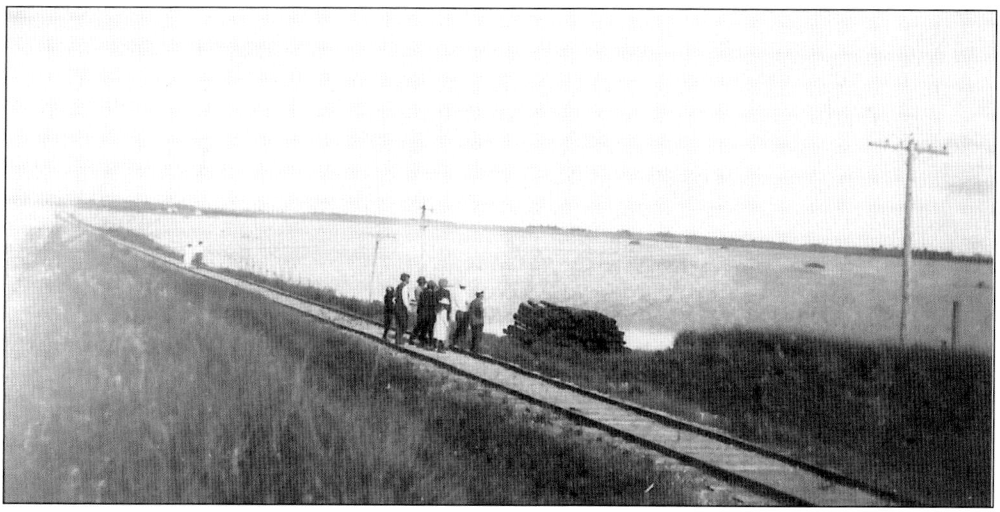

Silver Lake, located on the southeast edge of De Smet, has a long and interesting history. The Ingalls family arrived in 1879 to a "beautiful little lake full of water." Over the years, ditching efforts were made to drain Silver Lake into Lake Henry. During the 1980s, extensive rains filled the lake, making it a full body of water once more. Old-timers of De Smet recall learning to ice-skate on Silver Lake. Frozen rushes stood along the paths they skated on, and when they needed a rest, they would sit on a muskrat house.

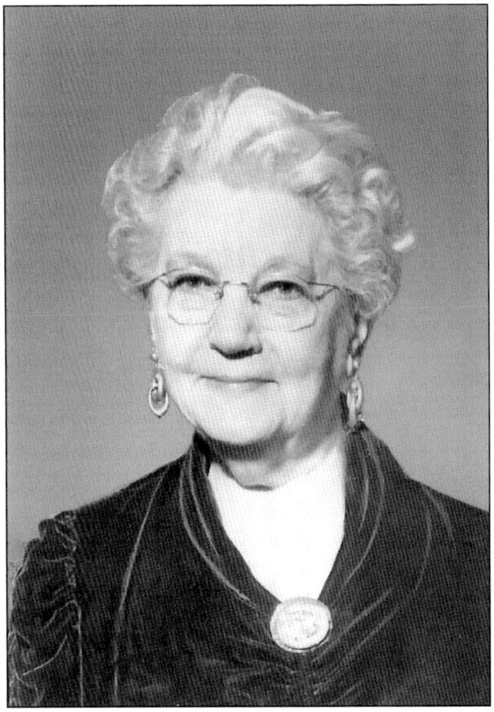

De Smet, South Dakota, became a literary landmark in the 1930s when Laura Ingalls Wilder began publishing her Little House books. Laura felt her childhood memories were "altogether too good to be lost," so she began writing her series of books. De Smet is the setting for five of her books, and with them she preserved the early history of the city.

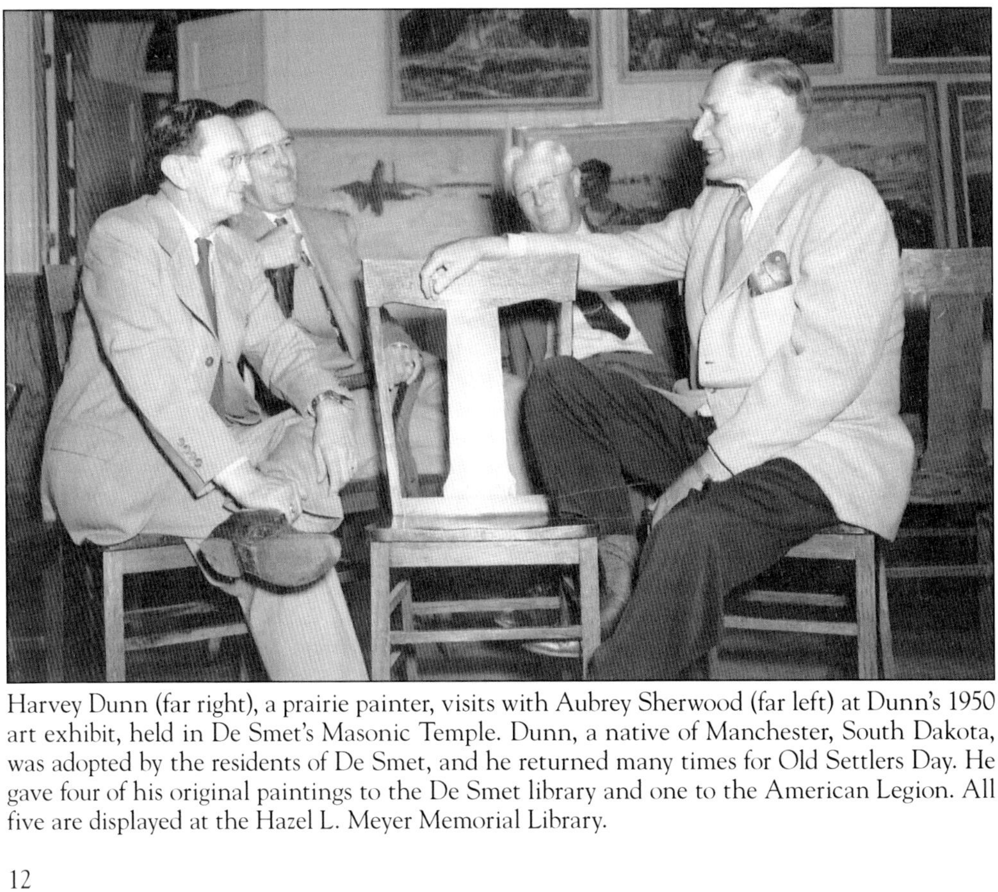

Harvey Dunn (far right), a prairie painter, visits with Aubrey Sherwood (far left) at Dunn's 1950 art exhibit, held in De Smet's Masonic Temple. Dunn, a native of Manchester, South Dakota, was adopted by the residents of De Smet, and he returned many times for Old Settlers Day. He gave four of his original paintings to the De Smet library and one to the American Legion. All five are displayed at the Hazel L. Meyer Memorial Library.

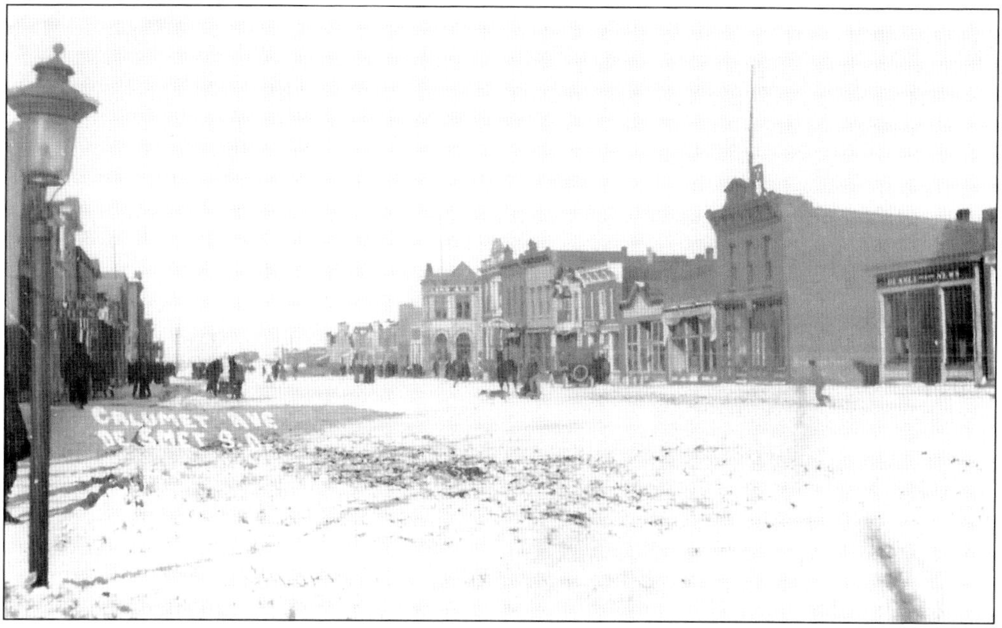

De Smet was a typical railroad town, with wooden sidewalks, gaslights on the main street, and barns in backyards for the milk cows. During the time that this image was taken, Robert Boast, a prominent resident and street commissioner, would not have to run a water truck to keep the dust from blowing down Calumet Avenue because the snow-covered street gave the board riders a clean trip to their destination.

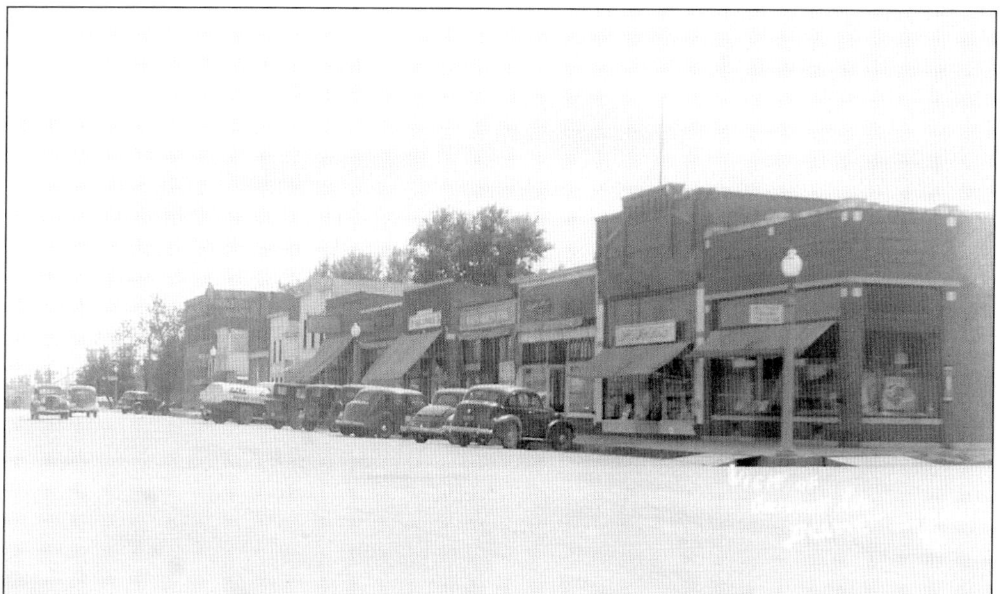

Main Street slowly emerged from early tar-papered, quickly built structures to those more fit to stand the test of time. This view is looking south from Second Street along the west side of Calumet Avenue.

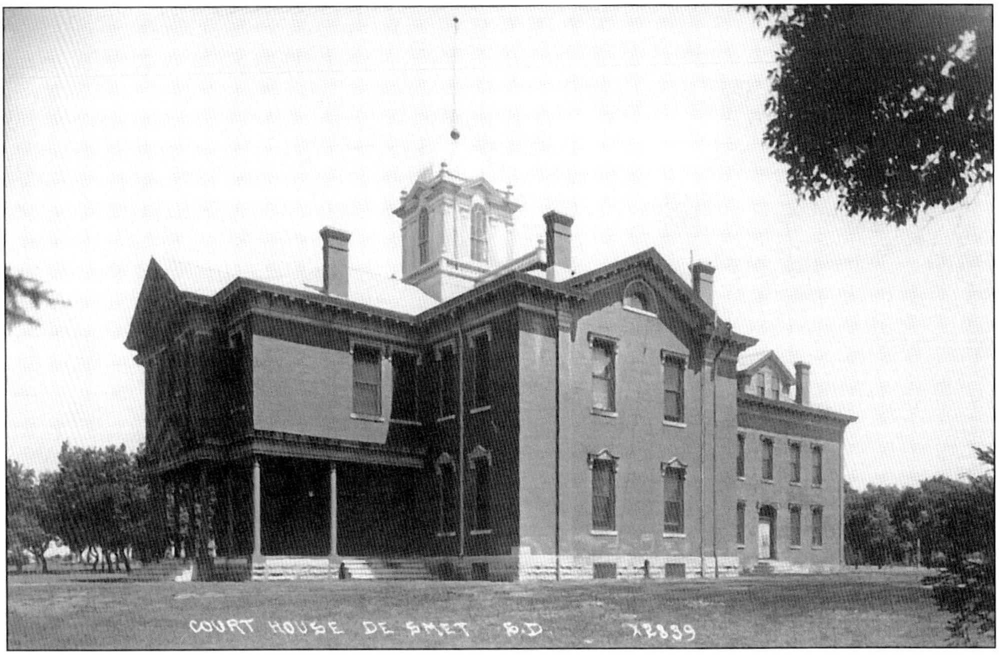

Kingsbury County was organized at the Amos Whiting homestead in 1880. The county was named for the Kingsbury brothers, who were prominent in territorial affairs. This stately courthouse was completed in 1898.

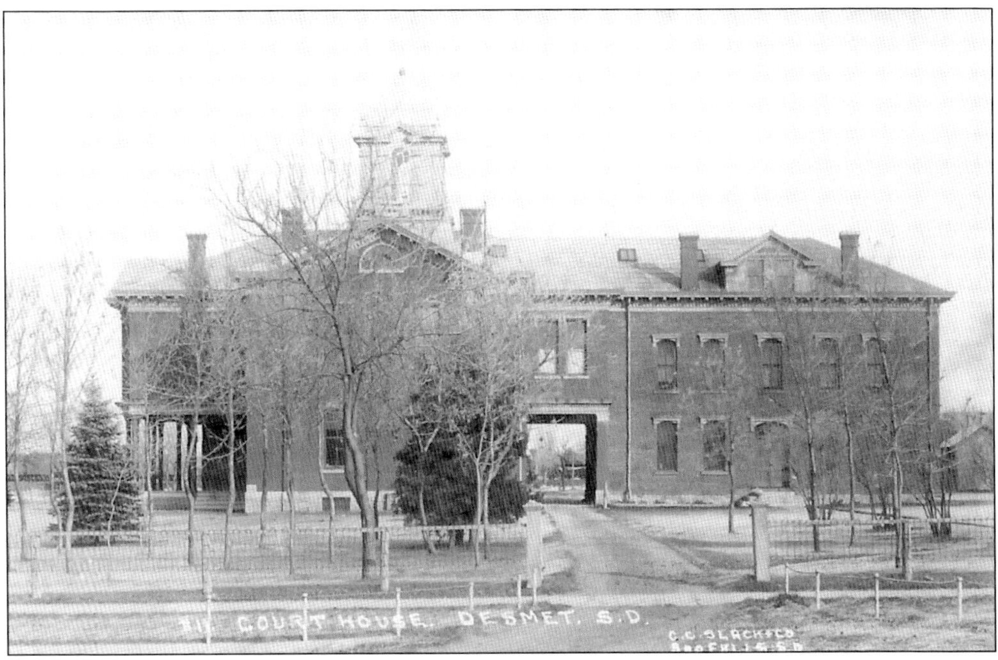

Momentum was taking the little town to greater places when it became the county seat in 1888. This austere courthouse was constructed for the people of Kingsbury County in 1898, and the west part was added in 1892.

When Nathaniel Thompson was put to death in 1893 by hanging, it was the first execution in not only De Smet, but in the state of South Dakota since its organization. Thompson stabbed Electa Bliton (Arlington) to death. R.H. Richardson was the county sheriff and made arrangements for the execution that took place in the jail yard, which was surrounded by a high fence to shut out proceedings from the public eye.

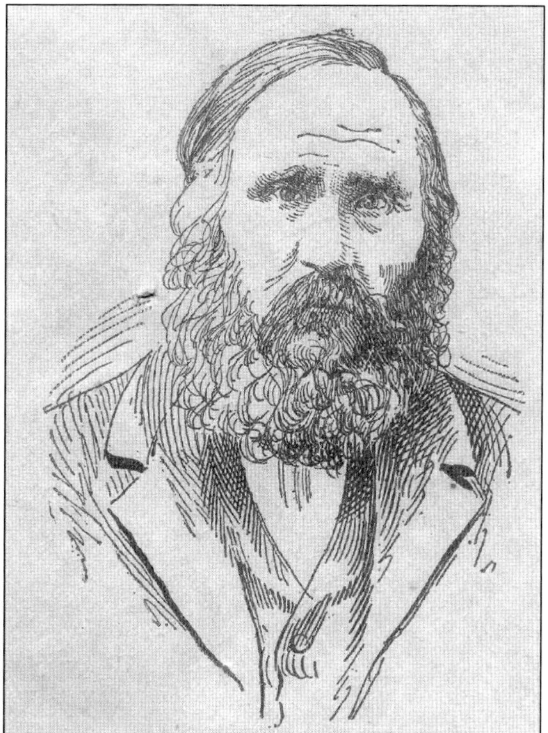

NATHANIEL R. THOMPSON.

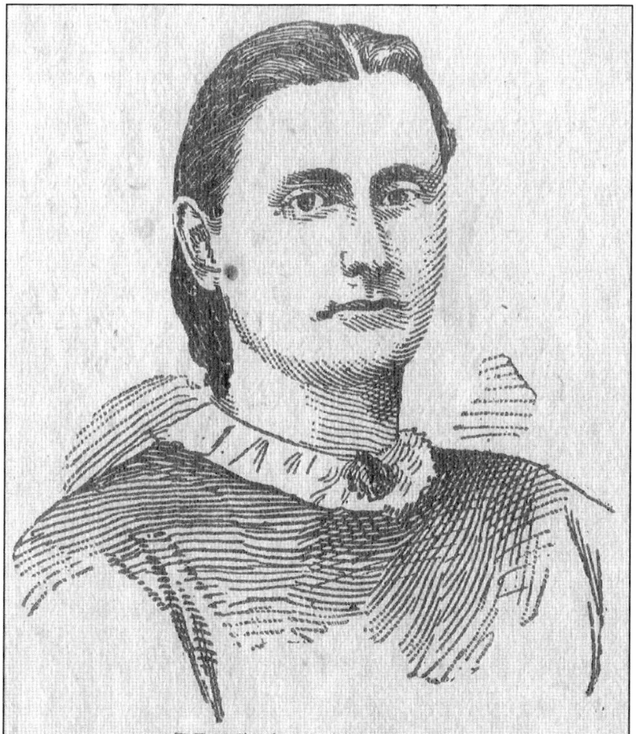

ELECTA J. BLITON.

Mrs. Thompson had filed for divorce because of cruel and inhumane treatment from her husband, Nathaniel, and his son. She was cared for by the ladies' benevolent society and housed at the home of Electa Bliton after being carefully examined by the commissioners of insanity, where her husband had taken her for treatment. The trial went on for more than one year.

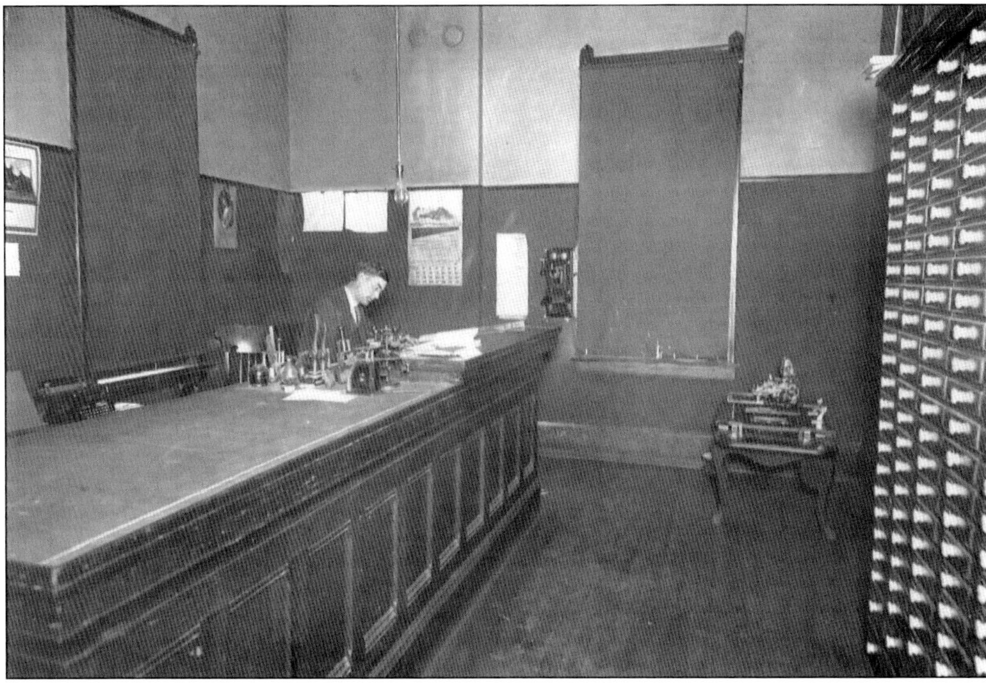

Shown here is the clerk of courts' office in the Kingsbury County Courthouse, De Smet, South Dakota. E.F. Ruskell served as the clerk of courts from 1915 to 1917 and appears in this picture. The wall calendar shows the date to be in September 1916.

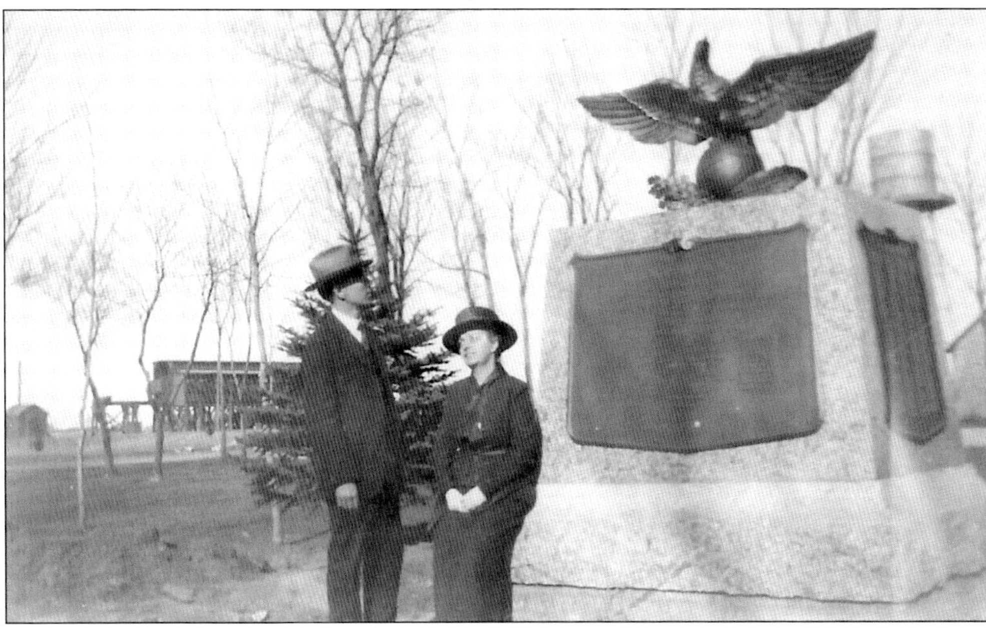

The cloud of war hung over De Smet in World War I. The first military draft since the Civil War called thousands of men into uniform. Enshrined on the World War I memorial (off the northwest corner of the courthouse) are the names of those who served from Kingsbury County. The plaque reads, "In Honor of the Boys from Kingsbury County, dedicated November 11, 1920." The couple shown here is unidentified.

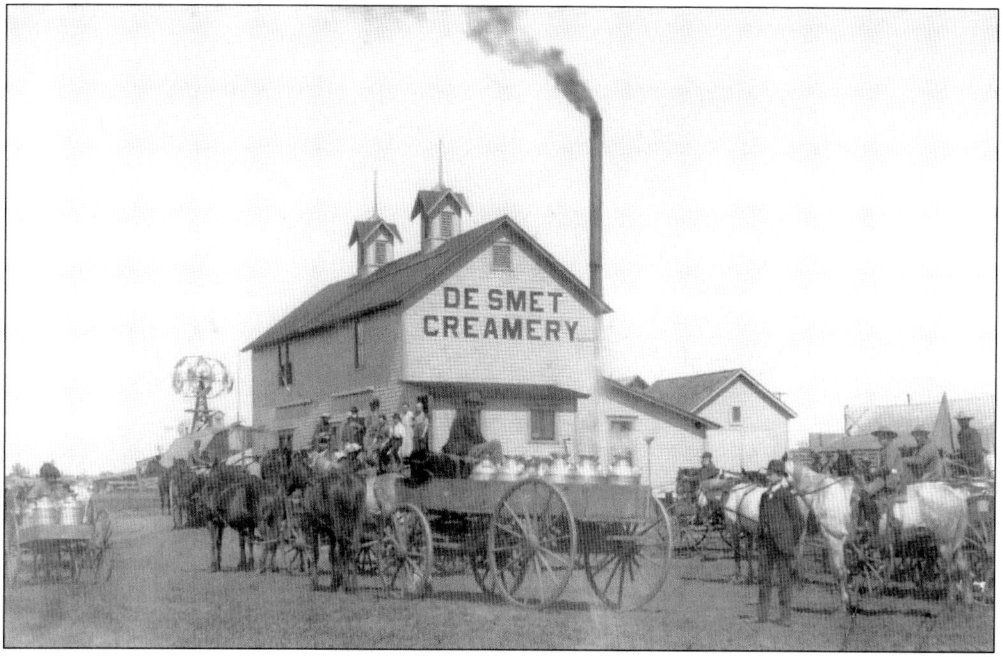

An important commodity, cream was a moneymaker, hence the nickname "Cream City" in early De Smet. Seen in this c. 1900 photograph are cans of cream being brought to the De Smet Creamery to be weighed and purchased by the creamery. Jack Distad, a butter maker, stands at the entry; C.P. Sherwood stands in suit and hat in the foreground. The O'Keefe Building is on the right.

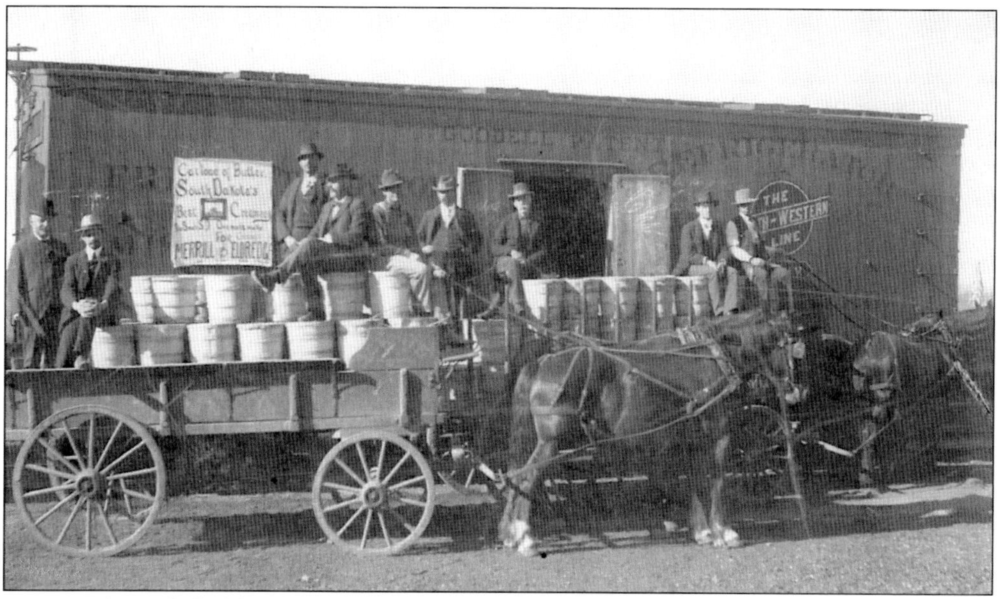

Bringing firm, chilled butter from farm to market was the intent of the North Western Line as it had a carload leaving De Smet in the Goodell Patent refrigerator car, headed for Merrill and Eldredge. It is hard to believe all the wooden buckets hold butter. Pictured, from left to right, are ? Stewart, C.P. Sherwood, unidentified, A.L. Waters (sitting), unidentified, Frank Andrews, A.L. Griffin (chief butter maker), Harry Hubbard, and unidentified.

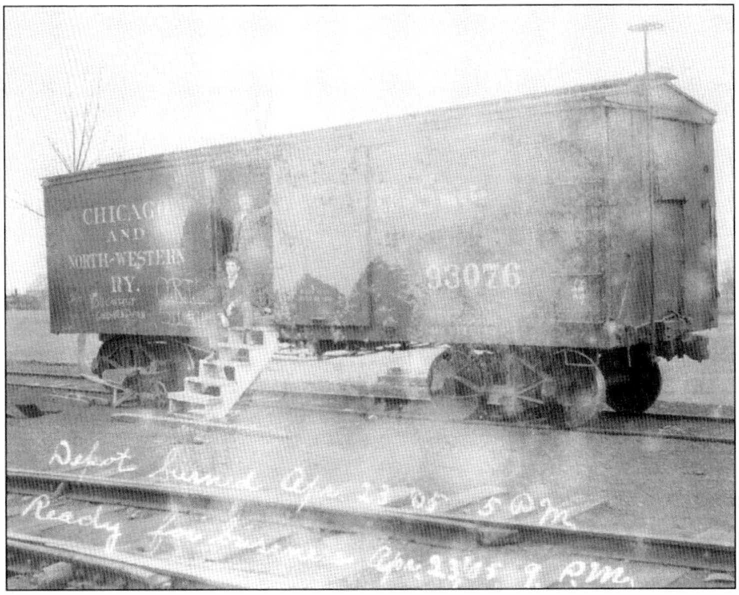

This converted boxcar is open and ready for business, as usual. This unique depot was set up after De Smet's original, two-story building burned to the ground in 1905. The notation on the picture states the depot burned at 5:00 p.m. and the railroad was ready for business by 9:00 p.m. the same day, April 23, 1905.

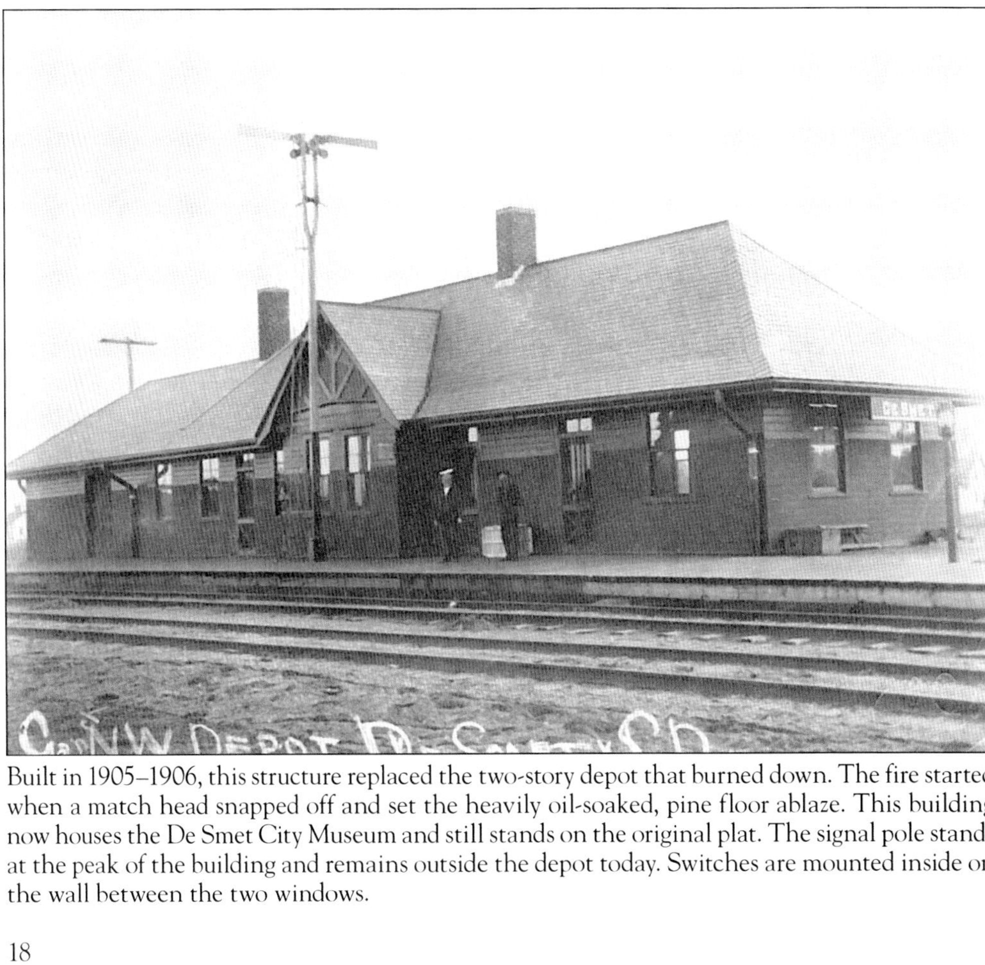

Built in 1905–1906, this structure replaced the two-story depot that burned down. The fire started when a match head snapped off and set the heavily oil-soaked, pine floor ablaze. This building now houses the De Smet City Museum and still stands on the original plat. The signal pole stands at the peak of the building and remains outside the depot today. Switches are mounted inside on the wall between the two windows.

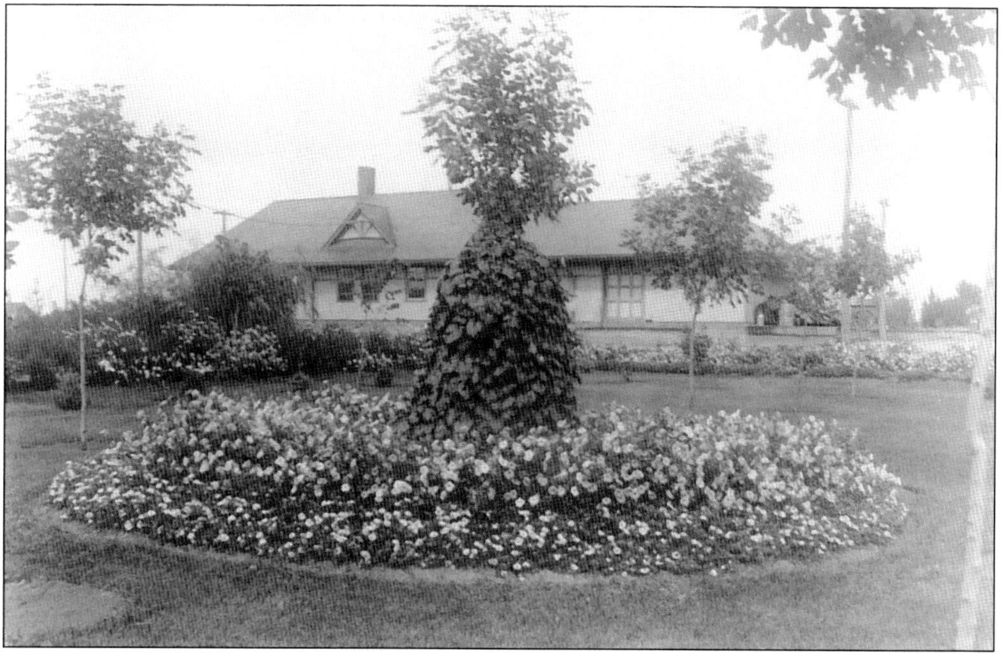

One conductor on the Chicago North Western Line remarked, "We'll be seeing the prettiest park on the line," meaning the railroad park at De Smet. Here, flowers circle a vine-covered tree while flowers line the perimeter and trees can be seen in the park itself. Many children recall playing hide-and-seek or other games in this park.

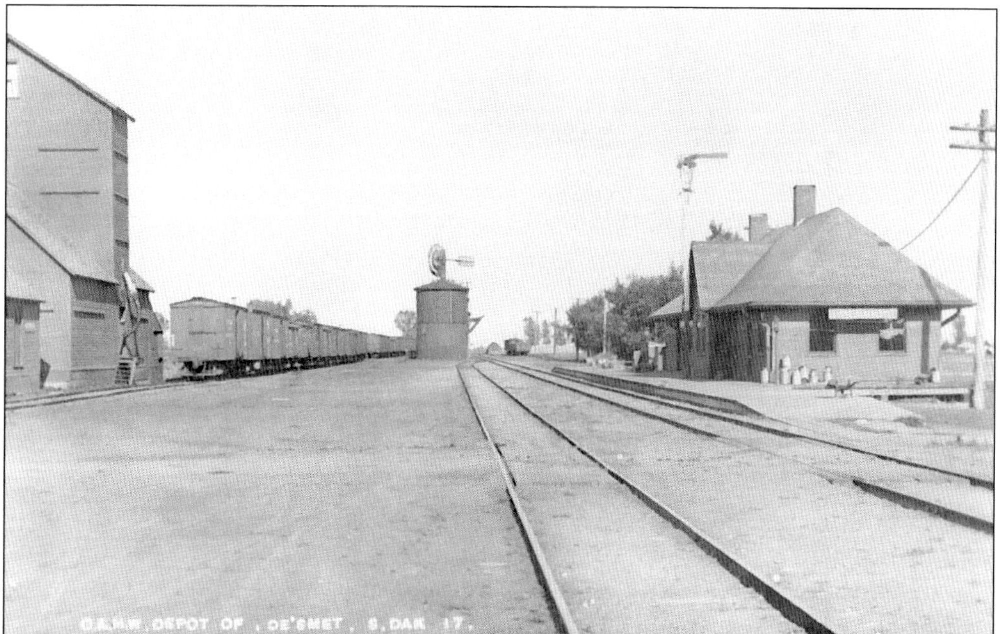

A wooden water tower, filled by the windmill, sits between the tracks on the northeast side of the depot, allowing for easy access for the steam locomotives to fill their tanks. A quarter of a million miles of railroad tracks crossed the nation in 1916, the peak of the train's popularity as a means of travel.

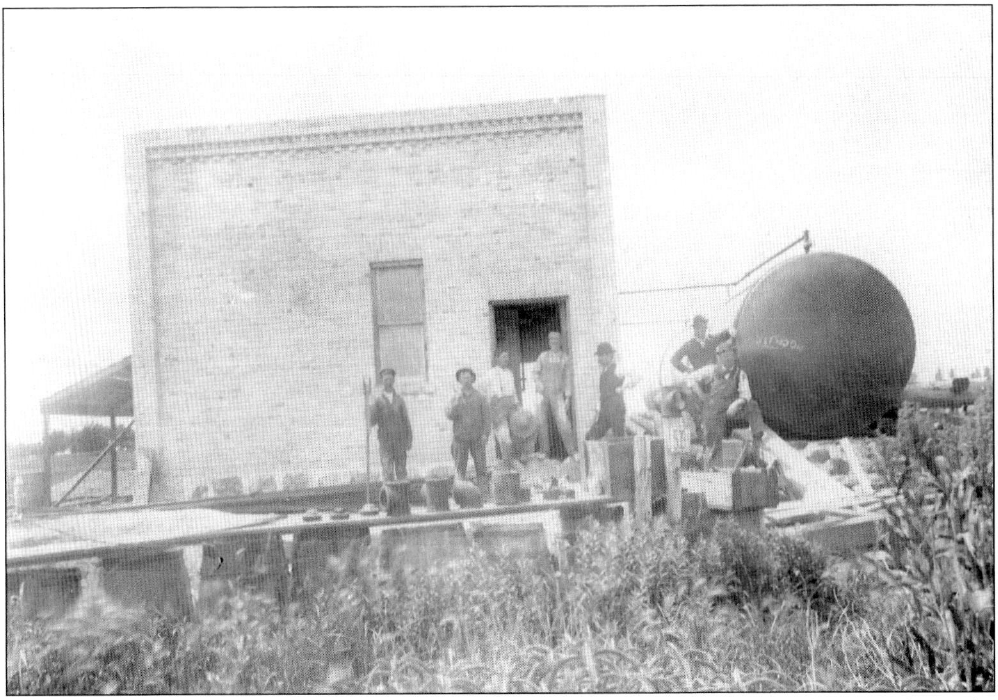

In 1903, the city's gas plant provided the means for the homes, businesses, and streetlights to be kept alight. An early news article states the plant was located in the former auto sales building (now the vicinity of the fire hall on Highway 25). The oil, burned to make gas, was shipped in by rail and piped to the large tank seen on the right side of the picture.

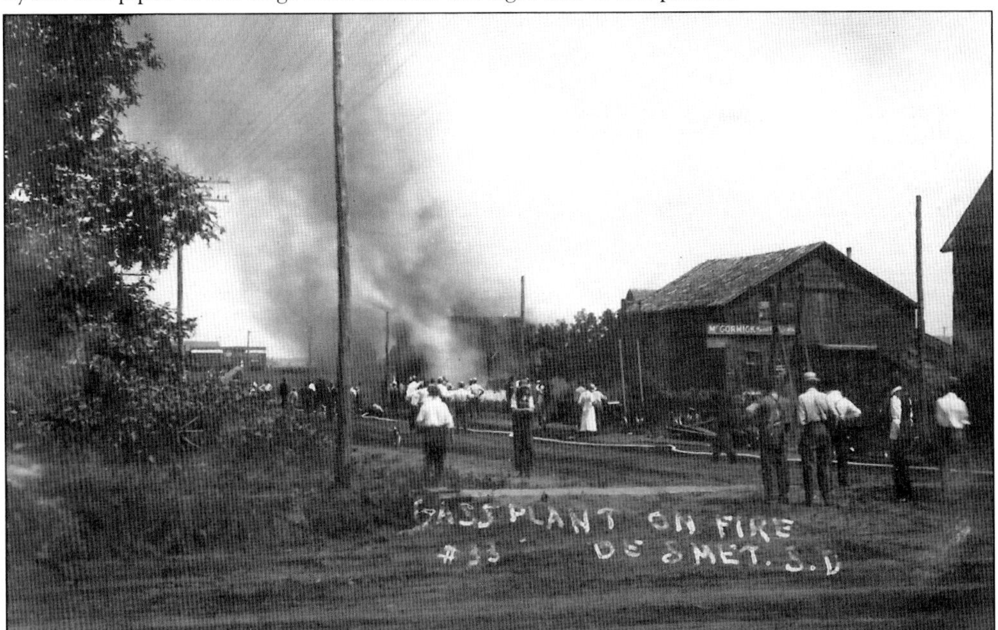

Belching smoke, the city's gas plant is ablaze in 1904. Sediment and frost combined to fill up the mains so gas could not get through. However, some good comes from all, and the gas became more satisfactory due to the mains being cleaned after the fire.

In 1936, the WPA (Works Progress Administration) came to the rescue of De Smet's east-side Calumet Avenue sidewalks. Down the street, Mays Meat Market, a beauty shop, and the large Red Owl sign standing out from the storefront can be seen.

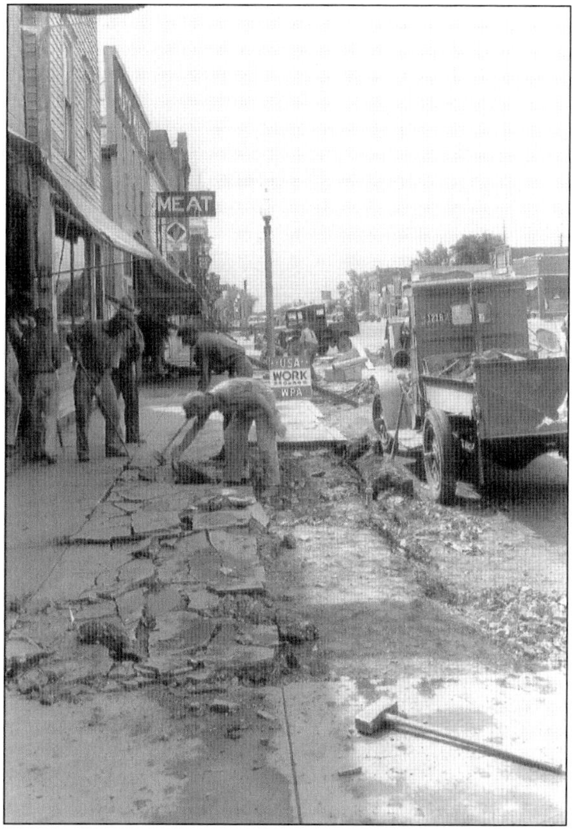

A dog never misses the chance to leave a lasting impression in fresh cement, and it appears the WPA men are diligently working on smoothing out the prints. There certainly appear to be many establishments that are readily selling libations. Across the street, a stately hotel occupies the corner, the Chevrolet garage has gas pumps, and the De Smet Lumber Co. sign is readable.

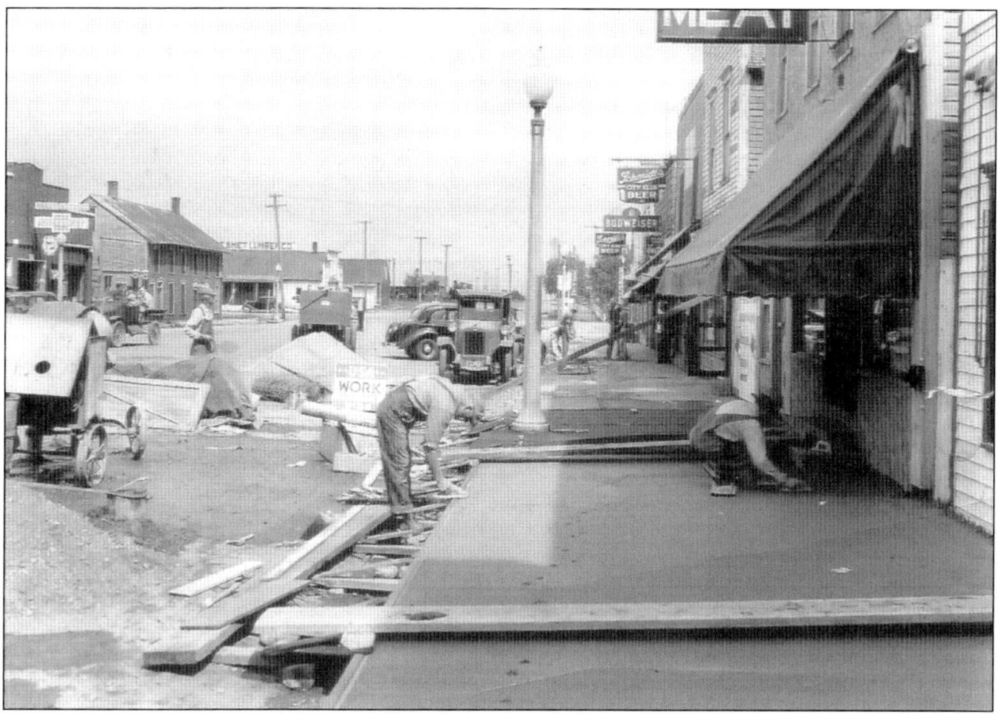

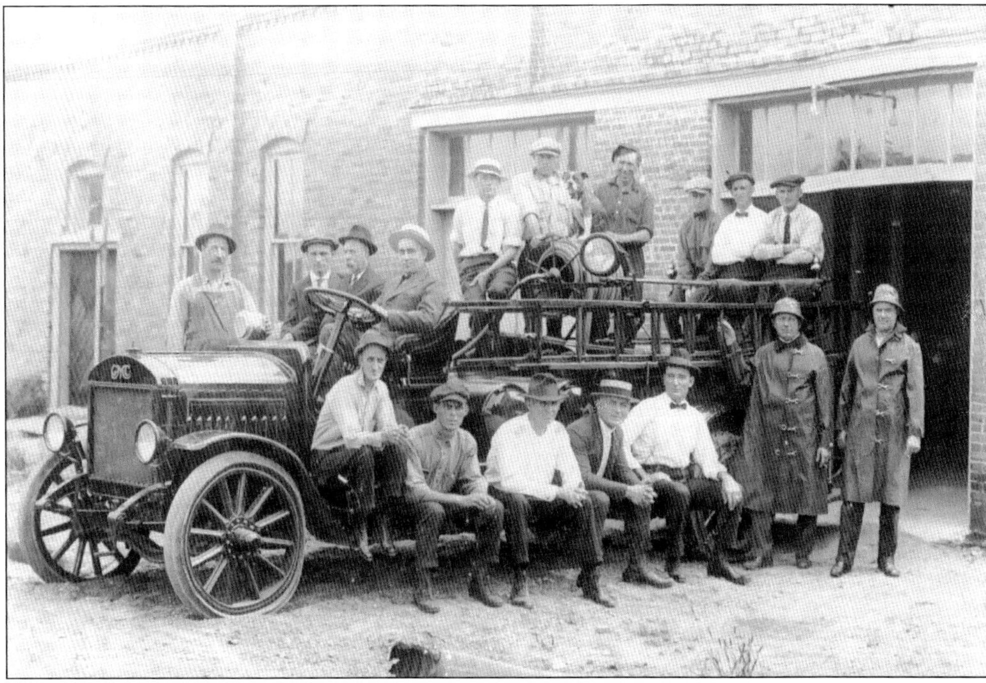

Shown here is a classic example of firefighting equipment and men in early De Smet. Few sounds are as frightening as the sound of the fire whistle; but thanks in part to Benjamin Franklin, who promoted organized firefighting in Philadelphia in the 1700s that set an example for the nation, these volunteers appear to be ready to handle the call.

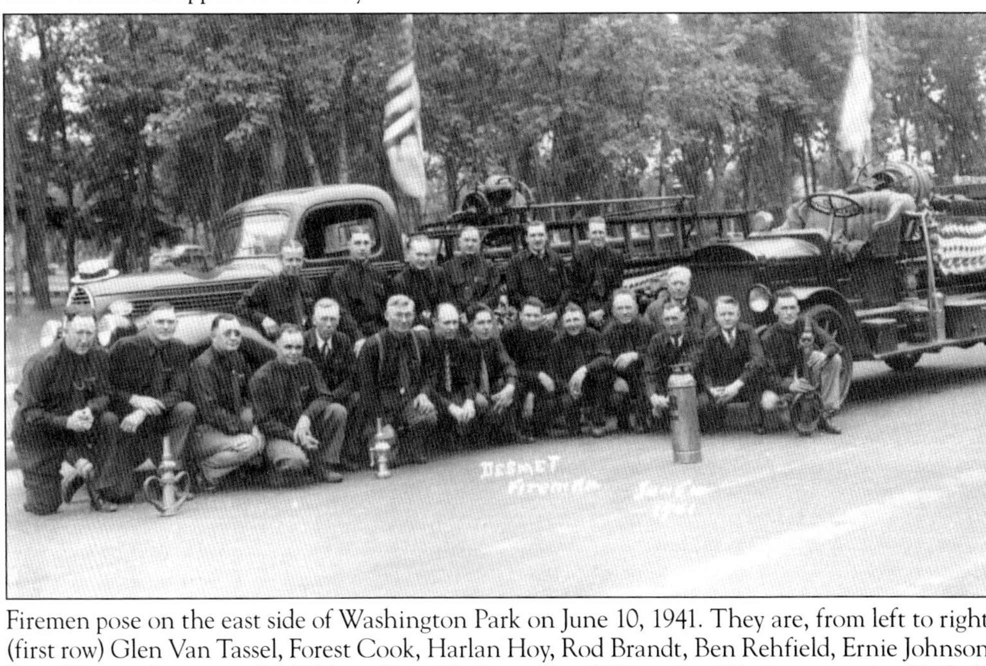

Firemen pose on the east side of Washington Park on June 10, 1941. They are, from left to right, (first row) Glen Van Tassel, Forest Cook, Harlan Hoy, Rod Brandt, Ben Rehfield, Ernie Johnson, Russ Hunter, Lawrence McKibben, Ron Graham, Ray White, Art Christensen, Art Enderly, Barney Hasche, Alfred Ryland, and Darrell Freeman; (second row) Ollie Schoonover, Theodore Smith, Reginald Smith, Ted Haughn, Doc Paul Tschetter, and Kerm Buchele.

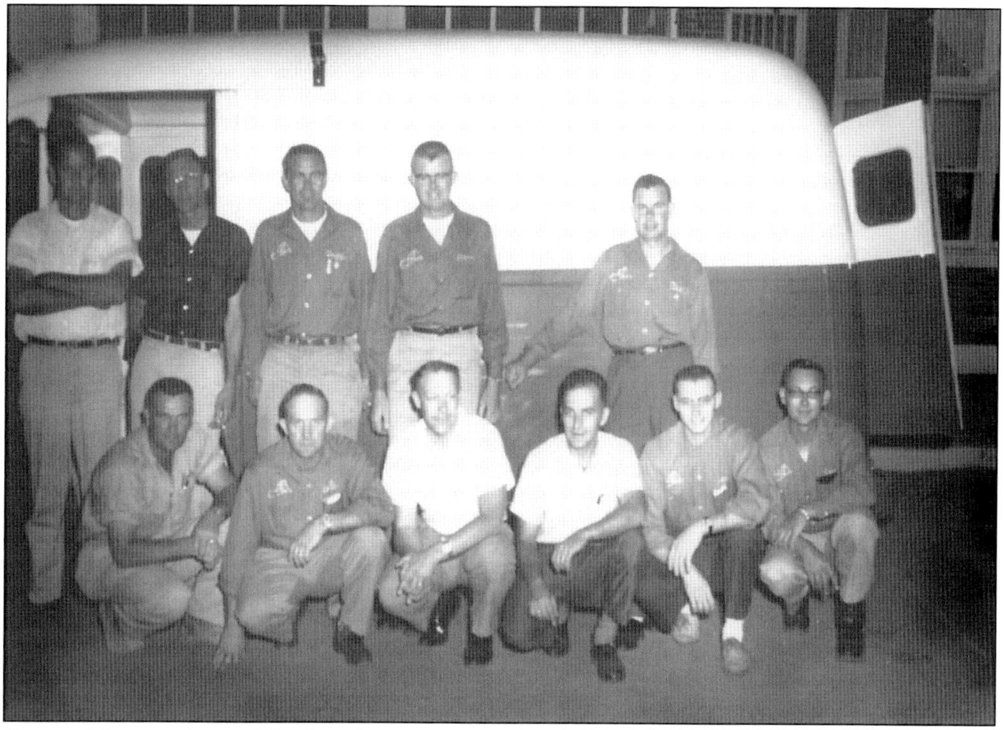

Some of the members of the fire department in the 1960s include, from left to right, (first row) Frosty Tibbetts, Dale Snyder, Dr. Robert Bell, Dr. William Hanson, Jim Burvee, and Leon Carpenter; (second row) Bill Purrington, Art Flindt Jr., Don Torgeson, Dave Harris, and Tex Myers. All have a relaxed look as they pose in front of the 1960s ambulance.

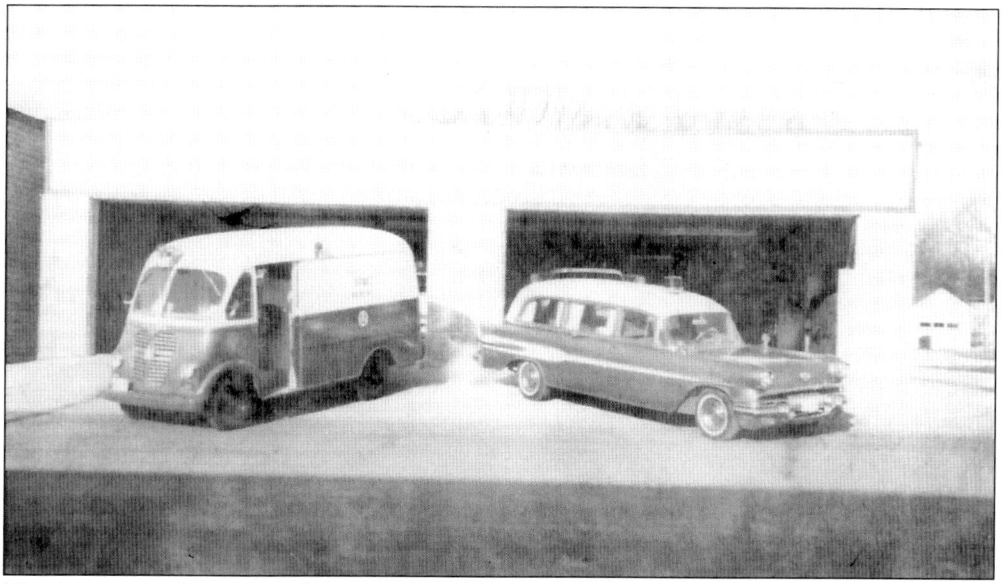

The department has come a long way from these two "new" ambulances, but the picture brings a ready smile to all who remember how the city thought these vehicles were "right uptown." The ambulance on the right is a former hearse that was given to the fire department by local mortician Marvin Ketelsen.

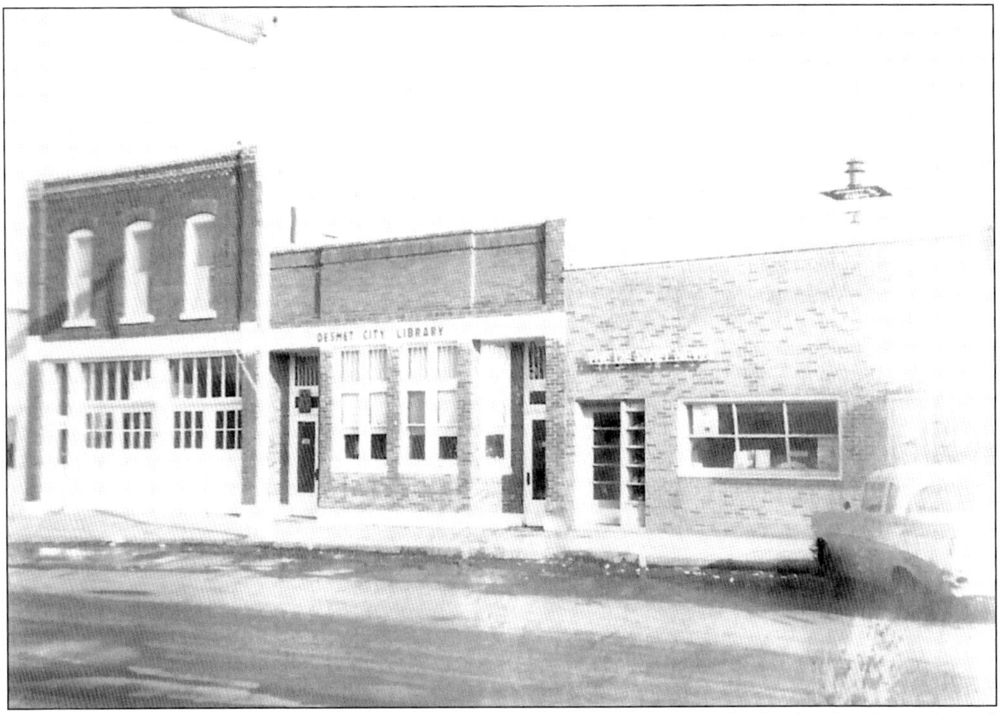

Organized fire departments have always been a must, beginning with the bucket brigade and continuing right on through today. The earlier trucks and gear were housed in the building to the left, on the east side of Calumet Avenue. The early library can also be seen just to the fire hall's right.

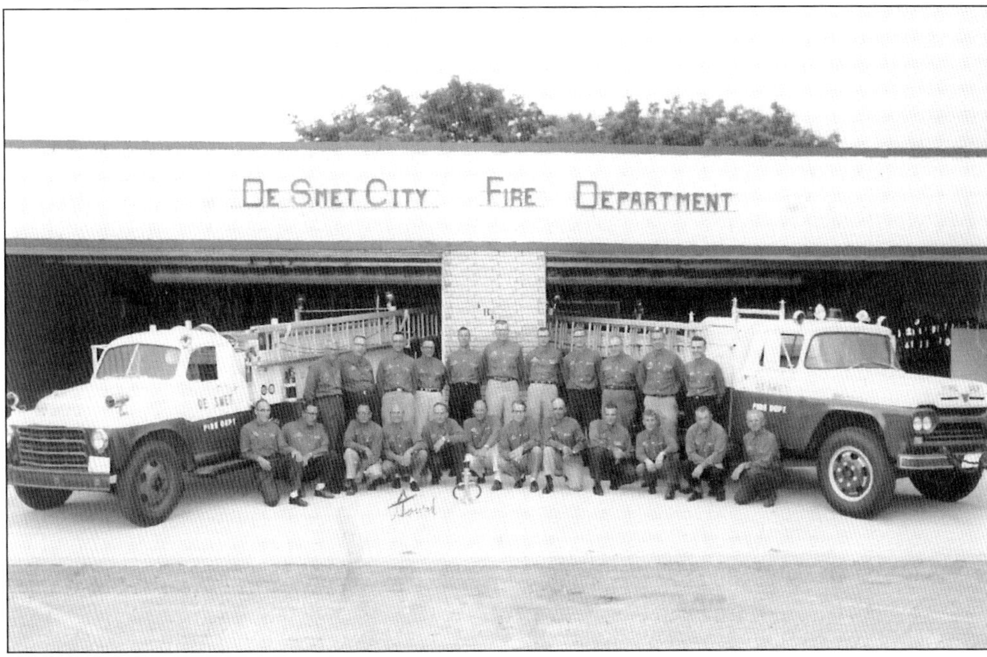

Volunteer firemen proudly stand before the fire station, built in 1964. Though it is no longer the fire station, the building still stands in the 300 block of southwest Calumet Avenue.

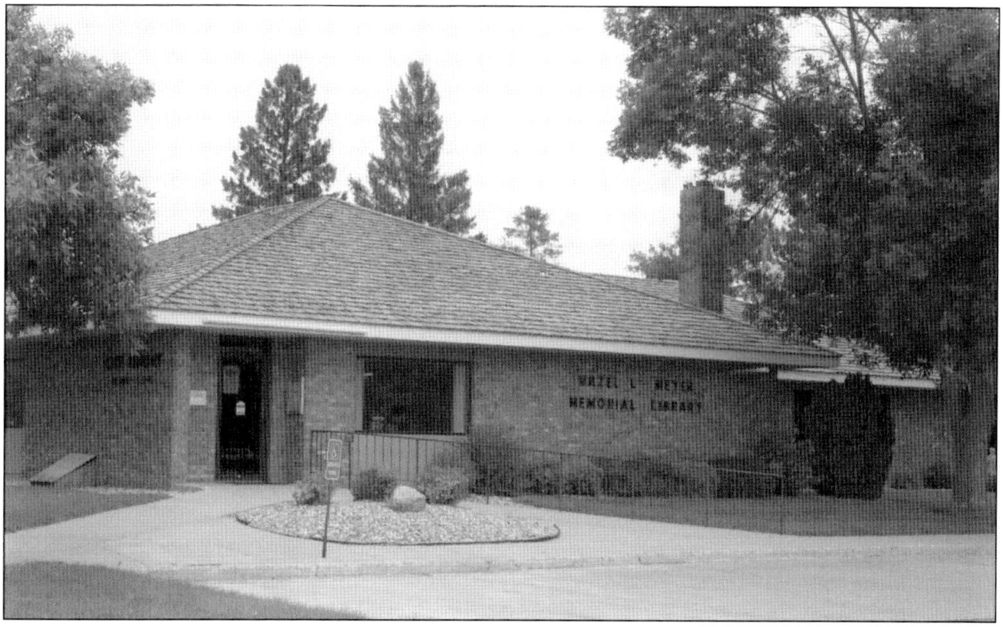

Relocated from a room in city hall after 31 years, the public library in De Smet was finally given a home at the Hazel L. Meyer Memorial Library. On the corner of Calumet and First Street, the land was donated by S. Neal Meyer and Roy Hanson for this new building site. Substantial funds from Meyer and his mother, Hazel, along with private donations and matching federal money, paid for the library in 1968.

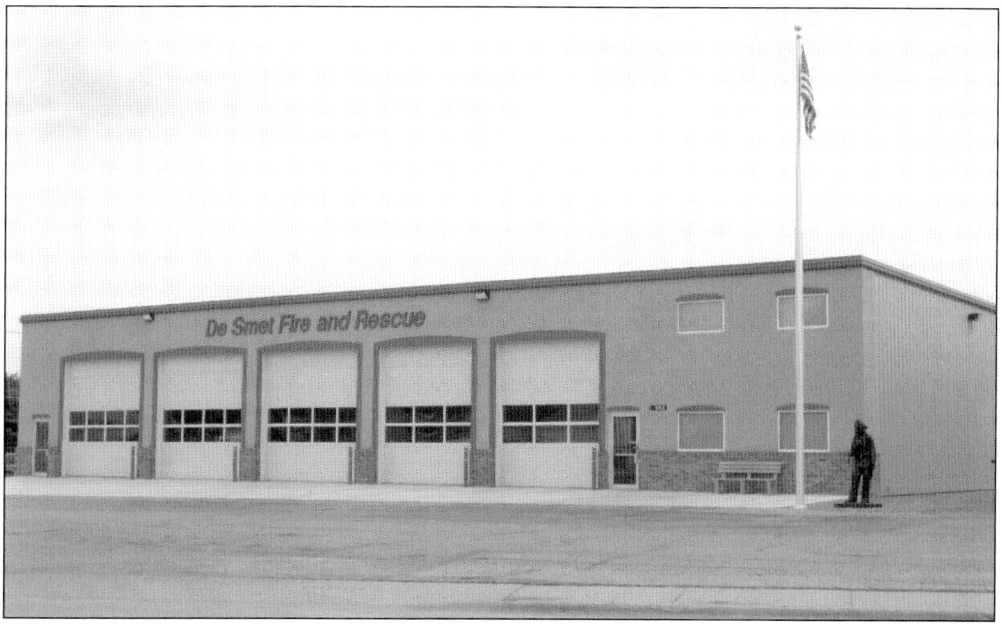

Part of the Firefighter's Pledge, "the love to serve unselfishly whenever I am called" took a new dimension on September 11, 2001, when an attack was made on the World Trade Center in New York. Each September 11, De Smet firefighters arrange a tribute in front of De Smet's fire hall in memory of firefighters lost in the 9/11 attacks. Built in 2010, it currently houses six fire trucks and two ambulances for the 30 volunteer firemen.

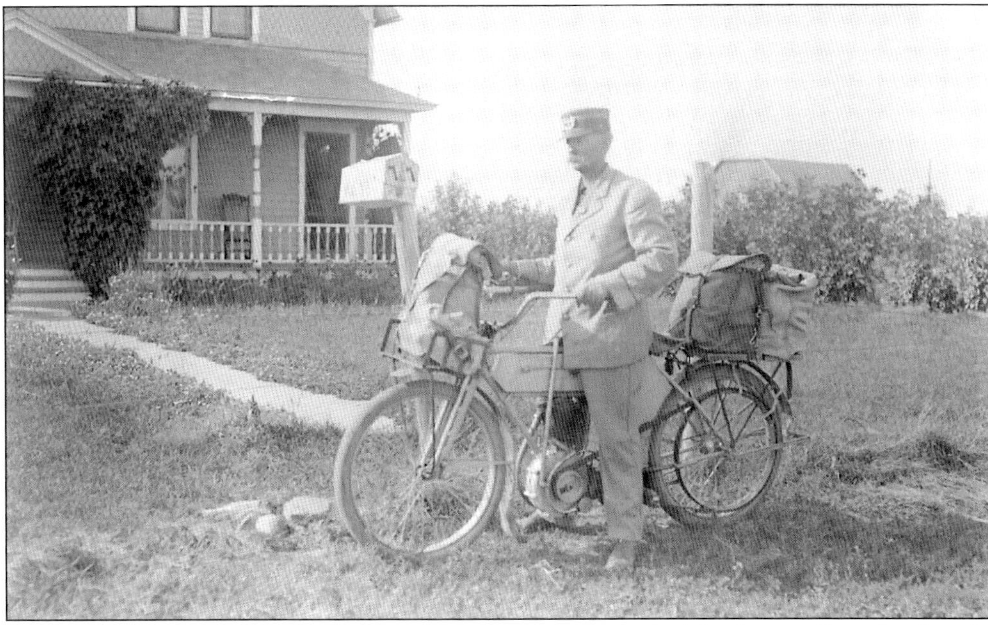

Life seemed good to many when a person could walk to the end of the front walk and gather the mail. This postal deliveryman has full bags on his motorized bicycle. De Smet applied for its first post office on March 24, 1880. To the authors' knowledge, the post office buildings have always been on Calumet Avenue or Second Street.

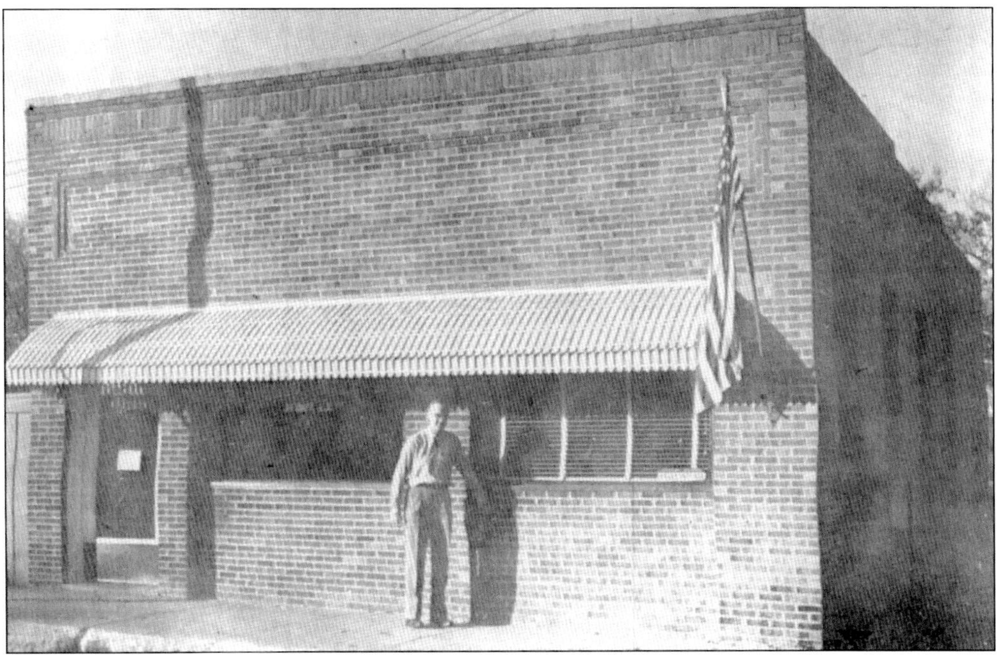

After 31 years, the flag came down at the old post office in 1960. Hollis Hill, postmaster, stands in front of the brick structure on Second Street. The post office moved to Calumet Avenue, where the Sturgeon Hotel sat at one time. Later years saw the old post office building serving the offices of Farmers Home Administration from 1960 to 1972, and as the dental office of Dr. Dan Slaight from 1972 to 2013.

Two

MEMORIES OF MAIN STREET

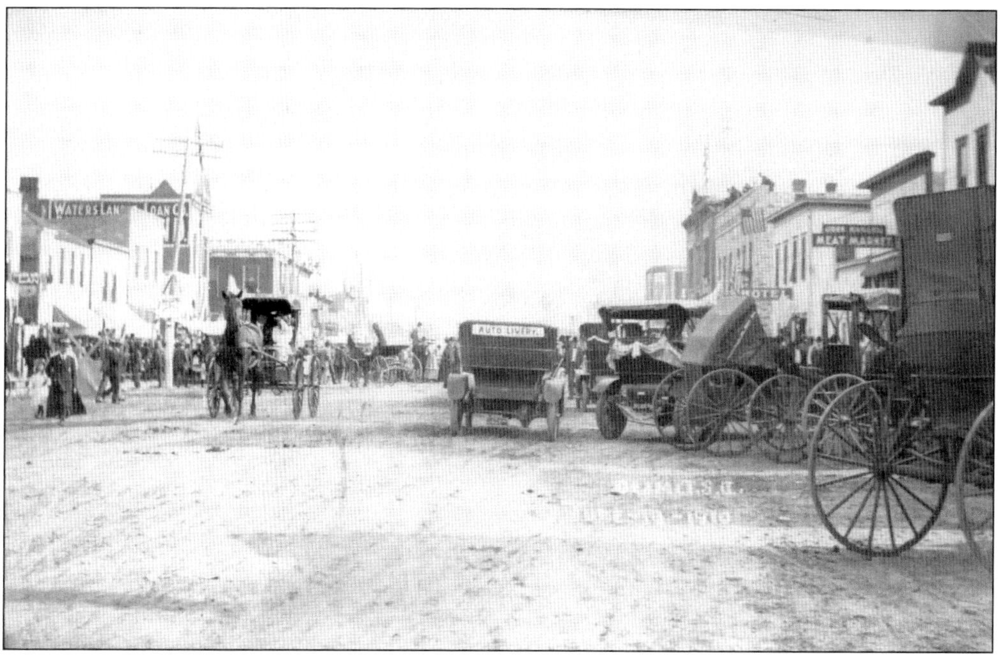

The growth and character of De Smet was influenced by the expanding West. A profusion of ethnic backgrounds built the "Little Town on the Prairie." As business opportunities arose in the town, folks took advantage by engaging in many different occupations. Due to the vigor and spirit of early settlers, the small town prospered, with irresistible appeal.

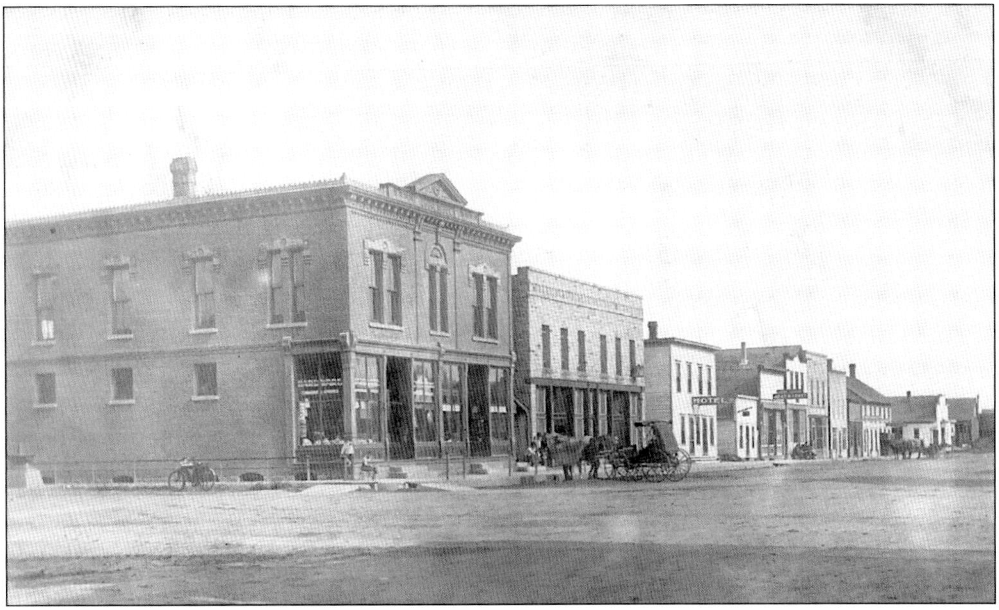

This imposing sentinel still stands at the corner of Calumet Avenue and Second Street. The Couse Building is located on a busy corner. Built in 1866, it was home to Miller Hardware, Bouchard and Son, J.C. Penney, and Ward's V Store. The grand structure housed the opera house on the second floor, and during the ensuing years it would be used for plays, graduations, basketball games, and other functions.

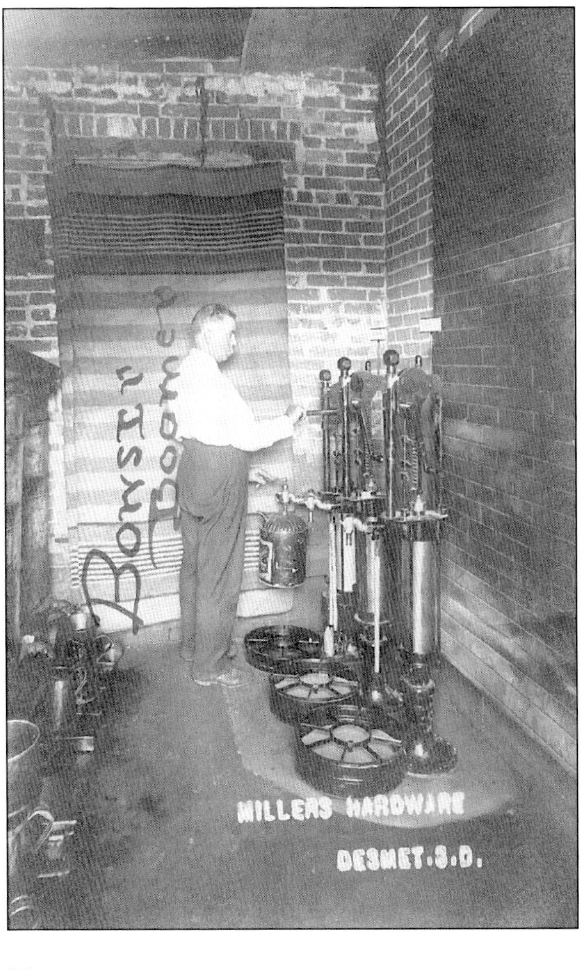

The shadow of De Smet's past lingers in this photograph of Miller's Hardware, on the northwest corner of Calumet Avenue and Second Street. Many opportunities arose in town, and Ig Miller took one to offer kerosene in his hardware store. The bricks are laid neatly on the right-hand wall, but an apprentice mason may have laid the back wall.

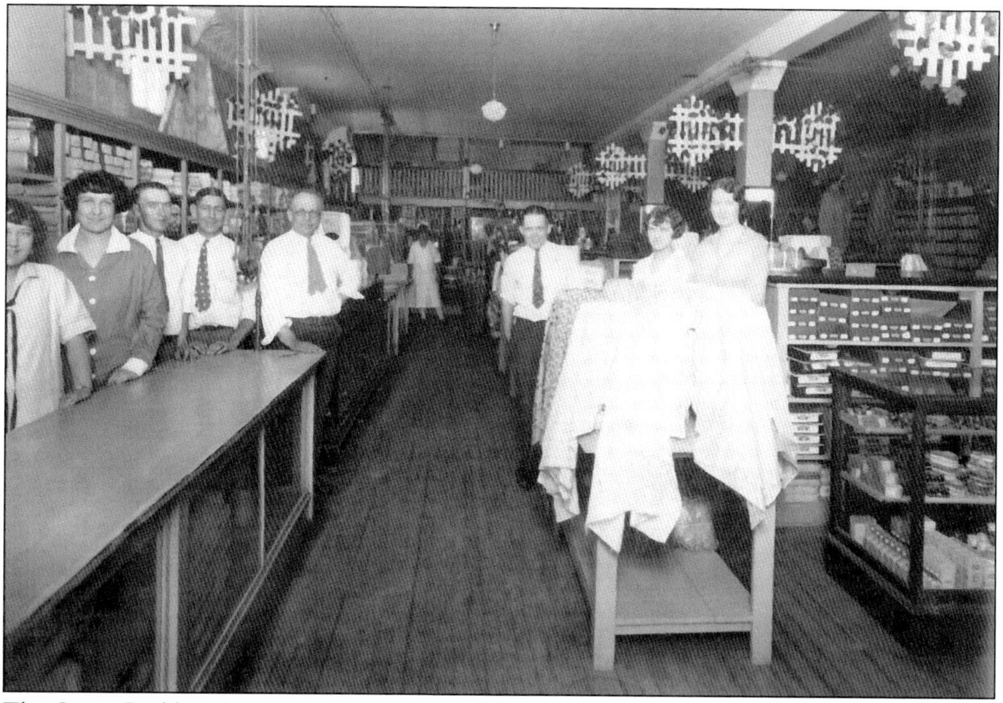

The Couse Building is seen here in 1923; Bouchard's employees in this picture are, from left to right, Lydia Evans, Viola Evans, Curtis Schultz, Clyde Riley (manager of the grocery department), E.J. Bouchard (owner-manager), Josie Block, Edgar Bouchard (bookkeeper), Florence Evans, and Edith Erckland. Attached to the counter is the "money cup," where the money was inserted, the chain was pulled, and the cup made its way to the bookkeeping department on the upper level behind the railing. Change was then made and returned.

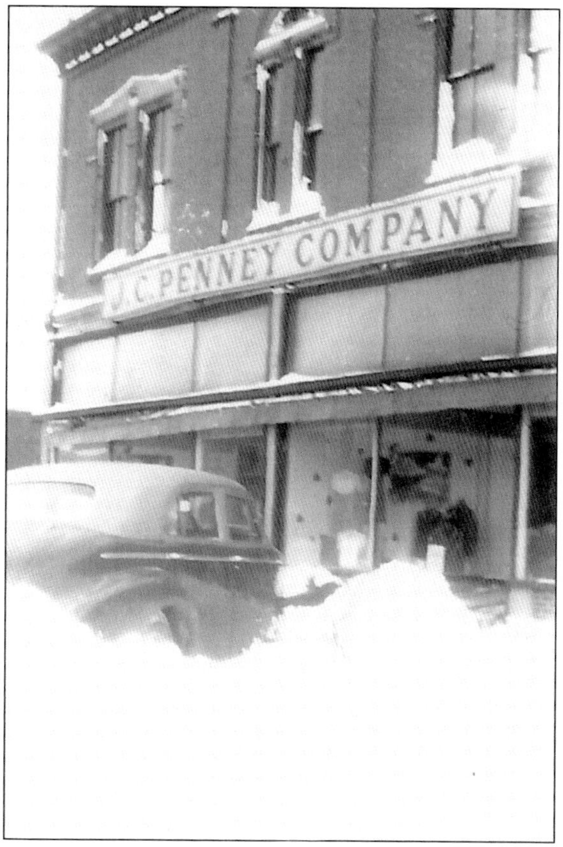

J.C. Penney arrived in De Smet in 1929. Placing its merchandise on the shelves of the former Bouchard Department Store, it was an immediate hit in the small town. Employees on this frigid, snow-piled day of 1943–1944 included Don English (manager), Al Kayser, Henrietta Hendricks, Marion Nienstadt, Beulah Lindsay, Vera Grotta, Elaine Coughlin, Rachael Moe, Pat English, Betty Bergstrom, and Elfriede Keiser.

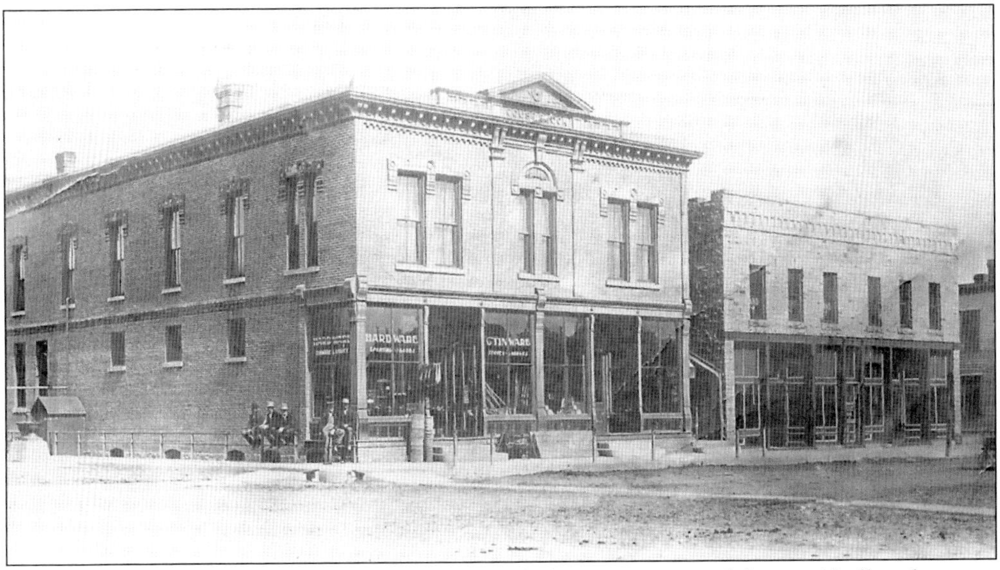

Take note of the second building on the right. Fred Floto, proprietor of this pool hall and tavern, offered an obvious place of enjoyment. It was built by a Mr. Healy in 1904 and sold to Floto.

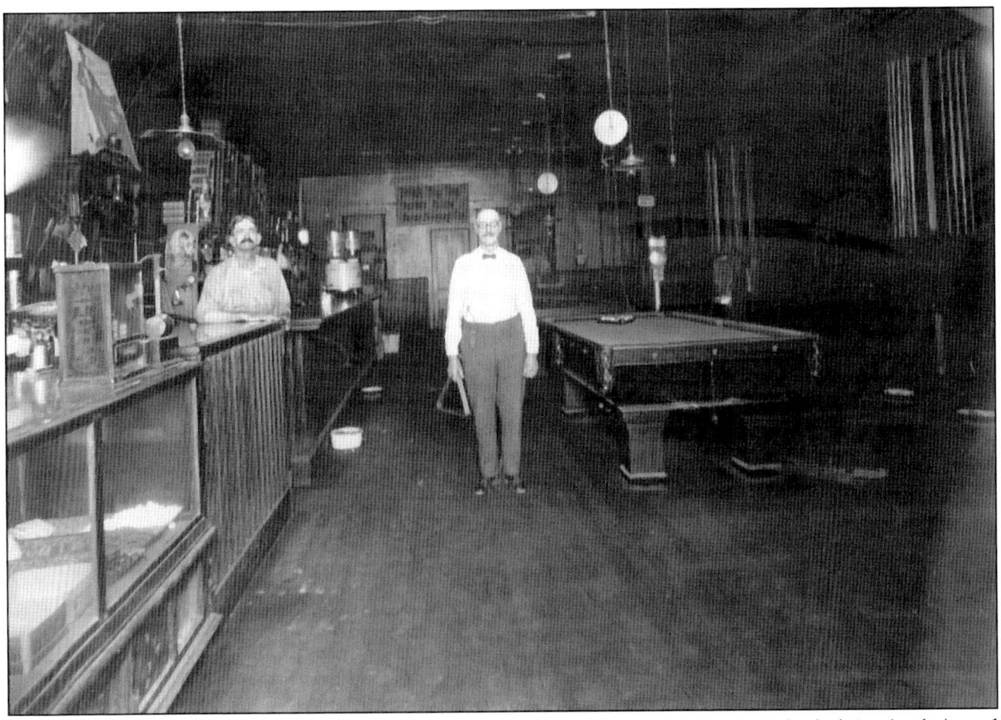

Klinkel's Taven is a business many citizens will be familiar with. William Klinkel Sr. (right) and George Klinkel purchased the tavern from Fred Floto (left) in February 1921. Klinkel's continued with the time-honored tradition of pool and libations.

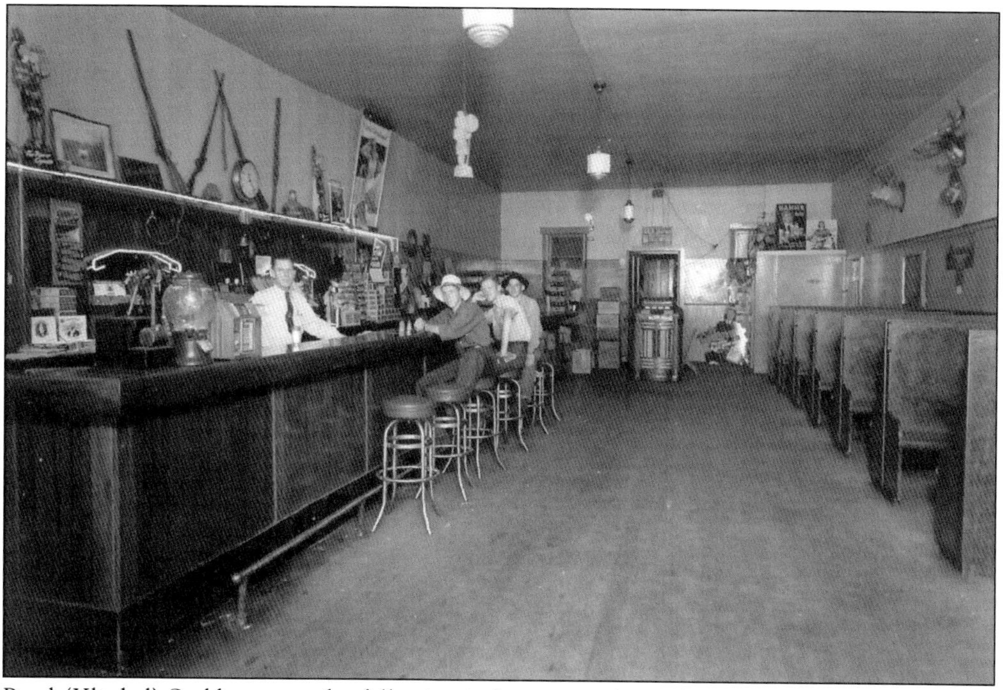

Pearl (Klinkel) Stubbe wrote the following information about this picture: "Klinkel's Tavern, August 14, 1942. George Klinkel behind the bar; on the stools: Walt Klinkel (front), Bob Klinkel and Richard Smith."

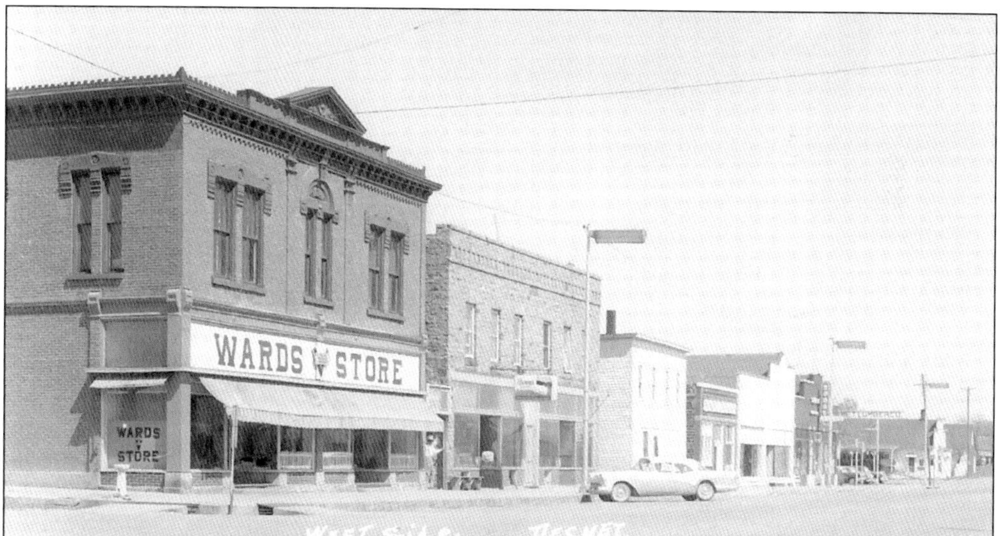

Walt and Alice Klinkel continued the Klinkel tradition by purchasing the tavern and pool hall business (second building on the right) in 1951 from Walt's sister, Pearl, and her husband, Bill Winsor. From 1958 to 1962, George Erger operated the business. Walt and Alice again entered the picture in 1962. Still standing on Calumet Avenue, the building has been owned and operated as the No Name Inn and the Dugout.

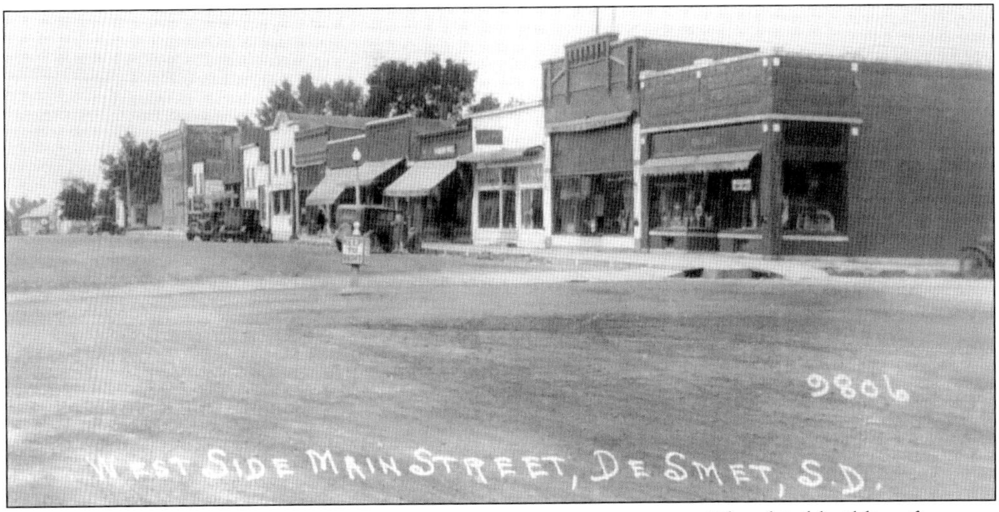

The third building from the right housed the store of Loftus and Broadbent, one of the oldest business establishments in De Smet. In 1930, Daniel Loftus was said to have one of the longest records as a local merchant.

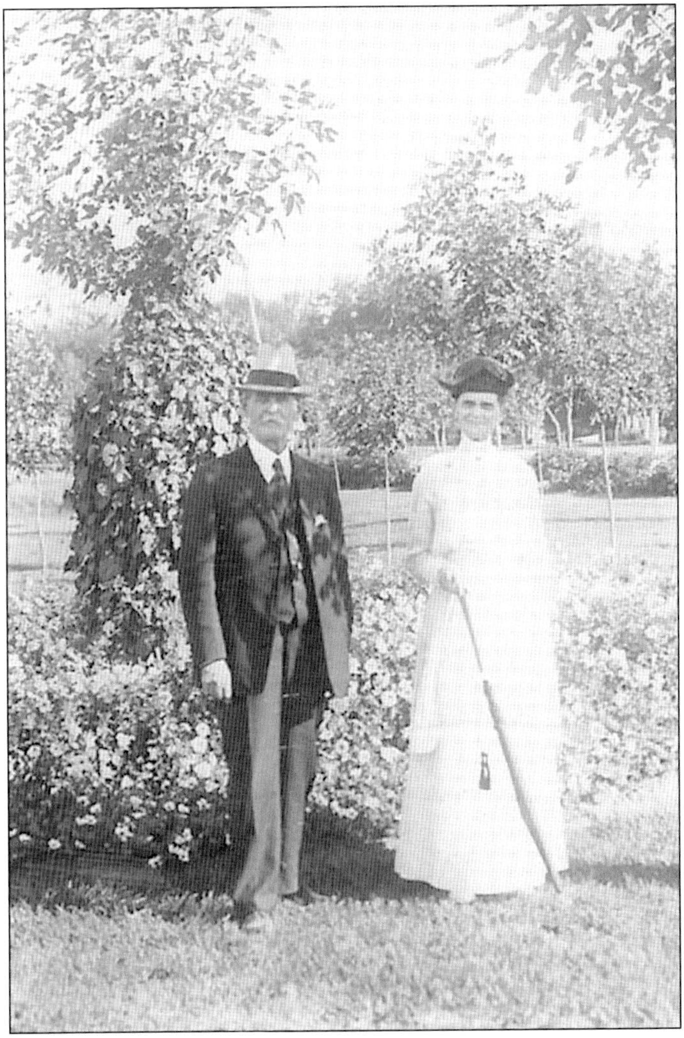

Posed in front of Railroad Park's floral circle, Daniel and Helen Kate Loftus have a colorful background for this sophisticated picture in the early 1900s. This gentleman was Loftus of Loftus and Broadbent.

Countless families bought their supplies in the little town at the Fuller Hardware. Families lived on the land, and this wagon stacked with sacks of feed or seed is evidence of the De Smet area being farmland. The cloth sacks could have been a joyful sight to the women, as they were used for clothing and other items made from the material once the sacks were emptied.

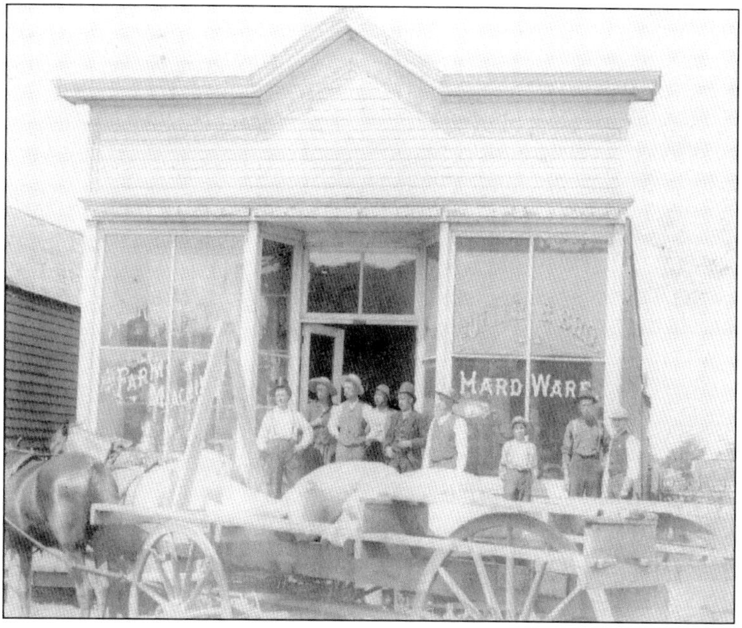

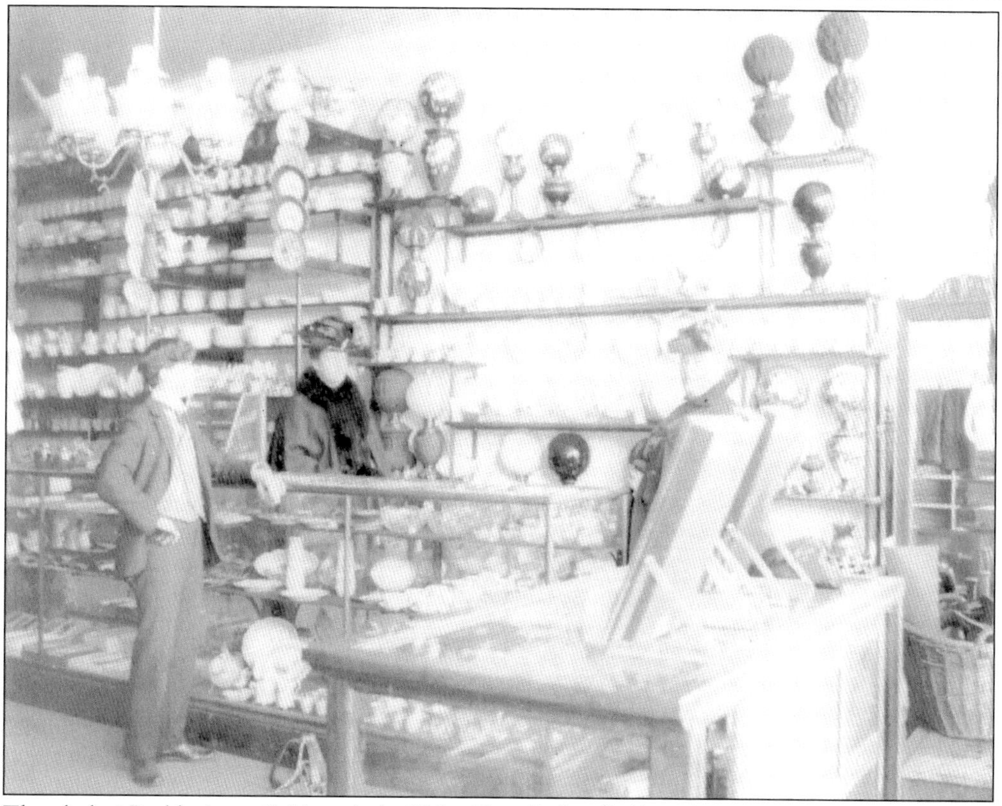

The clerk, ? Reddy, is available to help Chloe Dow Fuller (left) and Bersha Dow Dunn (right) in the Fuller Hardware Store, located at the corner of Second Street and Calumet Avenue. It has the distinction of being De Smet's first hardware store. Through the years, this was the location of Burkhart Bros., Tennies, and Buchele Drug.

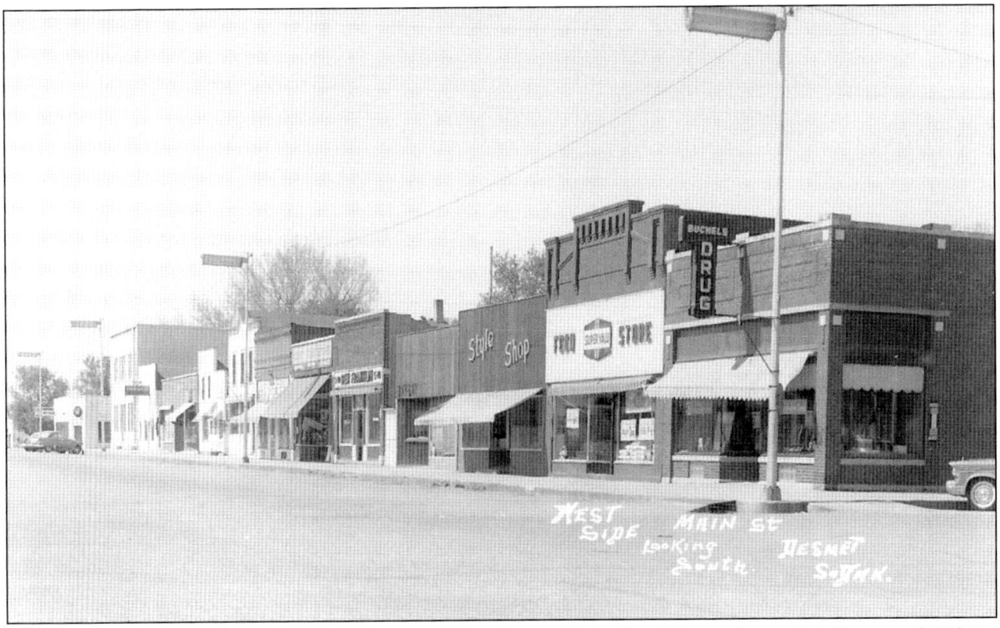

Two different worlds are seen on this page. The Super Valu Food Store (once Mallery and White Drug) appears to have changed very little structurally. Seen in this c. 1950 image are Buchele Drug, Super Valu, Style Shop, City Bakery, Ben Franklin, Coast to Coast, Peschl Locker, B.J. Hasche Insurance, a barbershop, Wika-Jensen Insurance, Floyd's Jewelry, Ryland's Men's Wear, Dakota Shoe Shop, Huisenga Appliance, and Dr. Scofield's dental office.

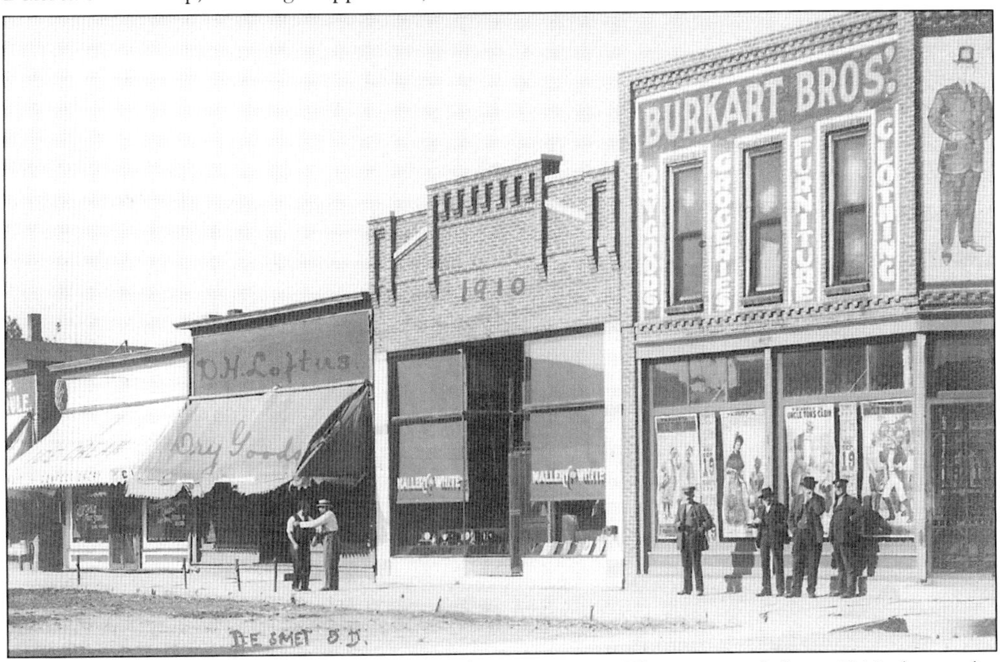

Merchants found a thriving livelihood in the new town. This postcard from 1910 shows the business places of Burkart Bros., Mallery and White Pharmacy, D.H. Loftus Dry Goods, Ice Cream and Confectionaries, and the Golden Rule. Notice the pineapple hanging over the awning of the ice cream store.

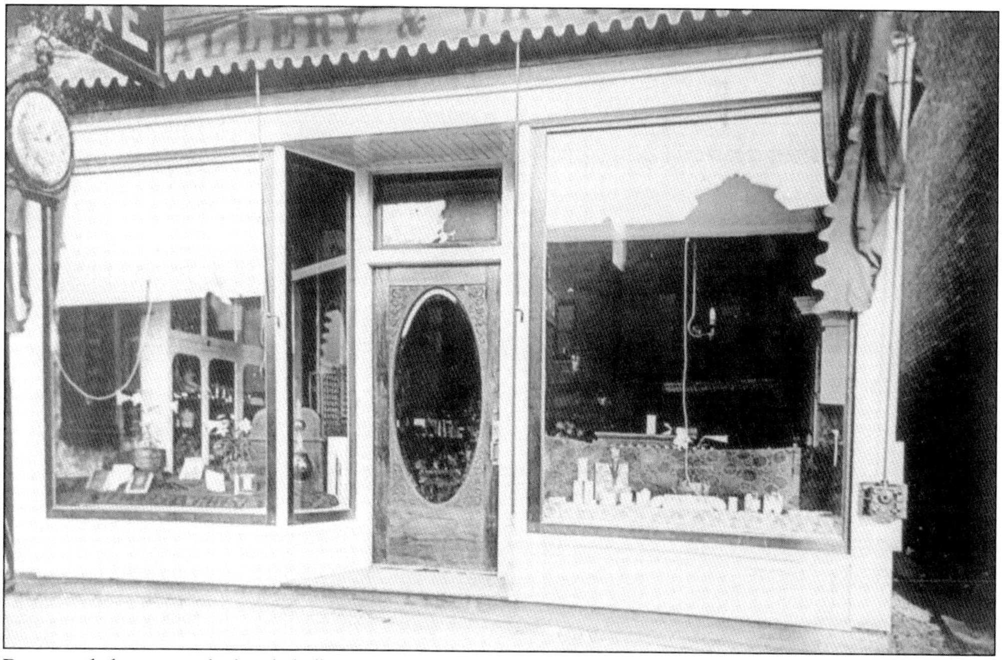

Recessed doorways helped deflect the cold of winter when they were opened, and Mallery and White Drug Store had a beautiful door with oval glass. Note the awning evidently installed after the 1910 postcard previously viewed. The mechanism to raise and lower the awning is at the right-hand side of the window. The hanging clock (left) is actually on a sign near the curb.

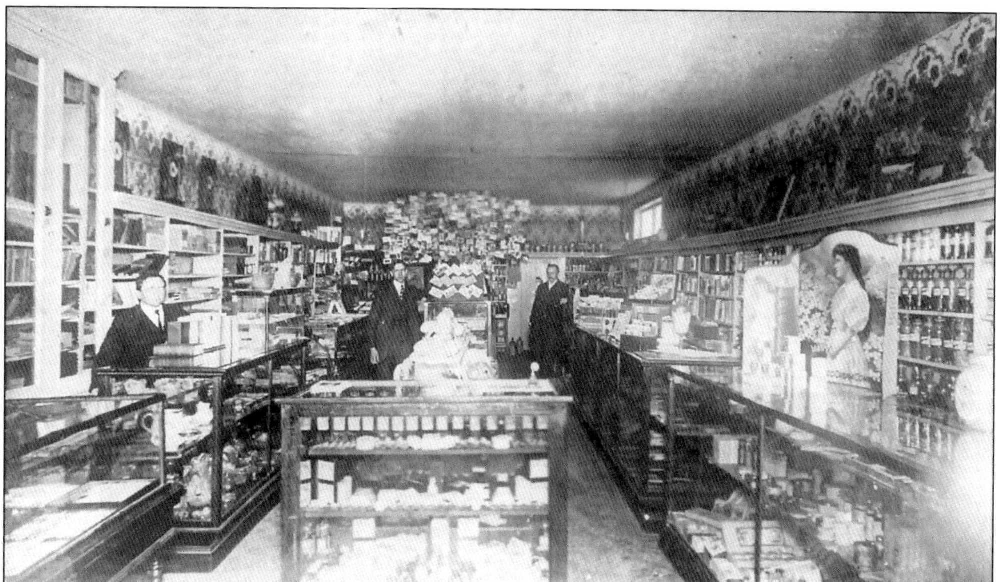

This is not just a simple pharmacy, but actually a magical place where every inch was put to good use. Around 1910, Mallery and White was located in the building most recall as the Super Valu Store, located on the west side of Calumet Avenue.

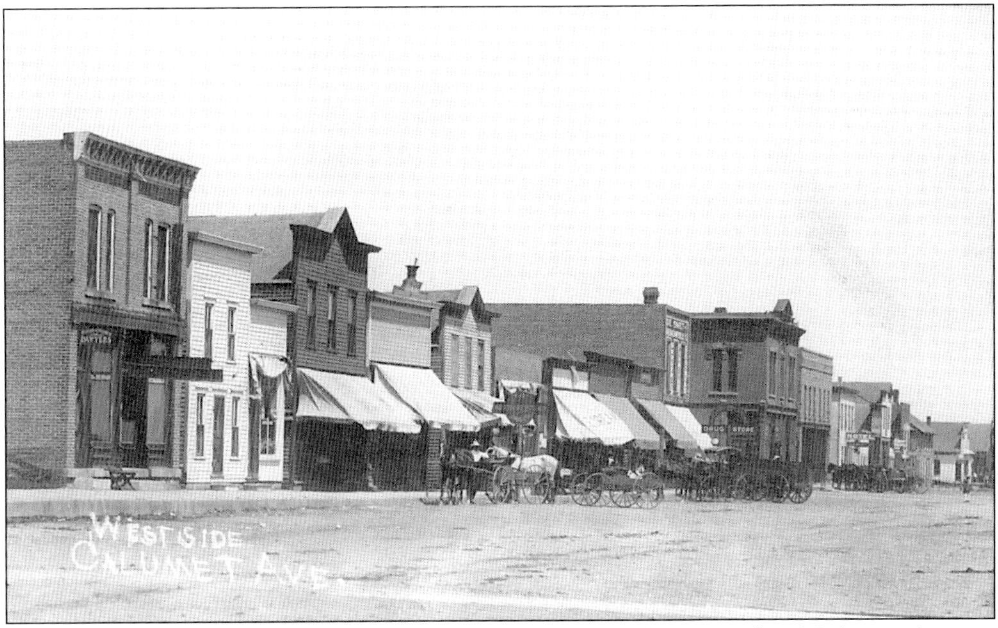

Note the businesses lining the second and third blocks on the west side of Calumet Avenue; included in this scene are law offices, the North Western Railroad office, Tinkham Furniture, Golden Rule, a confectionary, Loftus, Mallery and White, De Smet Mercantile, Miller Hardware, Floto Tavern, Spurgeon Hotel, and Meade Hotel.

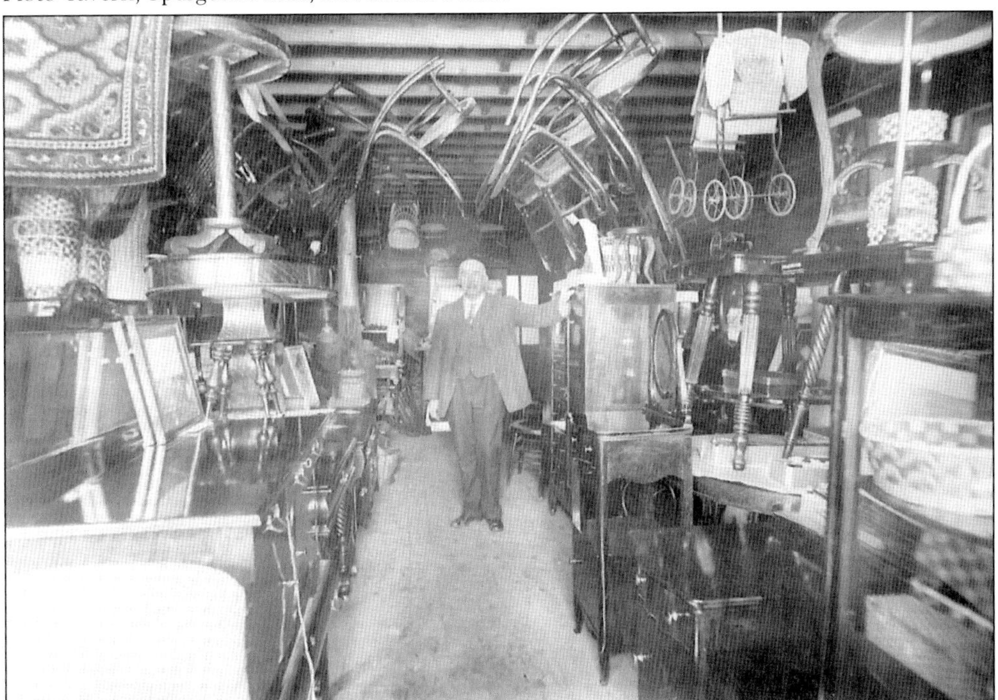

De Smet grew quickly, and C.H. (Charles) Tinkham was willing and ready to meet the demands for furniture. He stands in the aisle of his store, where it would appear as many items hang from the ceiling as sit on the floor.

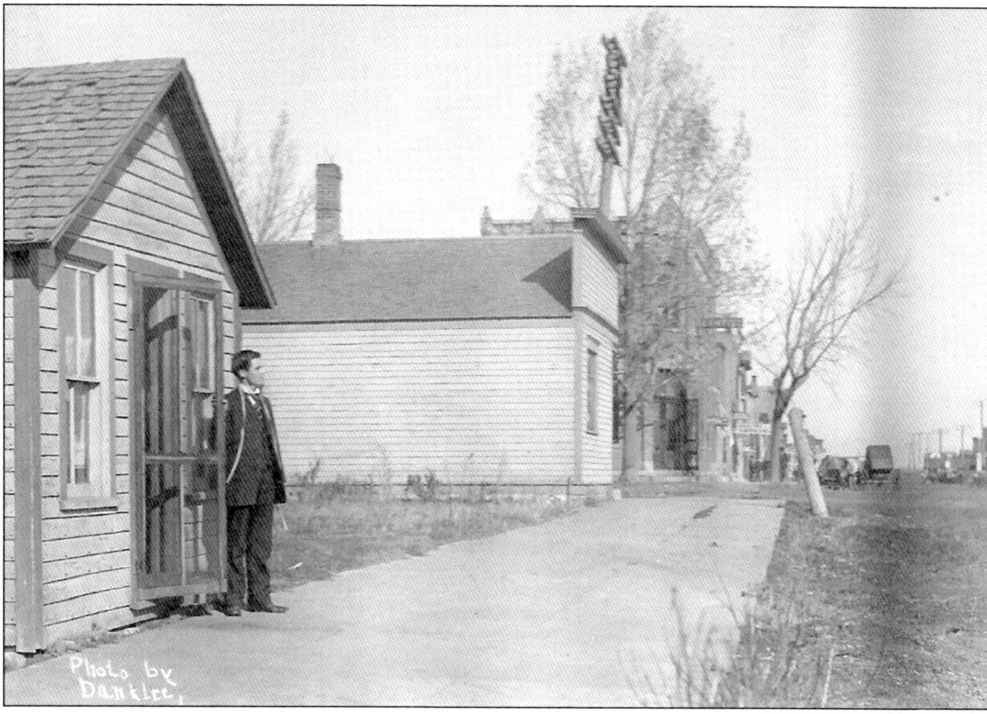

The era of the gentleman's tailor is today long gone in De Smet, but tailor Nelson stands here waiting for business. His trade is depicted by the tape measure hanging around his neck. Earlier, this was the home of Cooledge Photography. When the Jaycees razed the structure, they found tintypes from the shop. Located on the south end of Calumet Avenue on the west side, it was also the home of Alvin and Alice Klinkel for several years.

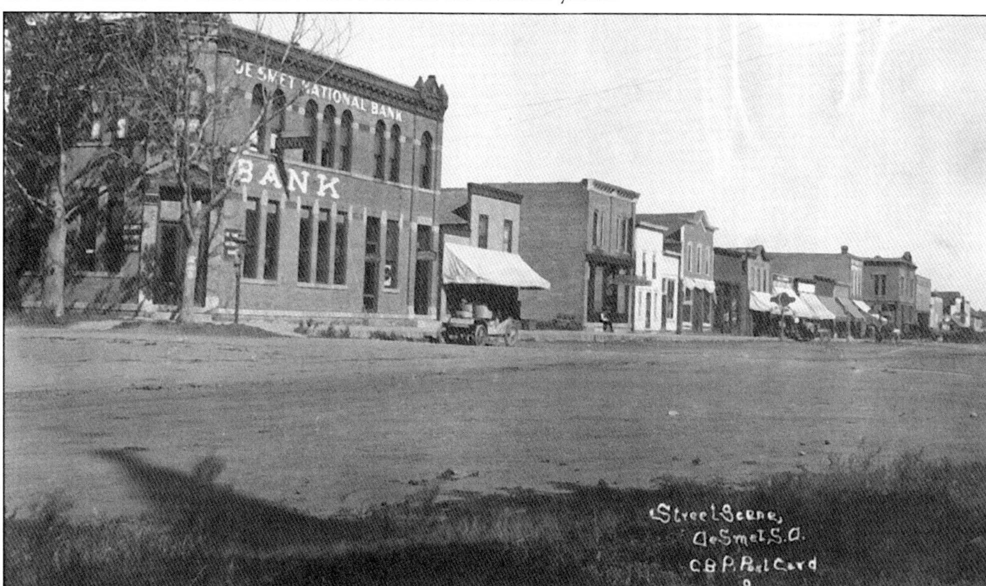

In the early 1900s, the De Smet National Bank (formerly Kingsbury County Bank) was located at the corner of Calumet Avenue and Third Street. The gaslight, standing on the corner, was lit in the evening hours.

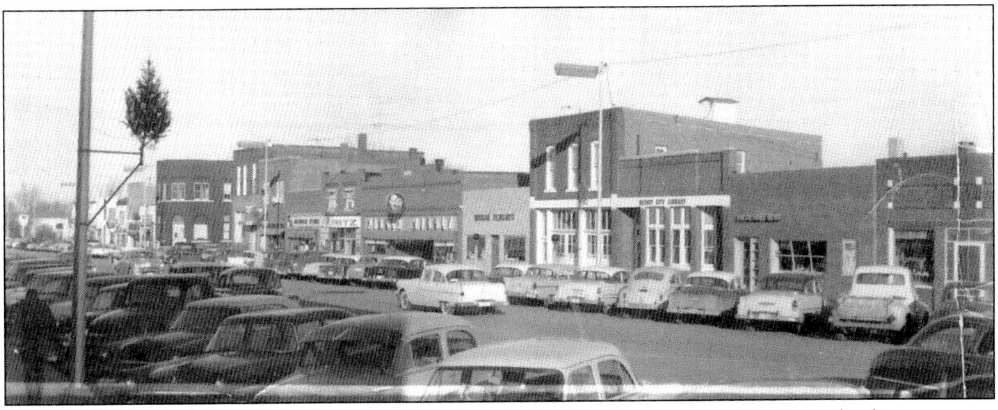

Piggly Wiggly was one of the first supermarket chains in the country. De Smet had its own, as shown in this picture of Calumet Avenue's east side. The De Smet Piggly Wiggly was short-lived, but there is no doubt from this picture that De Smet was a shopping hub. A Christmas tree on the lamppost may indicate a Christmas without snow that year.

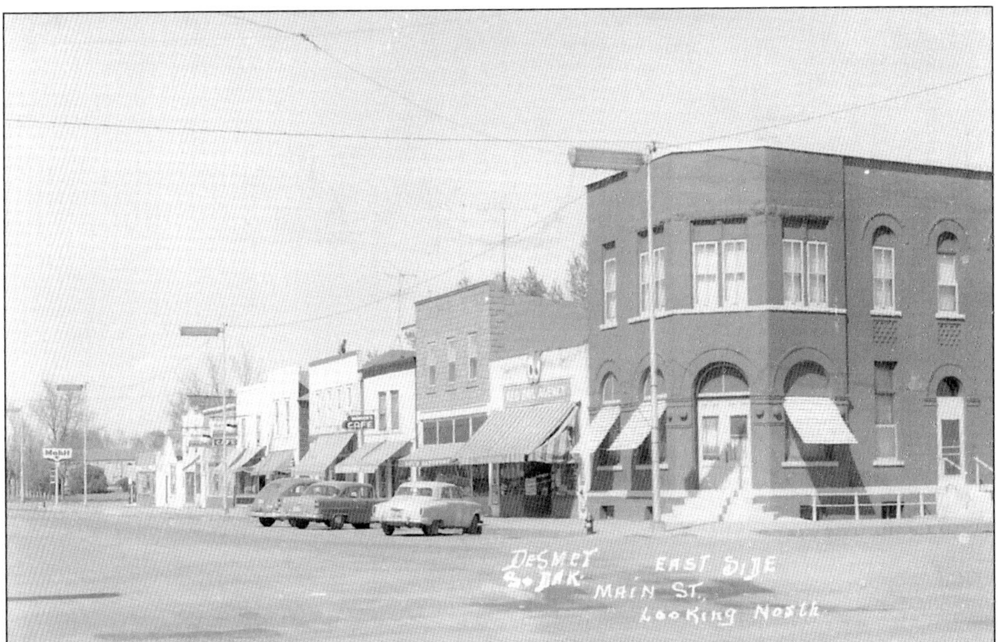

The "Friendly Red Owl" and Brick Coughlin invited people to shop at the Red Owl Agency on the east side of Calumet Avenue. De Smet folks could pick up their hatchery needs at Lou's Hatchery and have a cup of coffee with a piece of homemade pie at Howard Munger's Café.

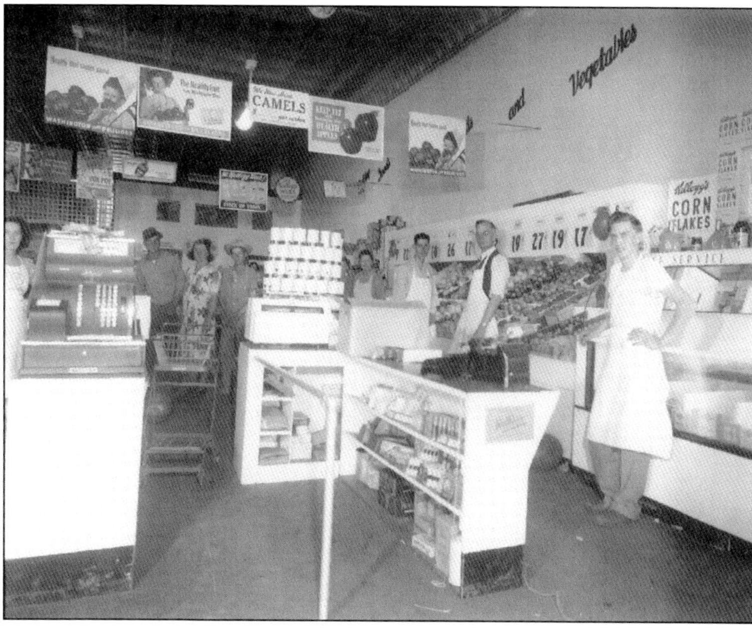

This c. 1940 photograph depicts the inside of the prosperous Super Valu store, owned by Henry Hinz. A shopper could lift the wire basket from the top of the cart and carry his or her groceries to the car. Don Wilkins is in the foreground. The other folks are unidentified.

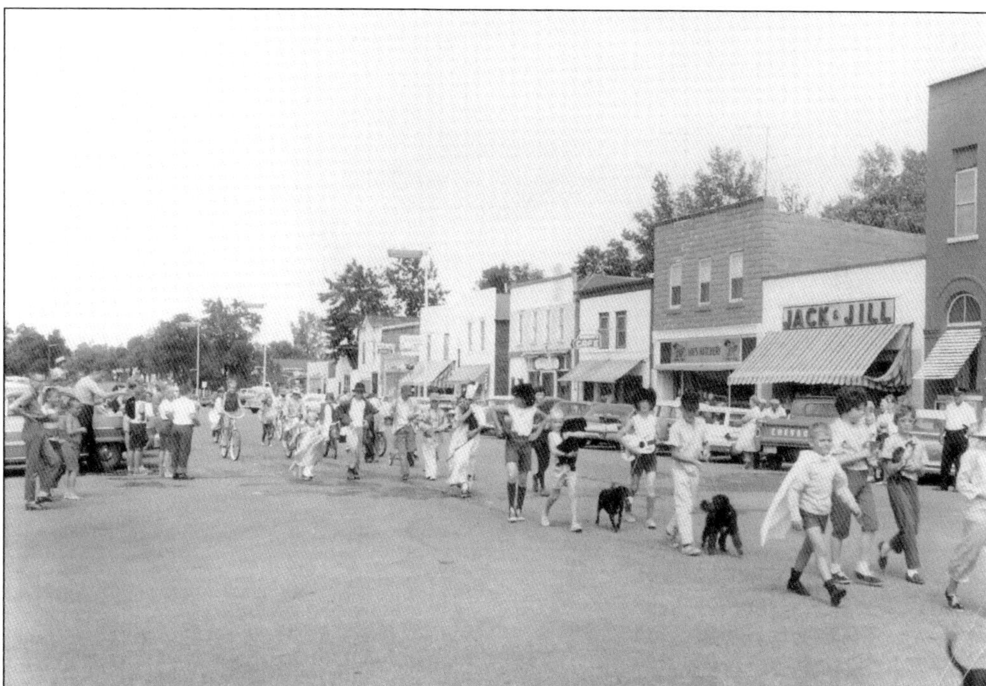

The Jack & Jill store sign has changed, but the building remains on the east side of Calumet Avenue. Along the street, from right to left, are Lou Wolkenhauer's Hatchery, Munger's Café, Connor's Café, a barbershop, Sy's Tavern, a bowling alley, a Laundromat, a dry cleaner, and Schoonover Sports. On the right, chief of police Laurel "Bill" Ritenhaur watches over a parade of children, pets, and bicycles. Gary (left), Connie (center), and Cathy Penney are at the front of the picture.

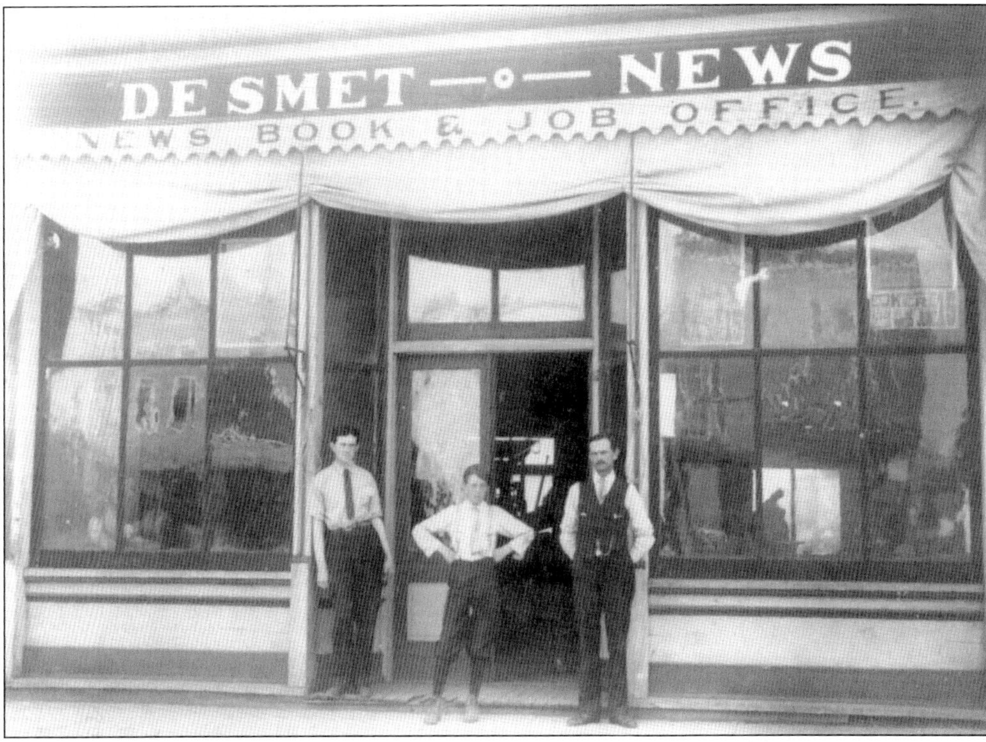

Kingsbury County's first newspaper, the *Kingsbury County News*, arrived here in 1880. The first owners were Jake Hopp and George A. Matthews. Other gentlemen and other newspapers evolved in De Smet, but at the turn of the century, Carter Sherwood formed the *De Smet News*. After 134 years, the paper operates under the auspices of Dale Blegen.

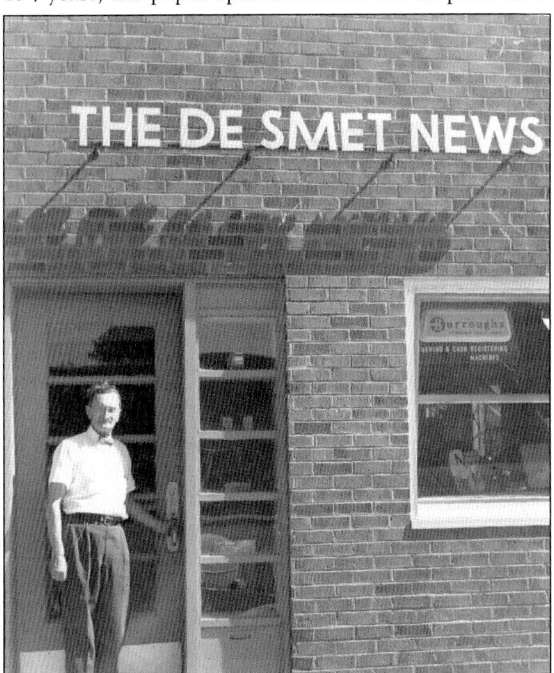

Many people touch lives, but Aubrey Sherwood touched the heart of De Smet with his newspaper and his friendships with author Laura Ingalls Wilder and painter and illustrator Harvey Dunn. He is seen here entering his place of business in the 1970s.

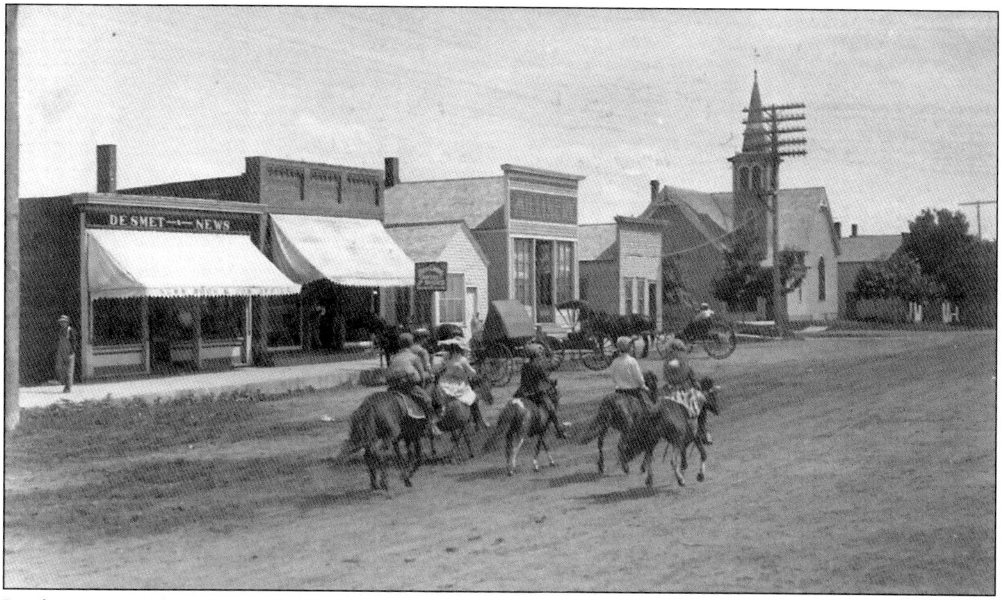

In this postcard, ponies are ridden down the middle of Calumet Avenue with the *De Smet News* office, the shoe store, a millinery establishment, telephone office, and the Evangelical church along the route.

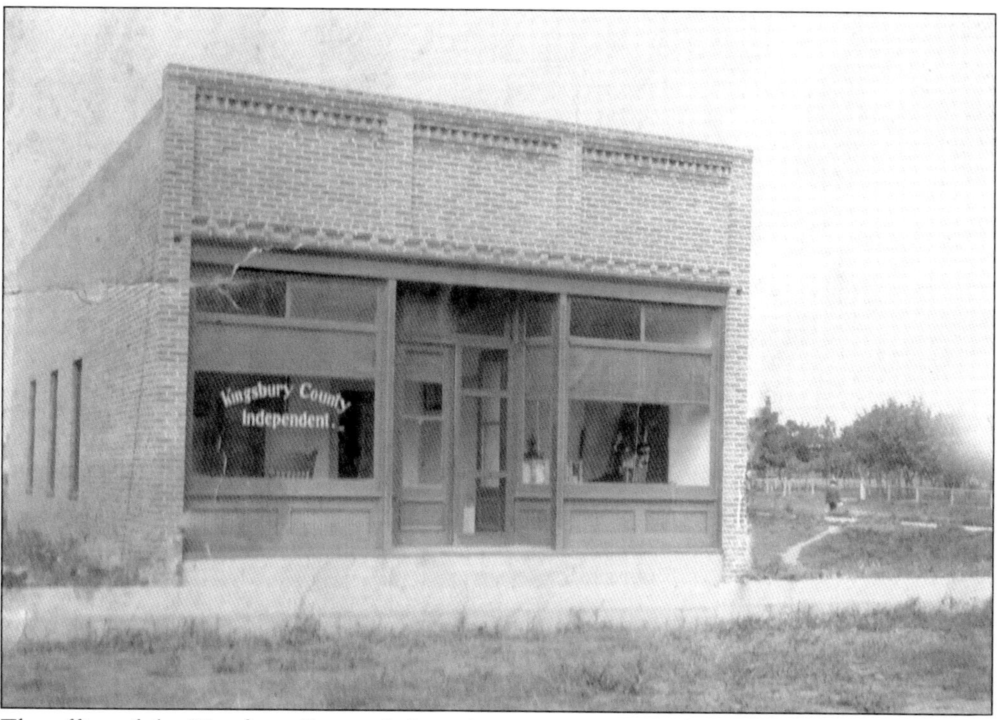

The office of the *Kingsbury County Independent* appears to stand pretty much by itself on the north side of Second Street. The *Kingsbury County Independent* was started by George Lattin in 1894. He sold out to Fred W. Wright (later a *De Smet News* employee) some years later, and Fred published the paper for 30 years. In later years, this building housed the Municipal Liquor store. On the right, an unidentified person can be seen walking toward the courthouse.

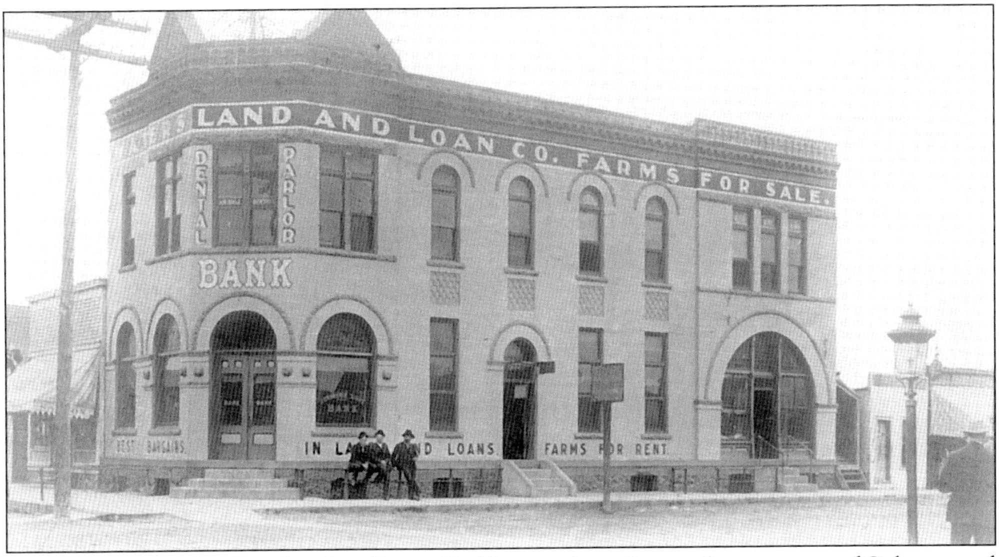

The much admired Waters Land and Loan Building anchors the northeast corner of Calumet and Second Street. Germania State Bank occupied a portion of the building, and customers could do business there by entering the double doors on the rounded front. A utility pole in front of Waters building and a gas streetlamp standing across the street indicate the changing times. An abstractor was also located in the building.

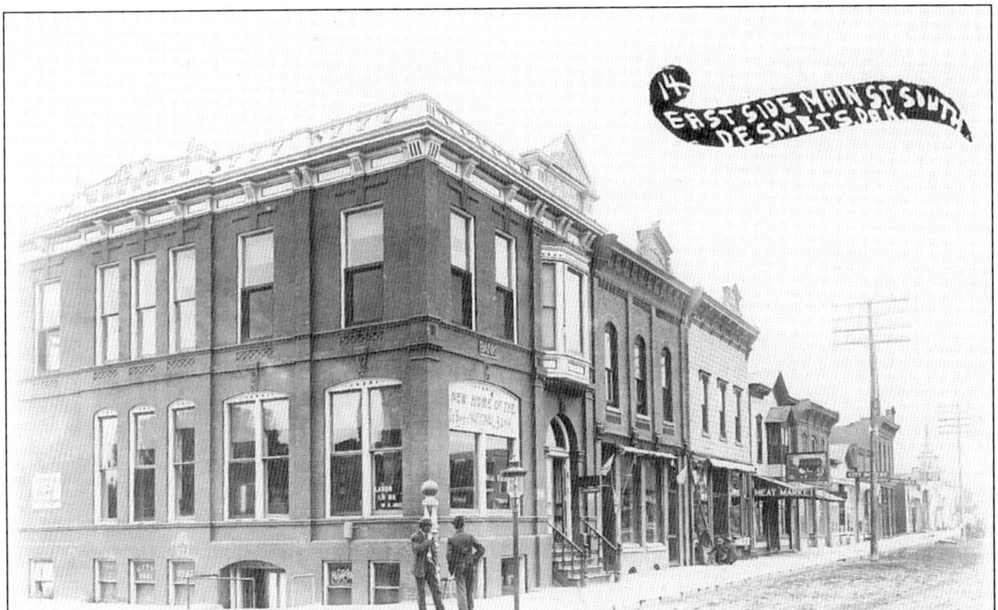

Anchoring the southeast corner of Calumet Avenue and Second Street is the "New Home of the De Smet National Bank." Over the years, it has lost some of its facade, but for all practical purposes, it looks the same today as it did over 100 years ago. The barber pole advertises the barbershop in the basement. The basement windows indicate that the City Dray office is located there also. For many years, it has been a law office for attorneys Green & Green and Gregg Gass.

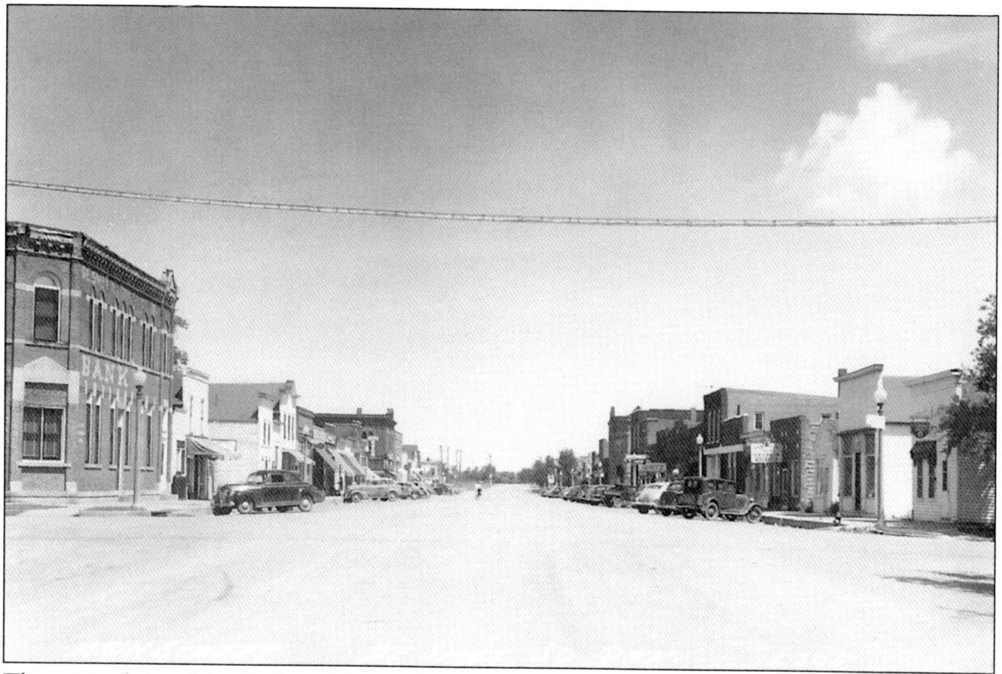

The original site of the De Smet National Bank was at the southwest corner of Calumet and Third Street. Noteworthy is the telephone office setting directly across the street on the east corner. Gas streetlamps have disappeared and electric streetlights and readily available fire hydrants reflect the prosperity of the growing town.

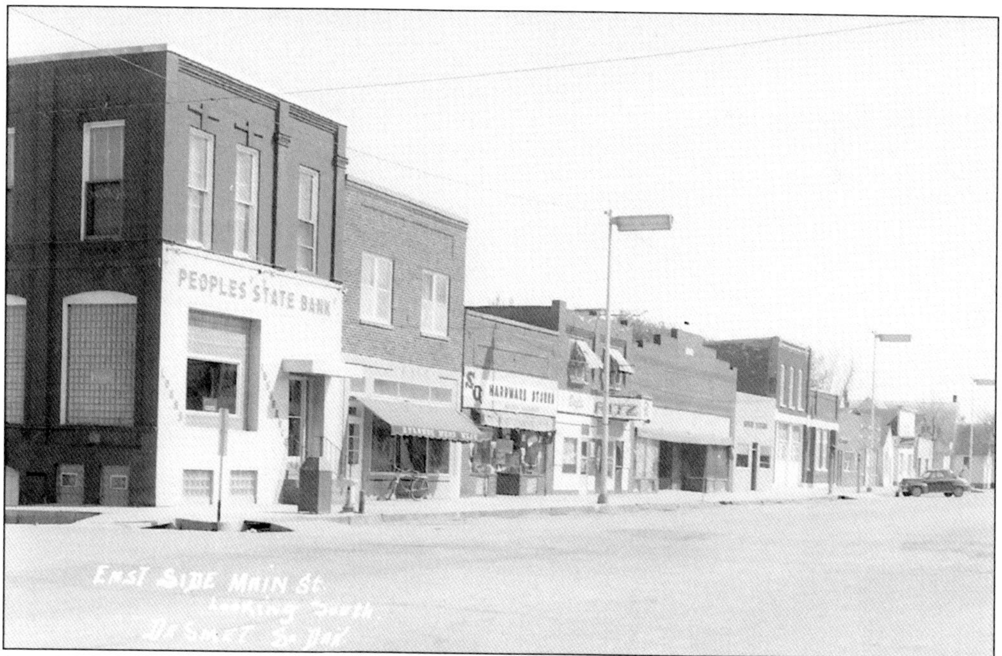

Peoples State Bank was on the move again. It withdrew from the former Waters Building and settled in the former National Bank building. As can be seen in this image, the metal-covered trash can helped with waste management. A water fountain was available for the public.

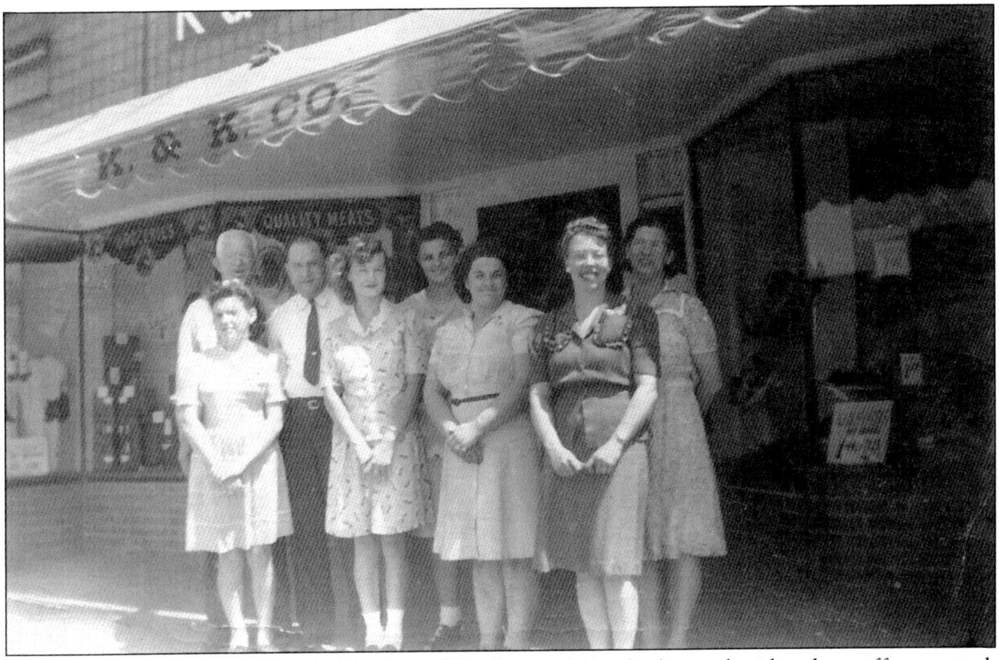

One-stop, no-frills shopping at K&K Store (Kutcher and Kutcher) was the idea the staff promoted. Standing in front of the store are, from left to right, (first row) Katie (Jacobs) Siver, Milt Fishgold, Florence "Sis" Burns, Katie (Renner) Jacobs, and Leona Brandt; (second row) Jack Luebs, Howard Schultz (hidden), Sina Woodbury, and Lottie McGarvie. This location on the east side of Calumet Avenue is now occupied by American Bank and Trust.

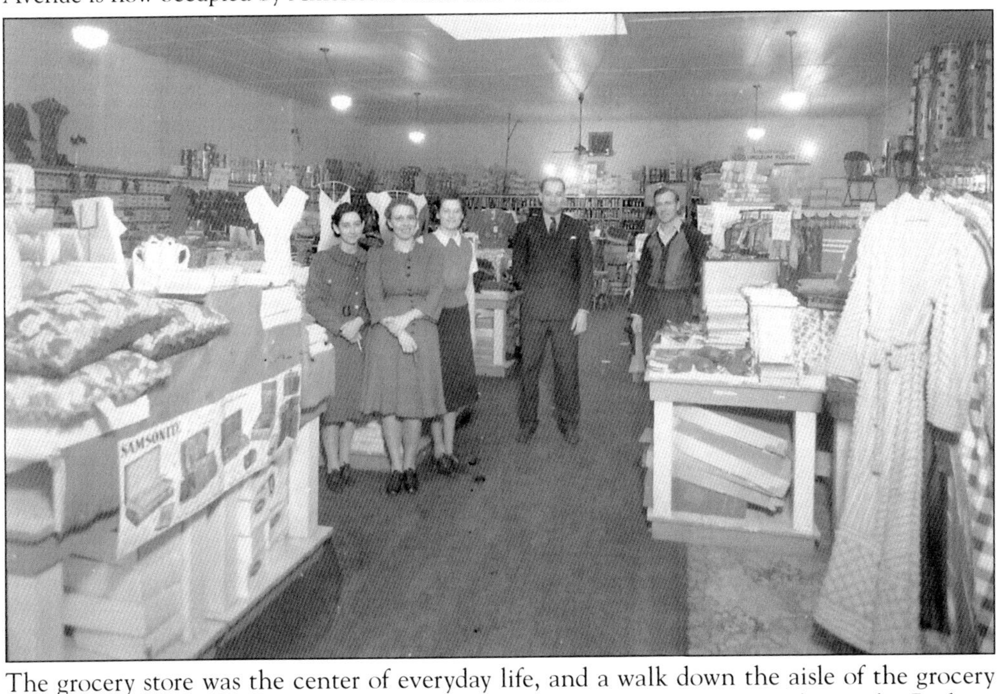

The grocery store was the center of everyday life, and a walk down the aisle of the grocery department in the K&K Store in 1940s could mean meeting, from left to right, Madge Rodney, Leona Brandt, Beulah Lindsey, manager Milt Fishgold, and Howard Schultz.

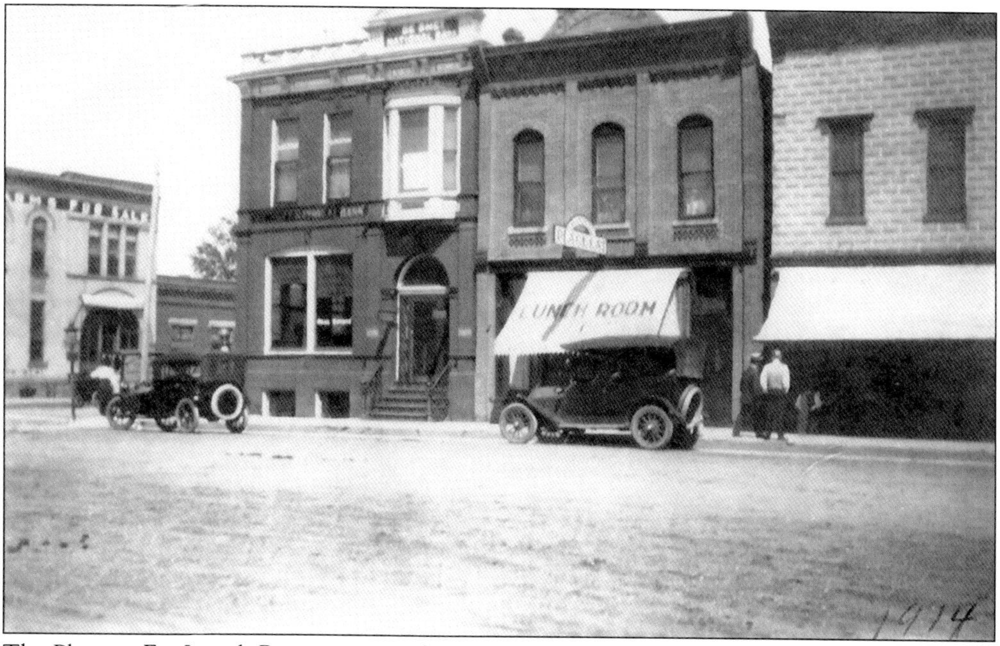

The Place to Eat Lunch Room was in a long-established building for many cafés, such as Burns Café and Gordon's Café, to name two. Lace curtains in the upstairs windows indicate that these are living quarters for the owner of the Lunch Room.

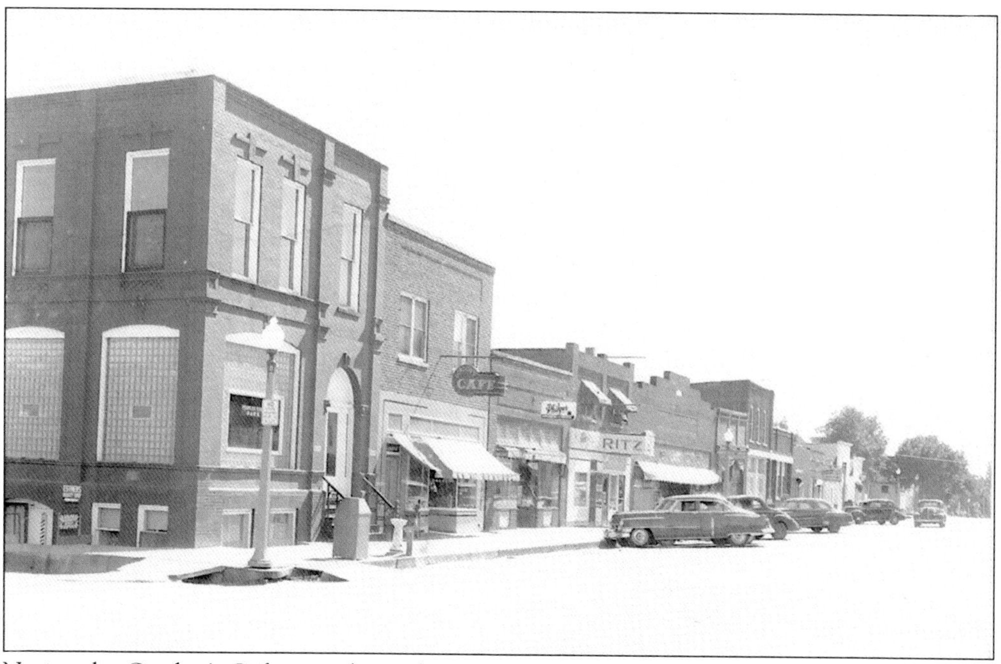

Notice the Gordon's Café sign above the awning of the second building. A heaping plate of shoestrings and a bottle of Coke cost 35¢ in the 1950s.

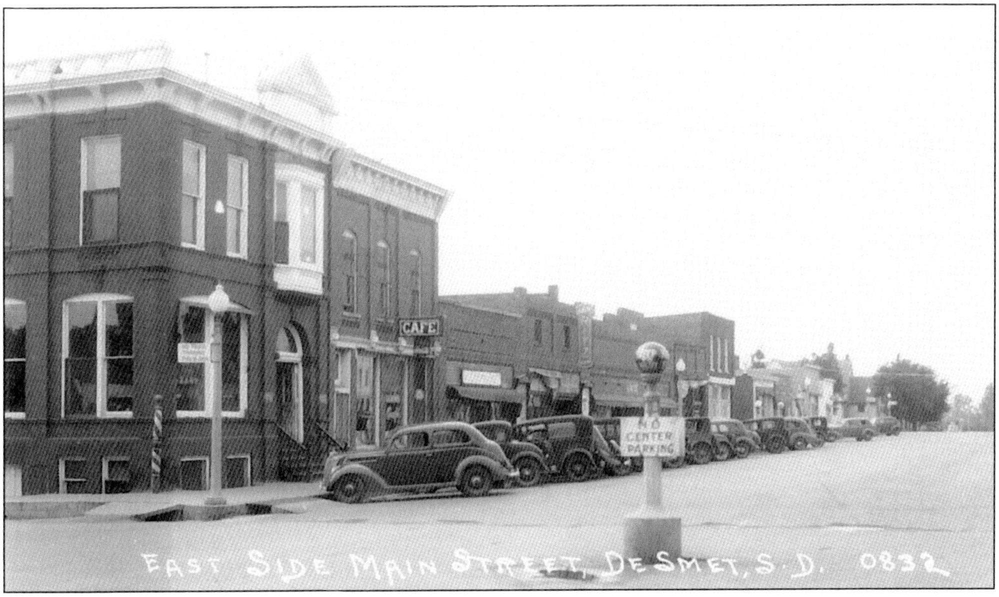

People definitely heeded the "No Center Parking" sign that stands in the intersection of Calumet Avenue and Second Street. Burns Café occupies the second building from the left in this picture, and Vick's Market is to its right. All the cars parked at the curb are reminiscent of a Saturday night's lineup.

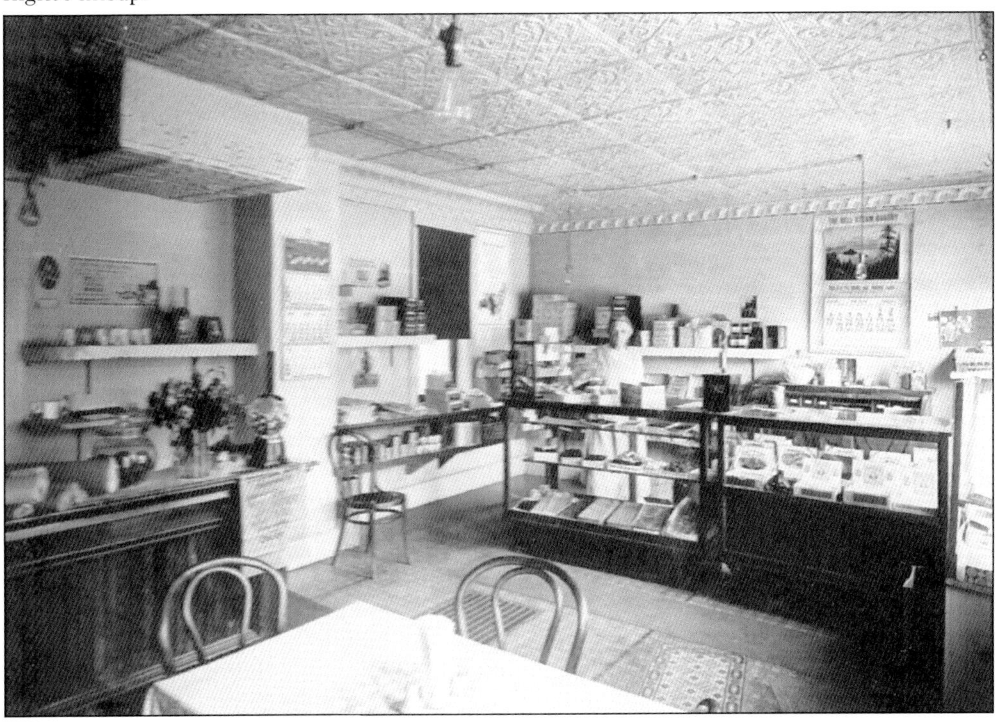

Carrie Ely stands behind her candy counter on a day in May. The round-bottom, bentwood chairs would seat customers having a meal or refreshments at her café in 1925. Future cafés in this location included those of Howard and Florence Munger (moving from the Ritz location to the south) and Lorane Washburn.

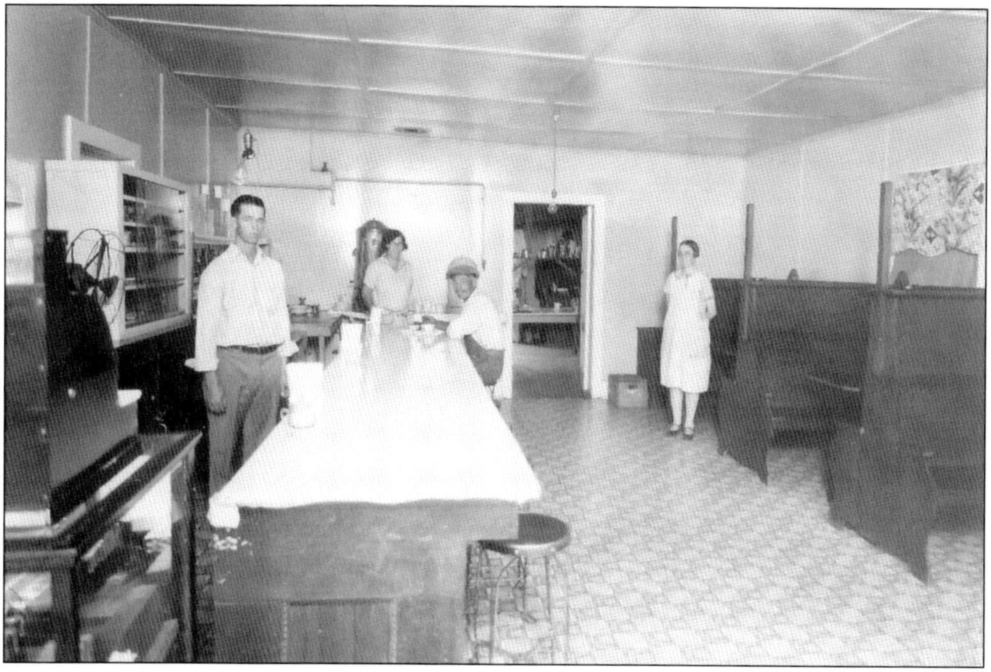

A Cavanaugh man is standing behind the counter of the Cavanaugh Café in this c. 1930 photograph. An unidentified lady stands at the end of the counter. Ed May occupies the counter stool, and Opal Liggett (later Mrs. Ed May) is shown by the booth.

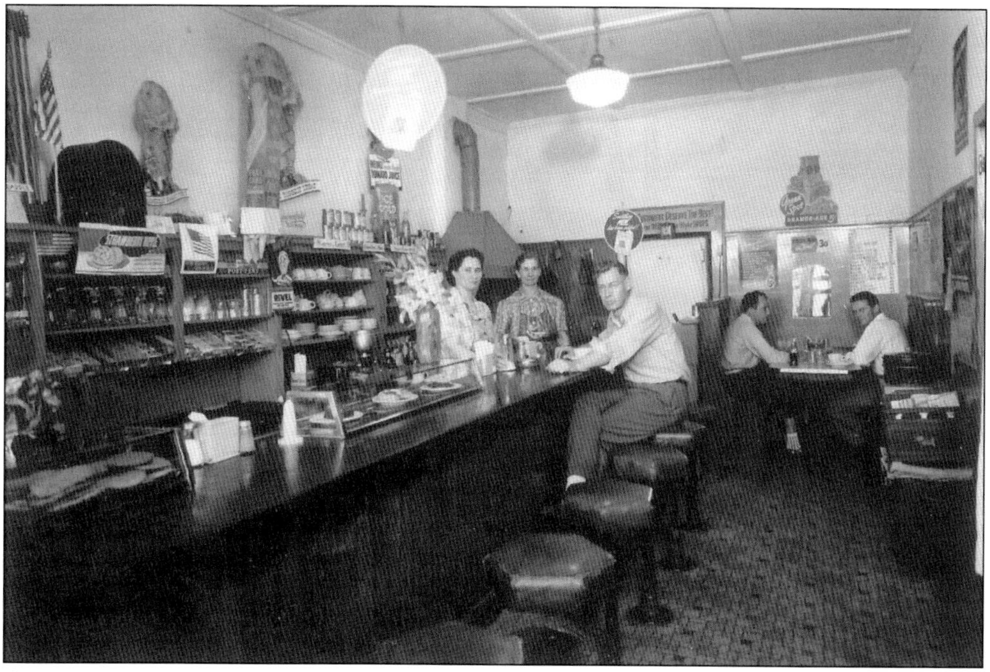

Once upon a time, Howard and Florence Munger operated the Ritz Café. In this 1942 image, Florence (left) stands behind the counter with Nora Luebs (right); Howard sits on the counter stool. An unidentified man is sitting in the booth with Harlan Seeley (far right), owner of the Ritz Theater just next door.

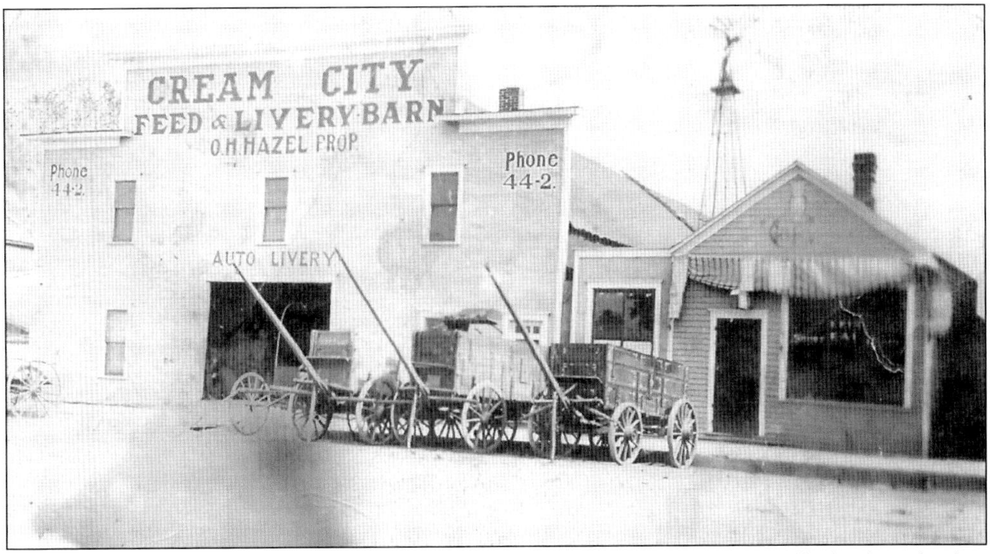

Early on, De Smet was widely known as "Cream City." Here, O.H. Hazel proudly displays the fact on his Cream City Feed and Livery Barn.

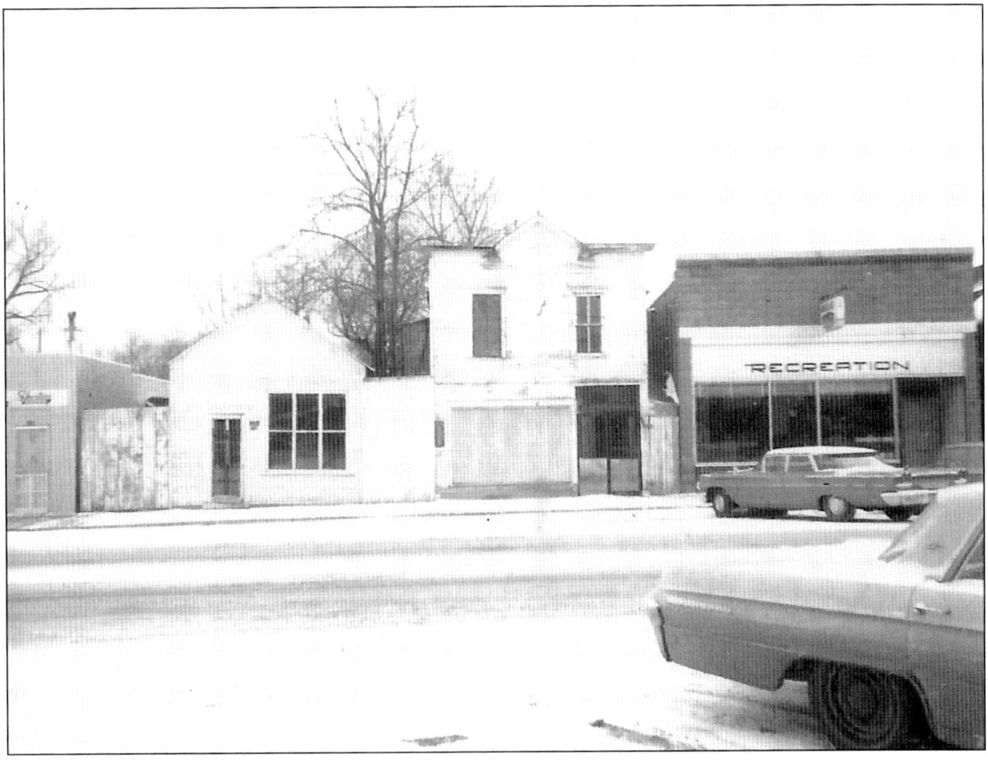

The small building with six windows and the tall building at center date back to at least 1883. Before they were razed, the small building was the De Smet Dry Cleaners, and then Dakota Arts and Countryview Catering. The tall building was Frank Schaub Harness and became NAPA, a Laundromat, and Wheaties. The "Recreation" building was owned and operated by various business owners—Cummins, Wehrkamp, Russ Schultz, Hilbert Schardin, and Mervin Schultz. Many will remember it as a bowling alley.

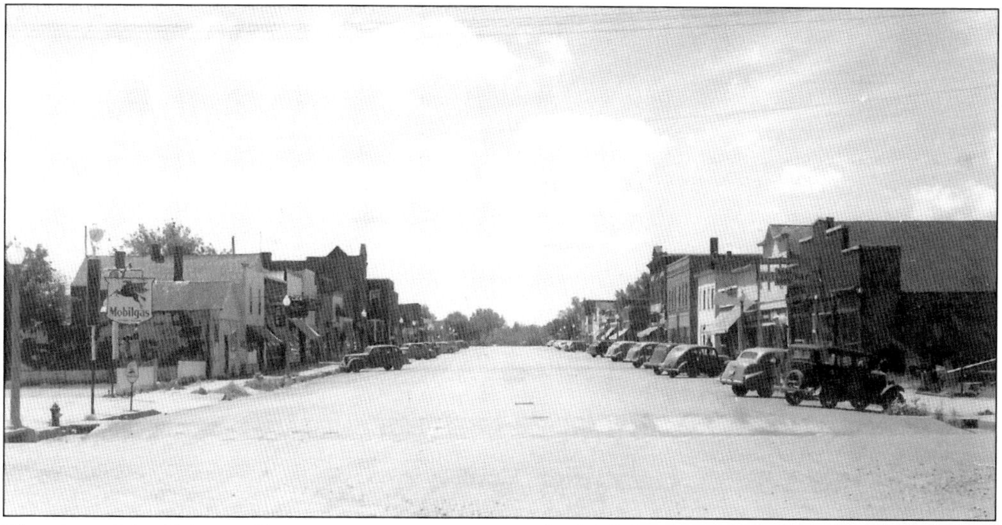

The sign of the flying red horse entices customers to the Mobilgas station that stood on the corner of Calumet Avenue and First Street. A couple of former Mobilgas men that come to mind are Glen Van Tassel and Roy Brusse.

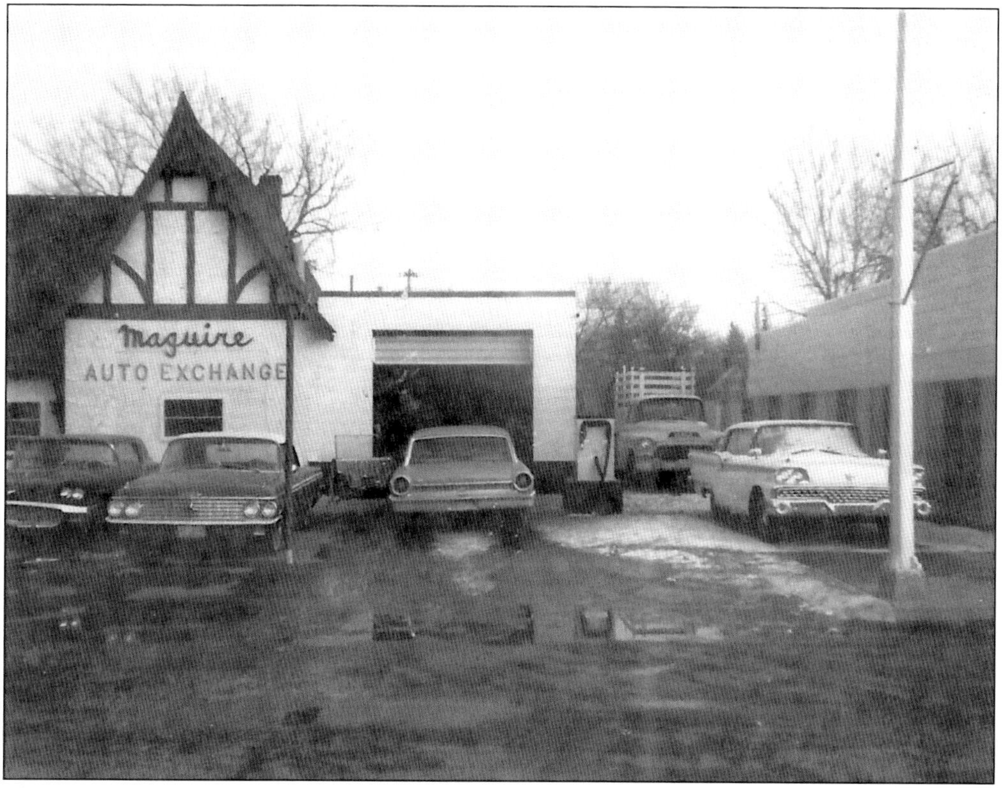

This quaint little building, which once housed the Mobilgas station, became Maguire's Auto Exchange, owned and operated by Bill Maguire. In later years, the site was home to several banks, including Farmers and Merchants, First Federal, Marquette, and Wells Fargo. Schoonover's Sport Shop is on the right; it was owned and operated by Ollie and Pauline Schoonover. Through the years, it was the Senior Citizen Center and Lynne's Lens photography shop.

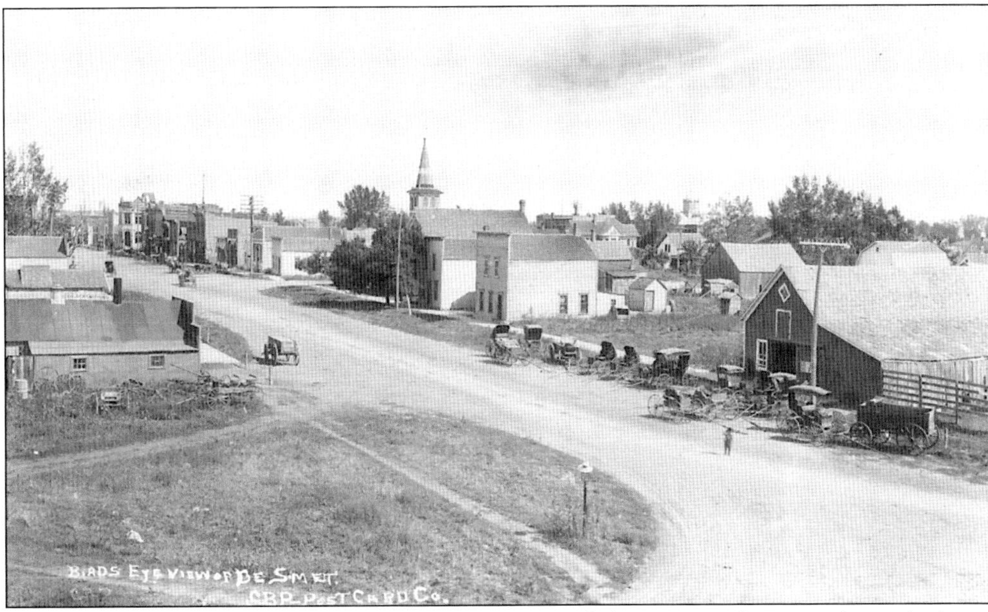

This timeless view of De Smet's main street, looking north from US Highway 14, shows the livery barn (mentioned in Wilder's book), a residence, the Evangelical church, telephone office, and the home of the *De Smet News* on the right; on the left is the blacksmithing shop, as the top of the sign reads. Gas streetlights and hitching posts are evident on the left, while the right side sports electrical poles.

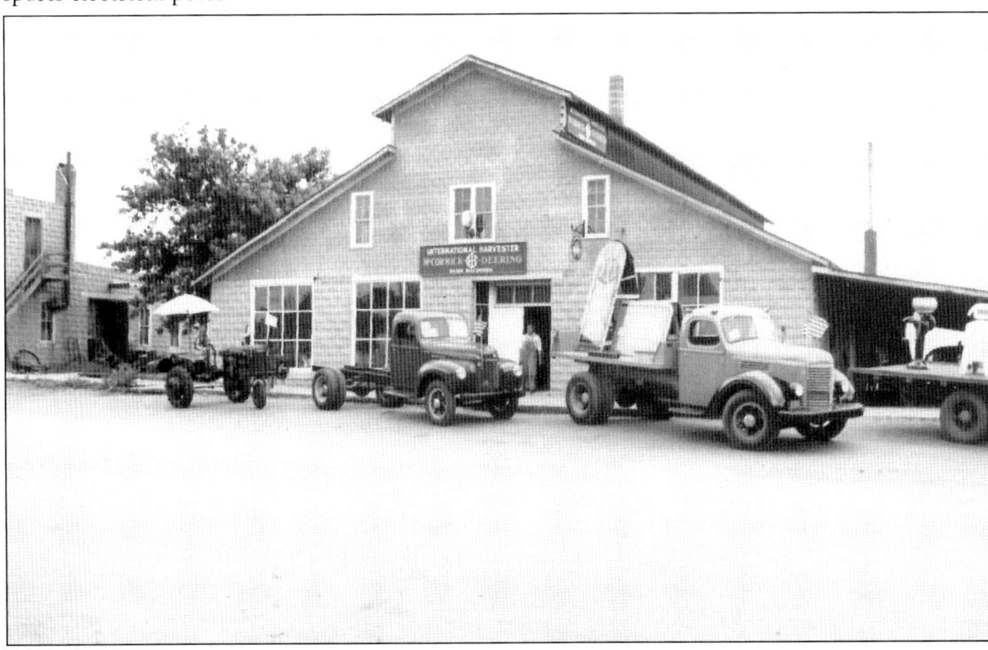

Rekindling the memory of the original O'Keefe Implement, this 1940s structure fronts a sign advertising "International Harvester McCormick-Deering" farm equipment. The way the trucks are lined up and with the cream separator and washing machine on the truck bed, it would be a good bet that folks are getting ready for the June 10 parade. Ernie Johnson's blacksmith shop can be seen just to the left.

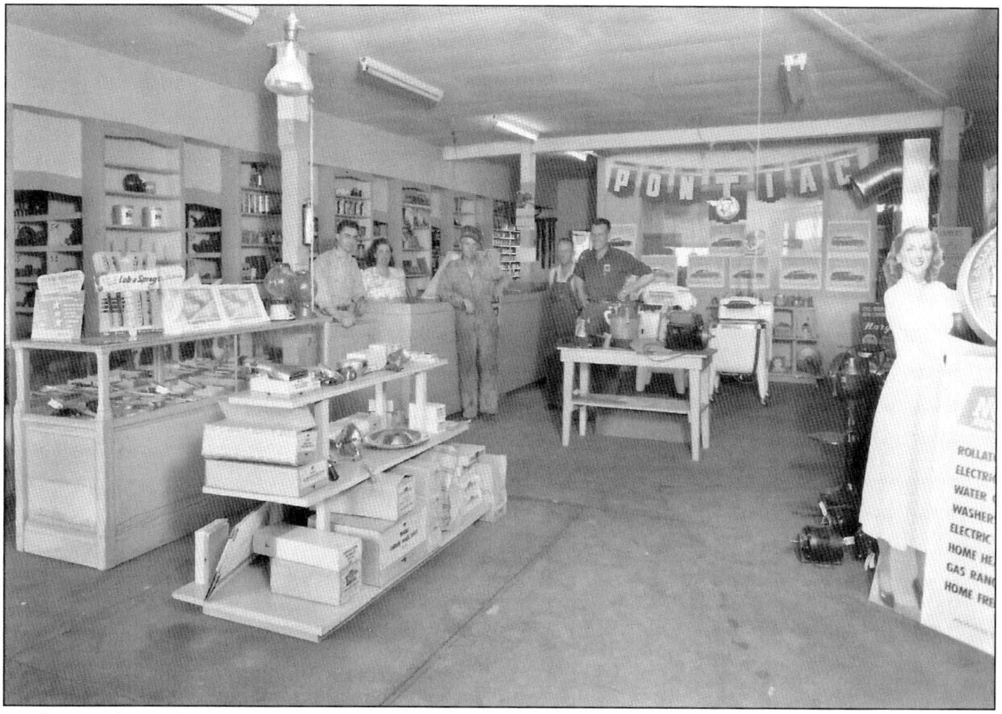

In this peek inside O'Keefe Implement, around the 1940s, the people include, from left to right, Thad O'Keefe, unidentified, Darcy Melstad, unidentified, and Gerald "Bud" Erickson.

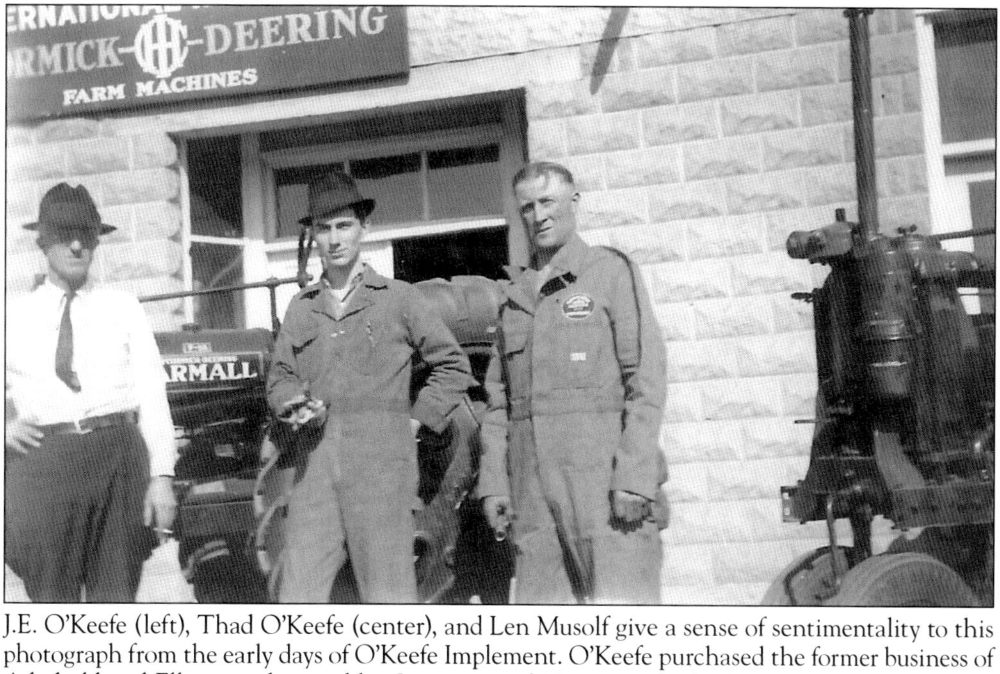

J.E. O'Keefe (left), Thad O'Keefe (center), and Len Musolf give a sense of sentimentality to this photograph from the early days of O'Keefe Implement. O'Keefe purchased the former business of Aderhold and Ellison and moved his International Harvester dealership from Yale to De Smet in 1938.

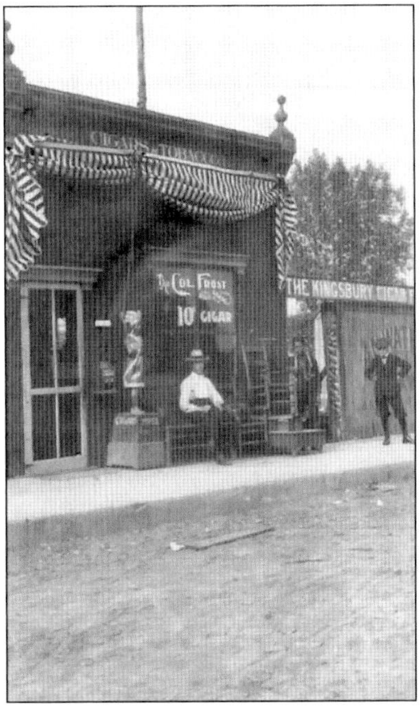

Kingsbury Cigar Factory was owned and operated by N.E. "Tack" Tackaberry. An unidentified gentleman sits in front of the store, perhaps waiting for a shoeshine. A.N. Waters owned the property to the right. It is believed that Tack's business sat on the south side of Second Street.

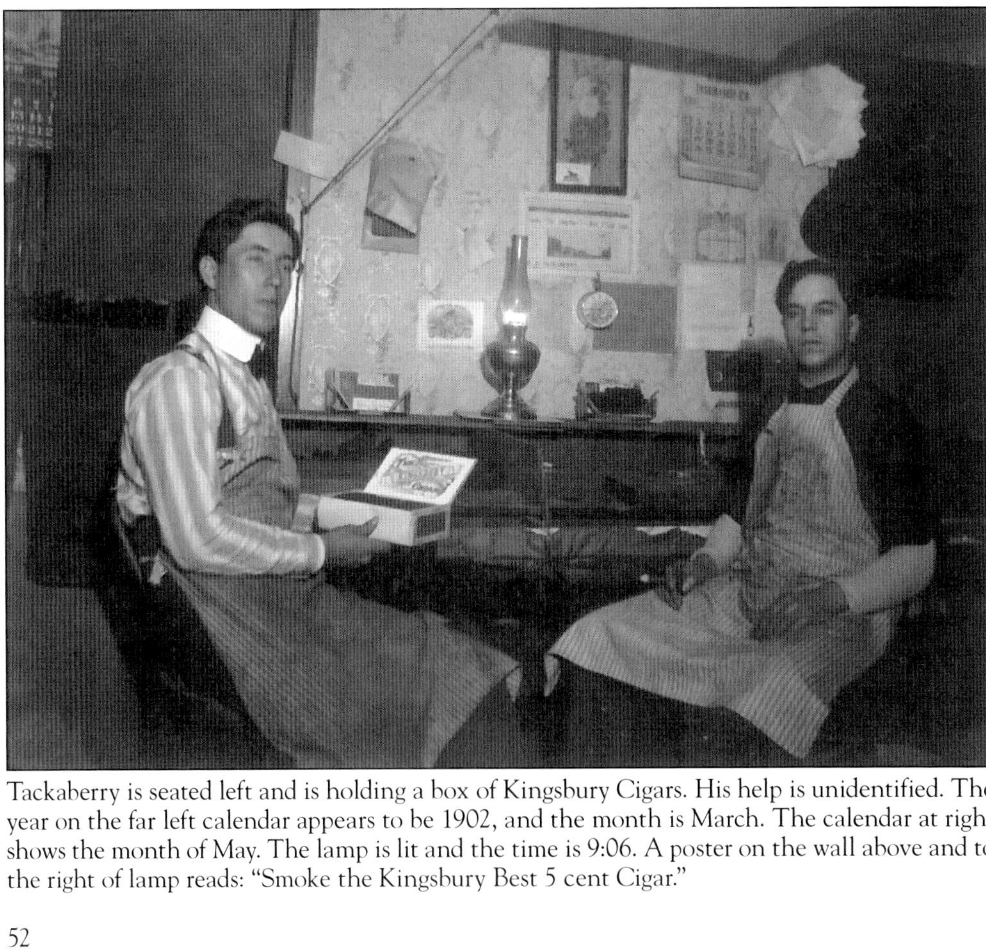

Tackaberry is seated left and is holding a box of Kingsbury Cigars. His help is unidentified. The year on the far left calendar appears to be 1902, and the month is March. The calendar at right shows the month of May. The lamp is lit and the time is 9:06. A poster on the wall above and to the right of lamp reads: "Smoke the Kingsbury Best 5 cent Cigar."

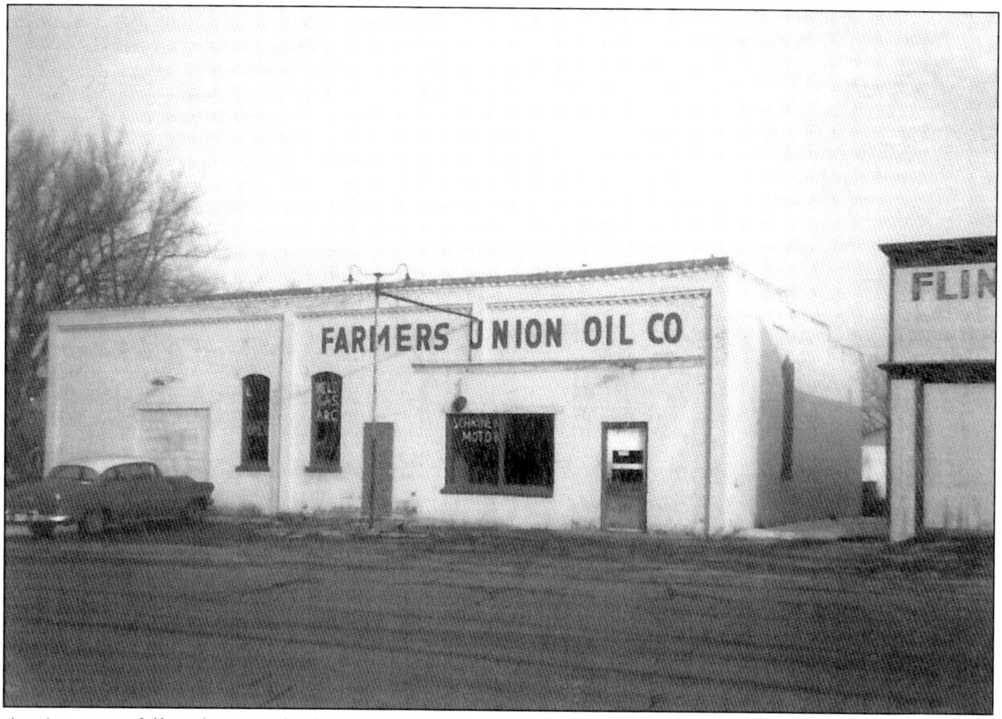

As America fell in love with the automobile, gas stations and repair shops sprang up like weeds. Farmers Union Oil Co., seen here in 1940, and Flindt's Garage became an active part of De Smet. These buildings were located on South Dakota Highway 25, on the left-hand side when coming from the north. FU Oil moved to the corner of Second Street and South Dakota Highway 25 in 1964; the Flindt's building was moved to the south of De Smet.

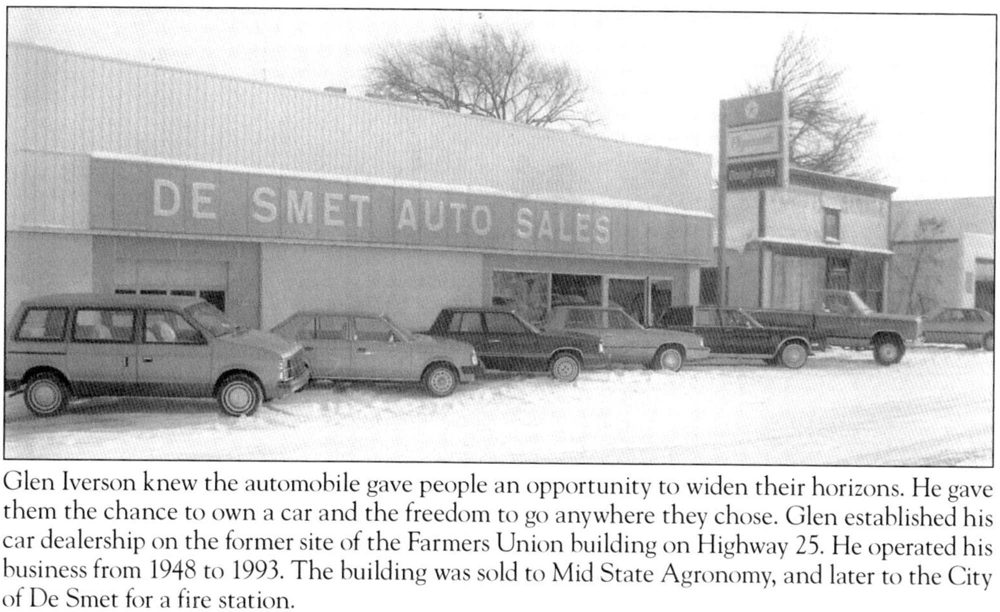

Glen Iverson knew the automobile gave people an opportunity to widen their horizons. He gave them the chance to own a car and the freedom to go anywhere they chose. Glen established his car dealership on the former site of the Farmers Union building on Highway 25. He operated his business from 1948 to 1993. The building was sold to Mid State Agronomy, and later to the City of De Smet for a fire station.

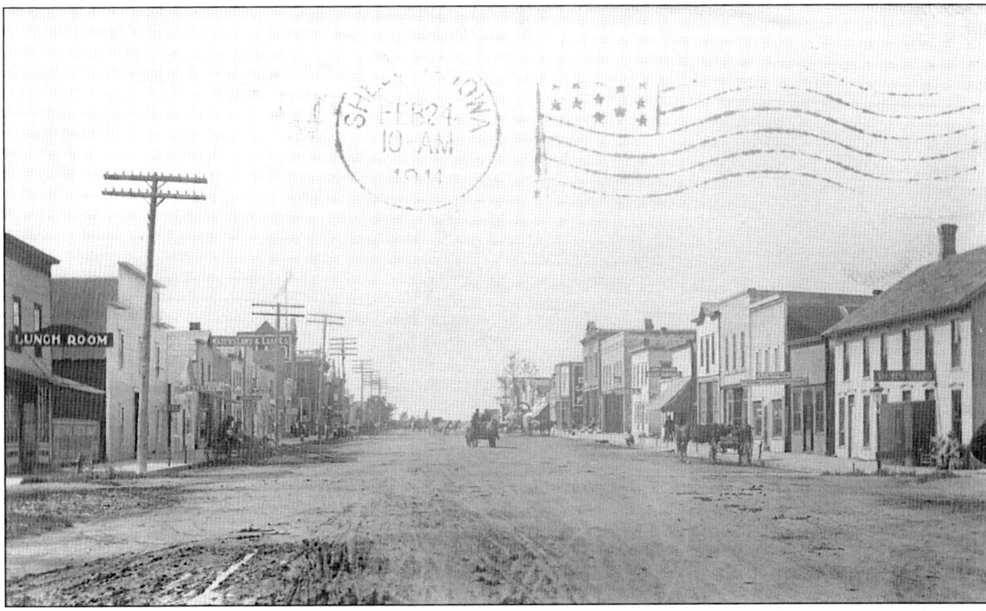

Rooms with a view—a view of Calumet Avenue, that is—could be rented at the New Grand Hotel, standing at the northwest corner of Calumet Avenue. Many know this hotel as the Meade, written about in Wilder's book *The Long Winter*. It was also at one time known as the Exchange.

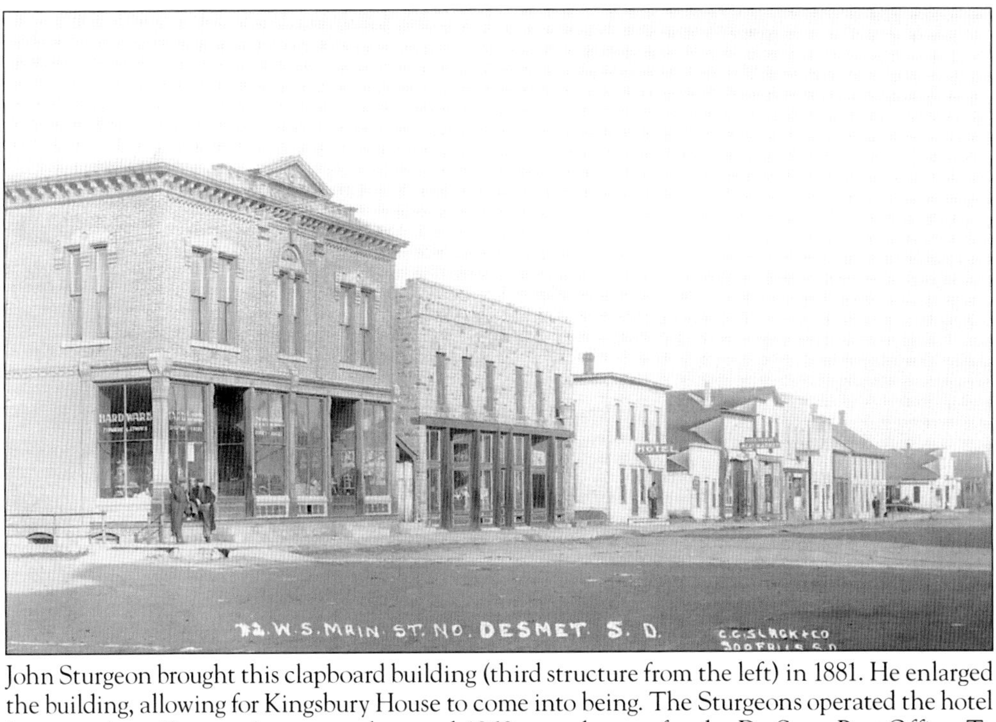

John Sturgeon brought this clapboard building (third structure from the left) in 1881. He enlarged the building, allowing for Kingsbury House to come into being. The Sturgeons operated the hotel for more than 50 years. It was razed around 1960 to make way for the De Smet Post Office. To its right is "Home of the De Smet DeLuxe Butter," the Farmers Creamery, established in 1928. Rigid sanitary laws forced the creamery to close in 1971.

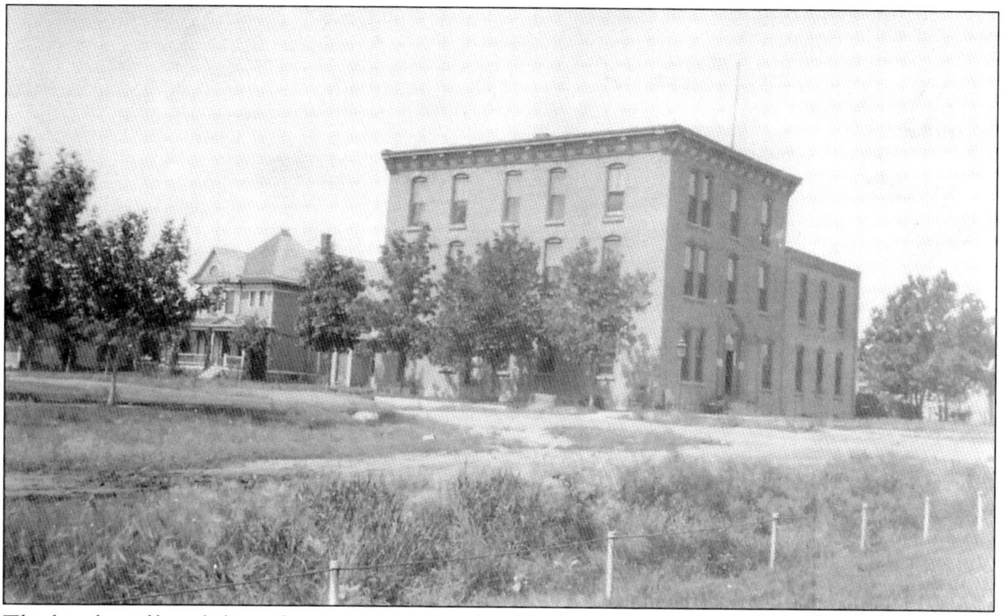

The heyday of hotels brought many guests to the Syndicate Hotel, located on the corner of Joliet Avenue and Second Street. The rear portion of the building was at one time the Garland House. Among early proprietors were Charles Ely, Pete Randklev, and the Moon family. The building was razed in 1991.

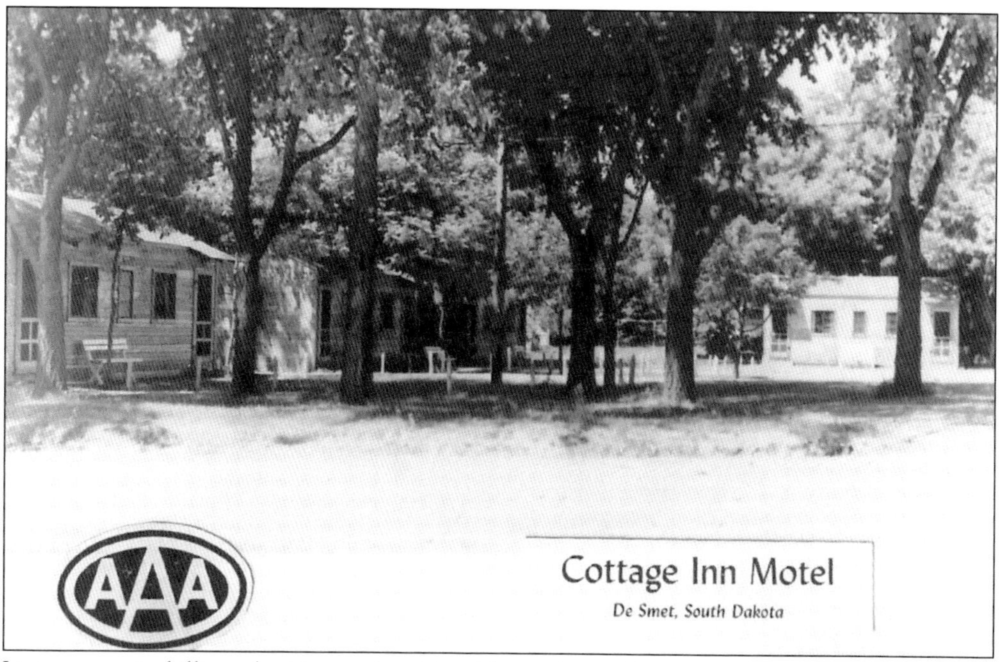

Living up to its billing, the Cottage Inn Motel has welcomed many guests, such as Laura Ingalls Wilder enthusiasts, vacationers, hunters, and fishermen. Established by A.J. Ryland, it has been family-owned and operated by the Myers family.

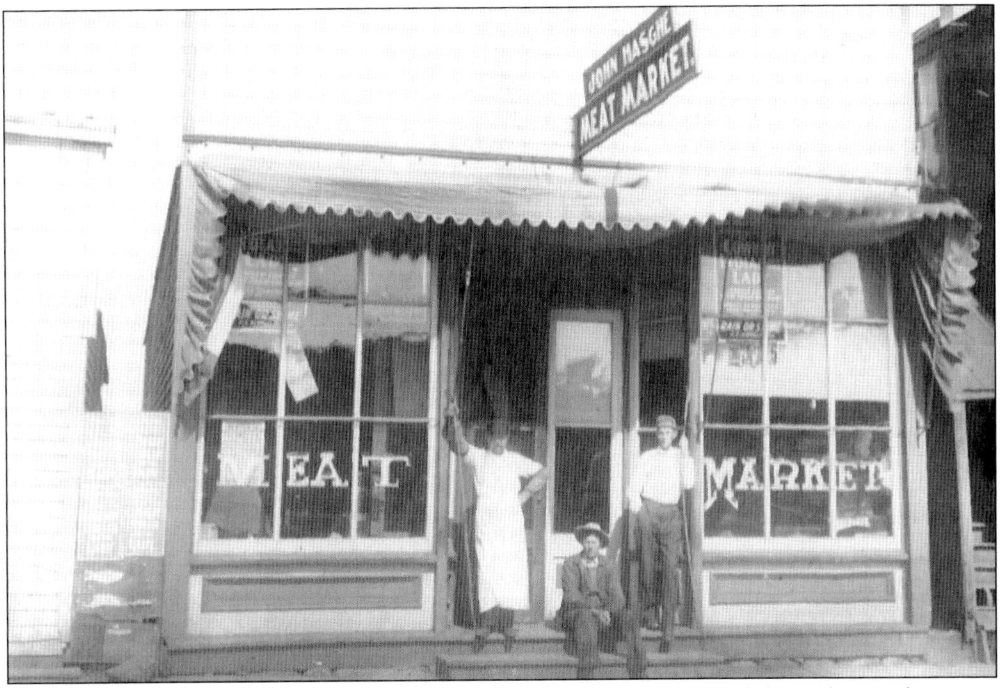

This image must have been taken in early summer, as the poster in bottom left window is advertising Old Settlers Day. John Hasche, left, is standing in front of his Meat Market in a pristine white apron. The gentleman on the left is unidentified.

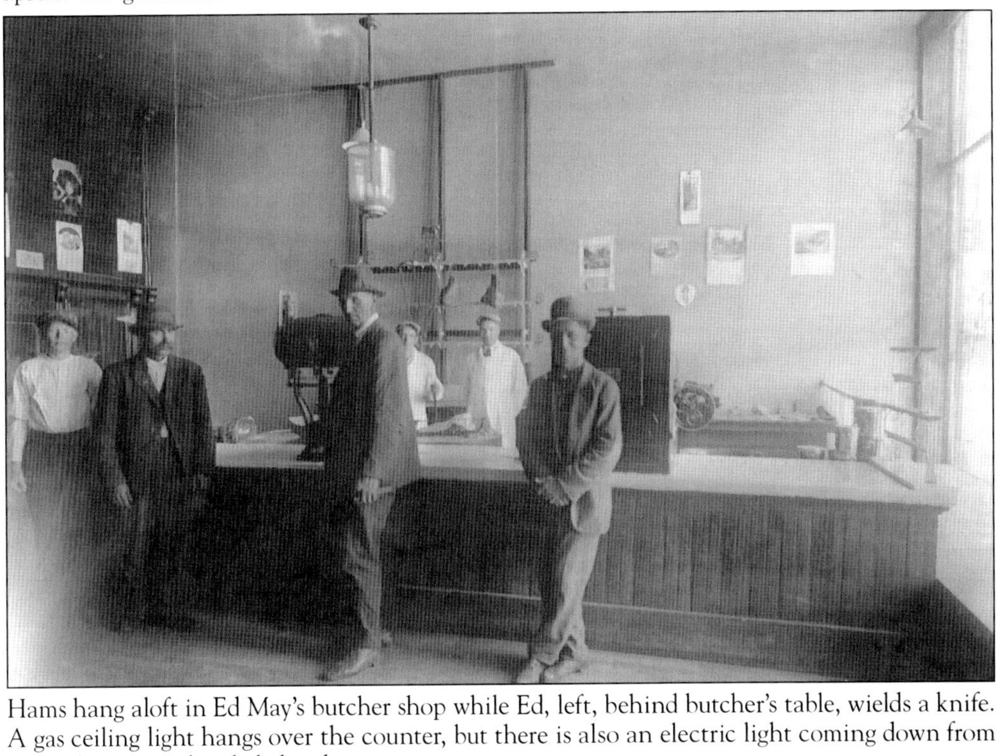

Hams hang aloft in Ed May's butcher shop while Ed, left, behind butcher's table, wields a knife. A gas ceiling light hangs over the counter, but there is also an electric light coming down from the ceiling immediately behind it.

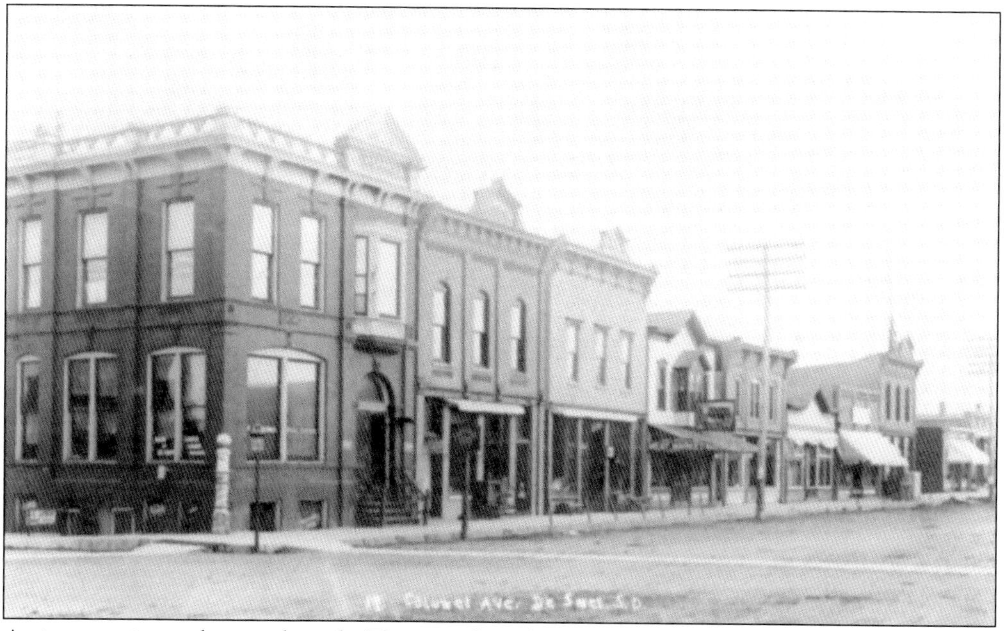

A picture paints a thousand words. This must have been the thought of the Rehfeld Meat Market proprietor when he hung the picture of a Hereford bull to pose majestically over the awning of the market. The barber pole at the corner of the J.H. Carroll Building immediately catches the eye.

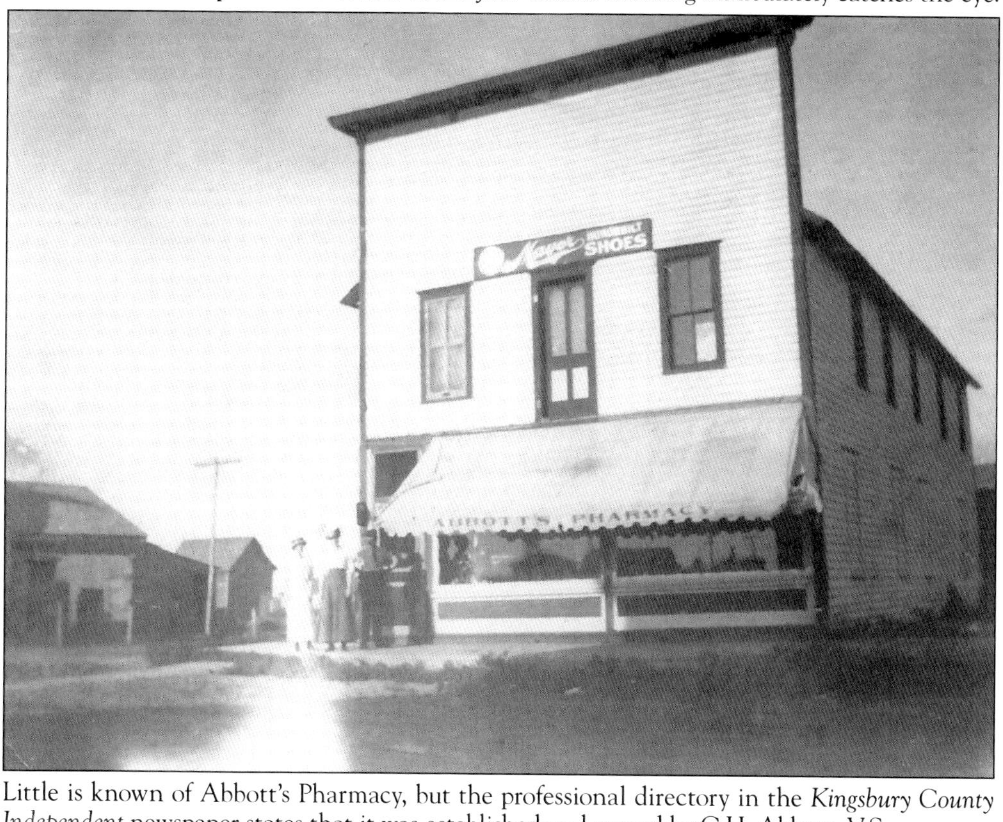

Little is known of Abbott's Pharmacy, but the professional directory in the *Kingsbury County Independent* newspaper states that it was established and owned by C.H. Abbott, V.S.

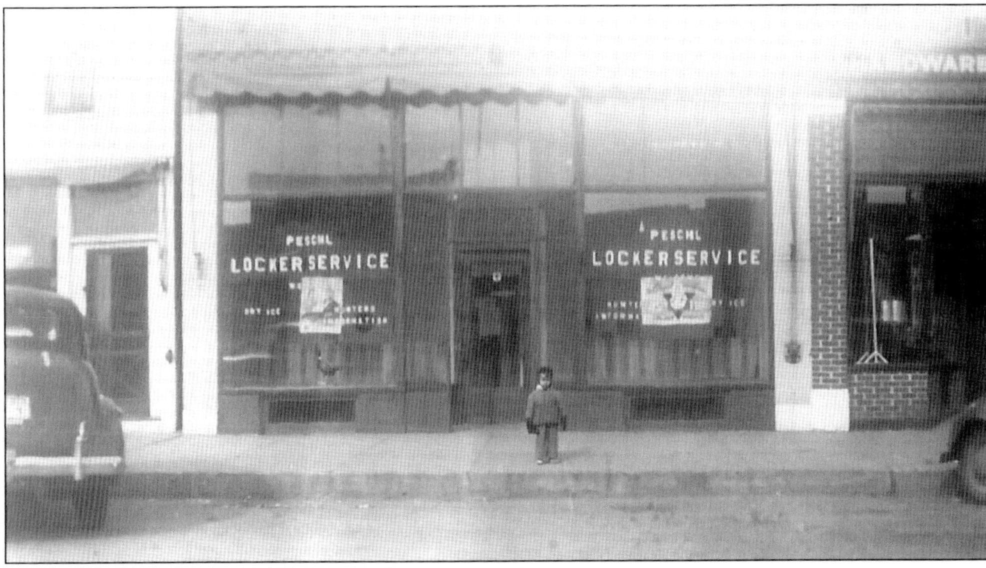

Originally constructed in 1888, the building in this photograph was home to Sasse Pharmacy and, later, Buchele Drug Store. Melvin Sorenson started the locker plant in 1945. Fred Peschl bought the locker service and operated it from 1946 until 1973. The window signs read "Hunters Information" and "Dry Ice," indicating the fall season and the reason why young Terry Peschl is dressed in his warm clothing.

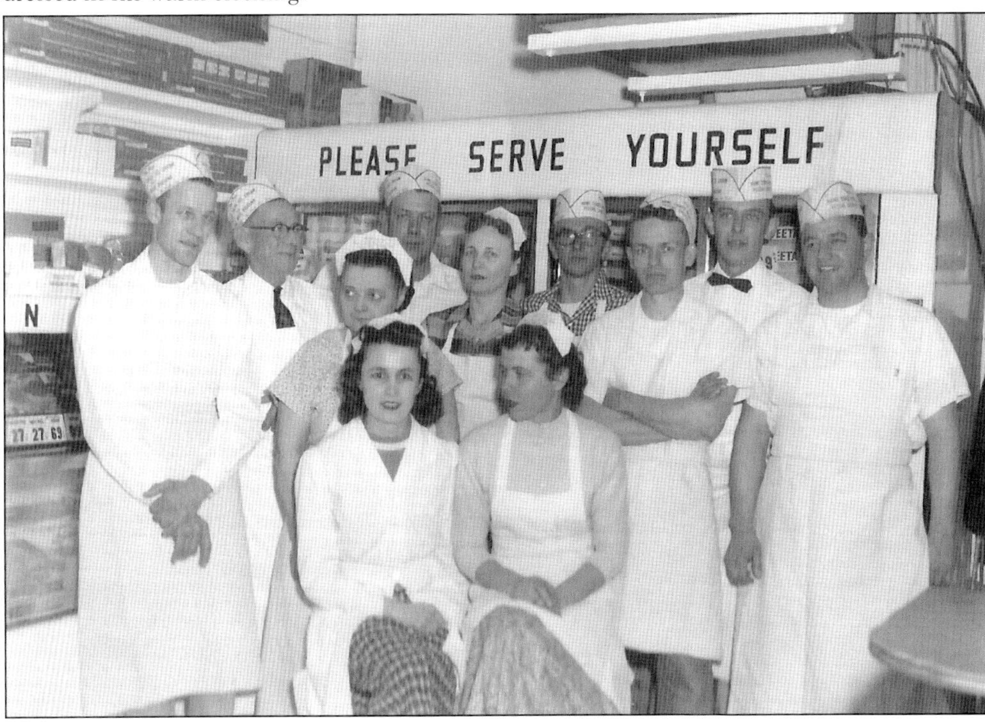

Though the sign reads "Please Serve Yourself," Fred Peschl was always willing to serve his customers, as were his employees. In this image are, from left to right, (first row) Marcie Peschl and unidentified; (second row) Cecil Heim, Margaret Schultz, Joe Johnson, and Fred; (third row) Earl Kickland, Clyde Riley, Carl Thiele, Billy Kickland, and Bob Johnson.

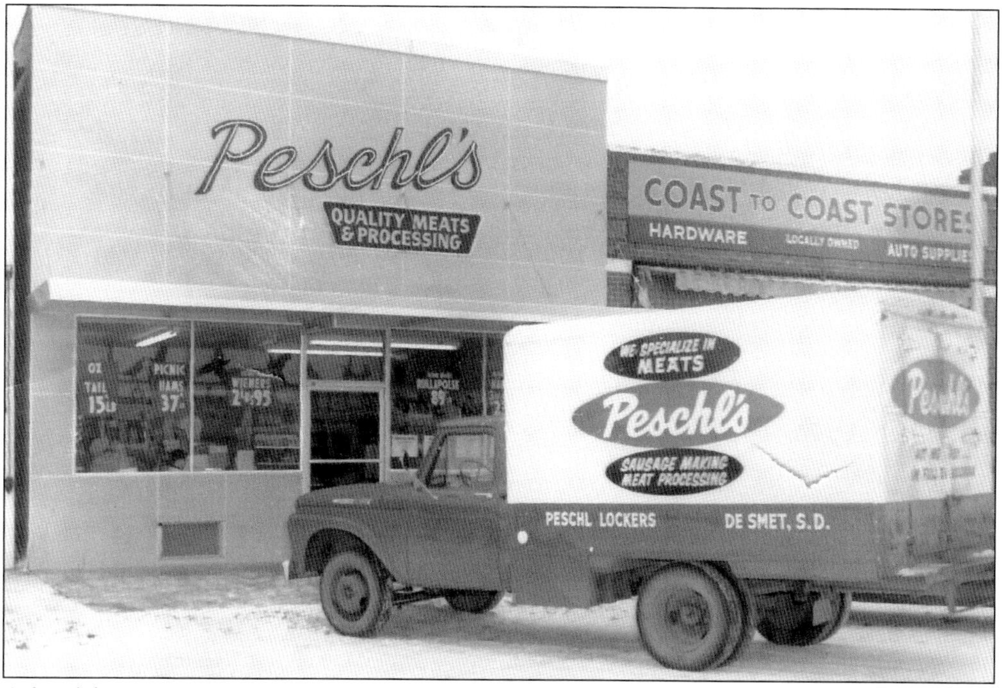

A face-lift was given to the Peschl building in the 1960s. A new truck with the admonition "Hit Me Easy . . . I'm Full of Bologna" on the back door is seen here; this phrase became Fred's mantra.

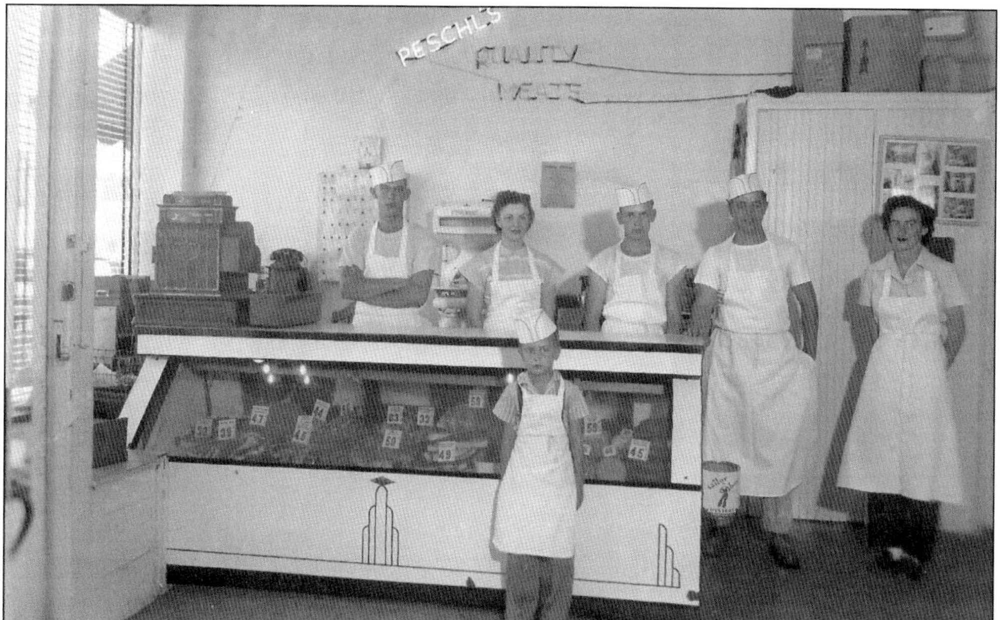

Inside the newly renovated Peschl building is freshly butchered meat on display. From left to right, Bob Johnson, Delores Aalbers, Joe Johnson, Fred Peschl and Shirley Garry are on hand to serve. Terry Peschl, standing in front of the meat counter, has his own apron and hat to wear. The keyboard behind the counter, to the left, holds keys to the lockers that patrons could rent to store their meats.

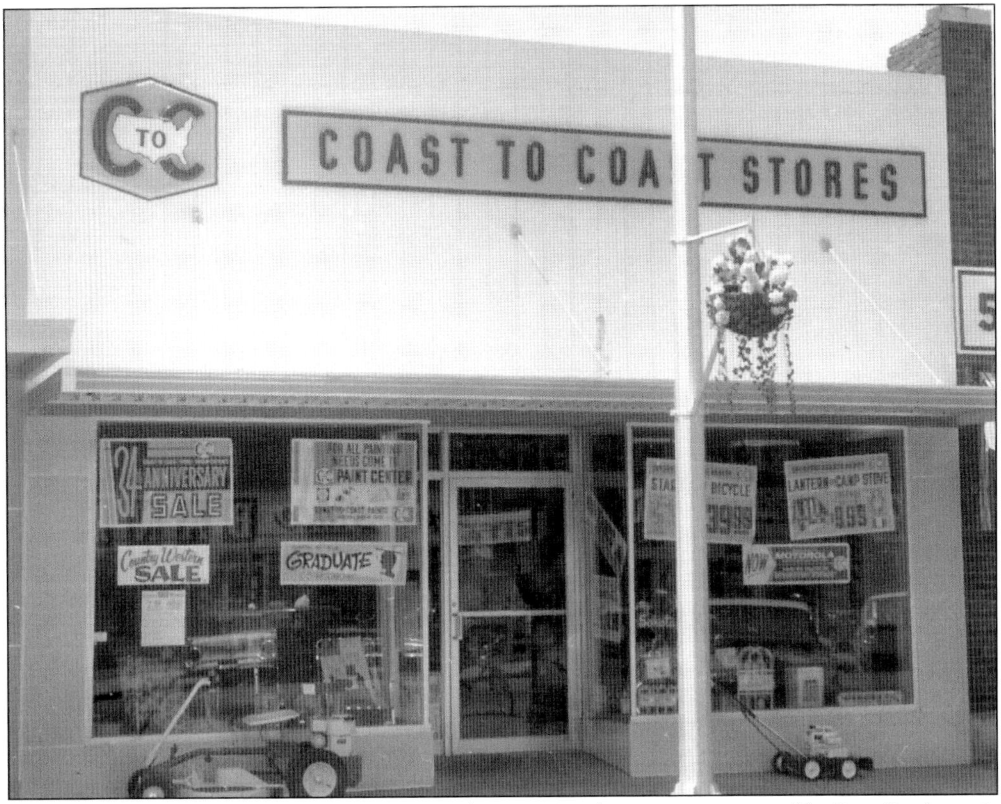

Fire took this business and building on March 2, 2002, when it was operated by Ron Beck, with Randy and LaVonne Bohn owning the building. Coast to Coast has been on the scene of De Smet's main street since it was established in the late 1930s. Some owner/managers have been Ellis Day, Warren and Lorraine Widman, Clarence and Eunice Mutschler, and Randy and LaVonne Bohn.

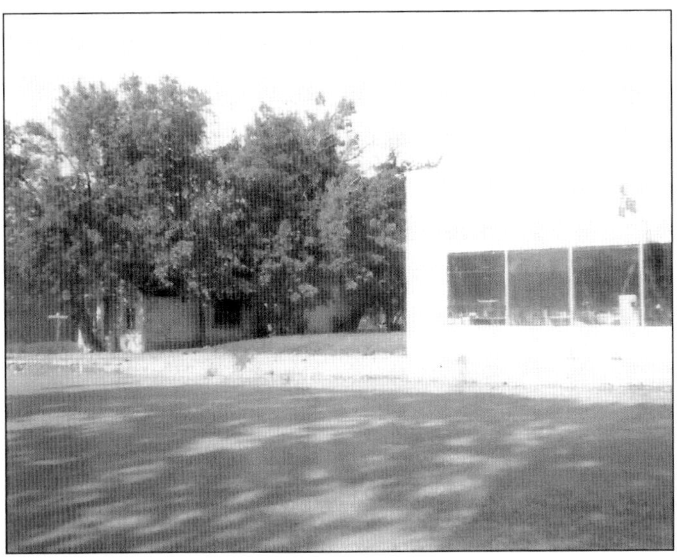

In this image, a former tailor's shop is snuggled among the trees. When it was razed, there were tintypes from the work of photographer Cooledge, who had his photography studio in this building before it was the tailor's shop. In later years, it was a private home. The display windows in Hyink's Furniture Store on the corner of Calumet Avenue and Third Street can be seen here.

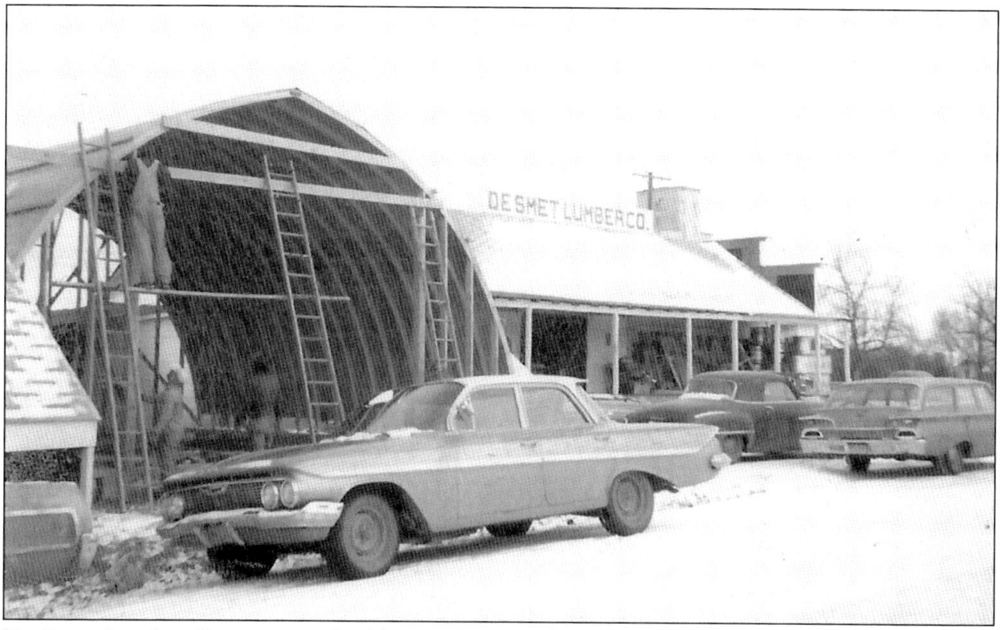

De Smet Lumber Company is building a Quonset hut to house more building materials. De Smet Lumber Company was established in 1932, when Bergstrom and Richardson bought out the Robinson Lumber Company. In 1961, the sole owner was Richardson; in 1966, the owners were Jim Kott and Elmer Johnson; in 1968, the sole owner was Johnson; but in August 1968, the business burned down. This is now the site of Dobson Chiropractic Clinic.

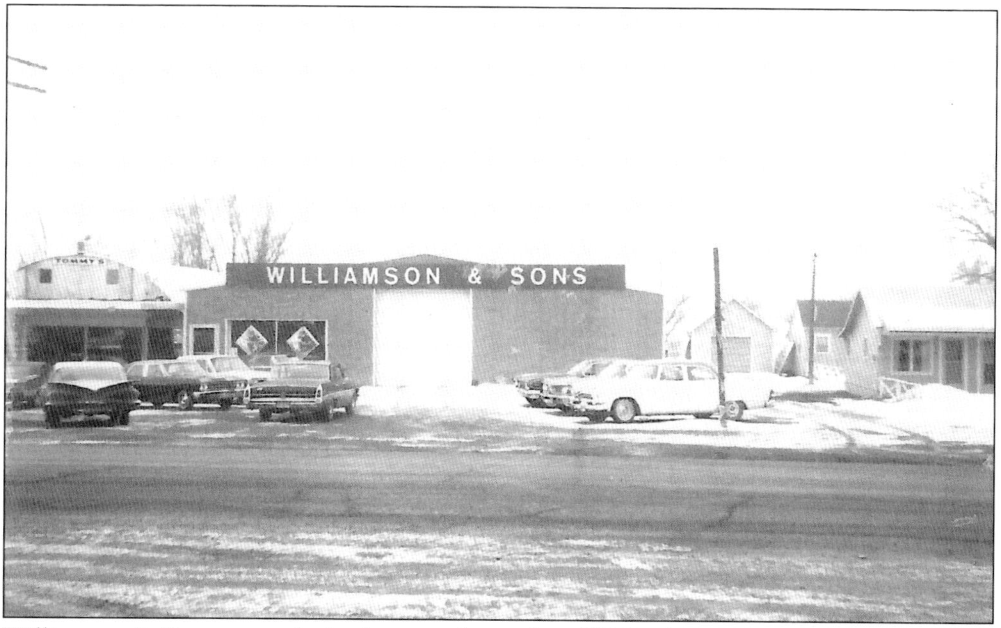

Williamson & Sons, a car dealership, was located on US Highway 14, just to the east of the Cottage Inn Motel. According to family, Tommy and Alice Williamson owned and operated the business for over 20 years. Tommy was the onetime owner of Tommy's Standard Service, which was located on the north end of Calumet Avenue, but he gave it up to sell the items that needed gas to run.

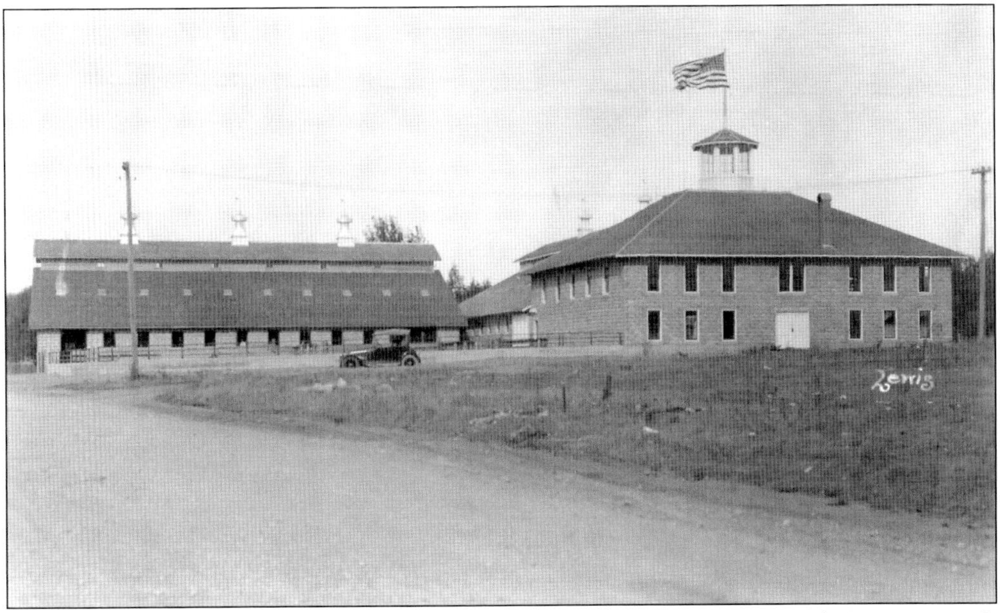

The pavilion was built in the early 1900s by the Kingsbury County Livestock Association. It was the pride of the community when purebred sales were at their height. It was purchased by Lars Carlson of Lake Preston in 1925, and H.O. and Harold Fritzel bought it in 1930. The barn to the left was torn down by owner F.L. Brewer in 1935. O.A. Erlandson's John Deere Agency is seen here in 1936.

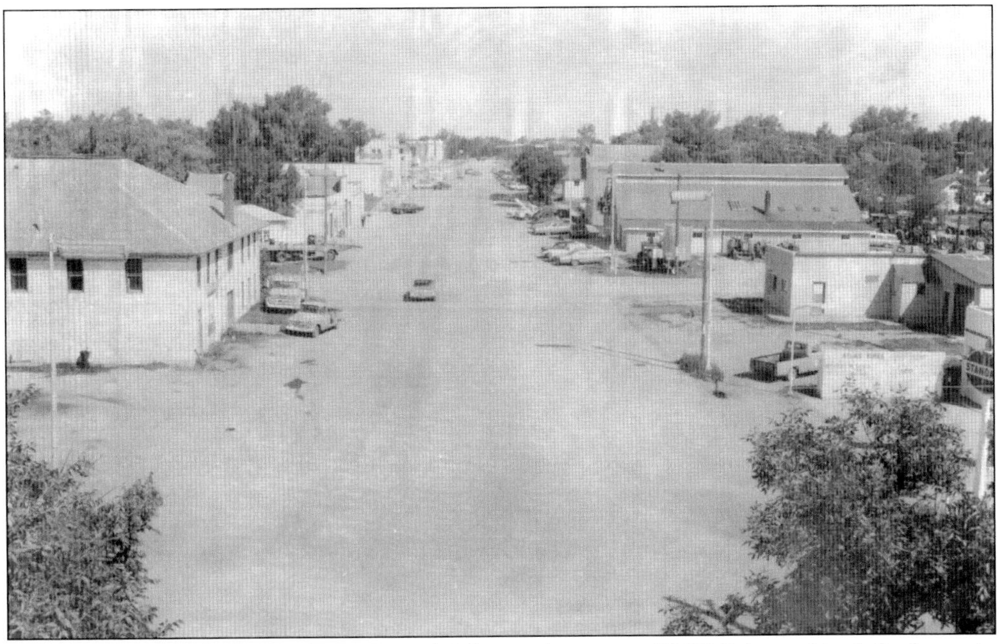

The pavilion complex sat on the corner of Calumet Avenue and US Highway 14, while the main building stood closer to Fourth Street. The last remnant of De Smet's Sale Pavilion was razed in 1976 to make way for the OxBow Café and General Store, built, owned, and operated by Tex and Jill Myers. In the intervening years of 1936 to 1975, Jake Kruse had an implement shop and car dealership at the site; Larry Stalheim and Kenny Hummel bought out Kruse.

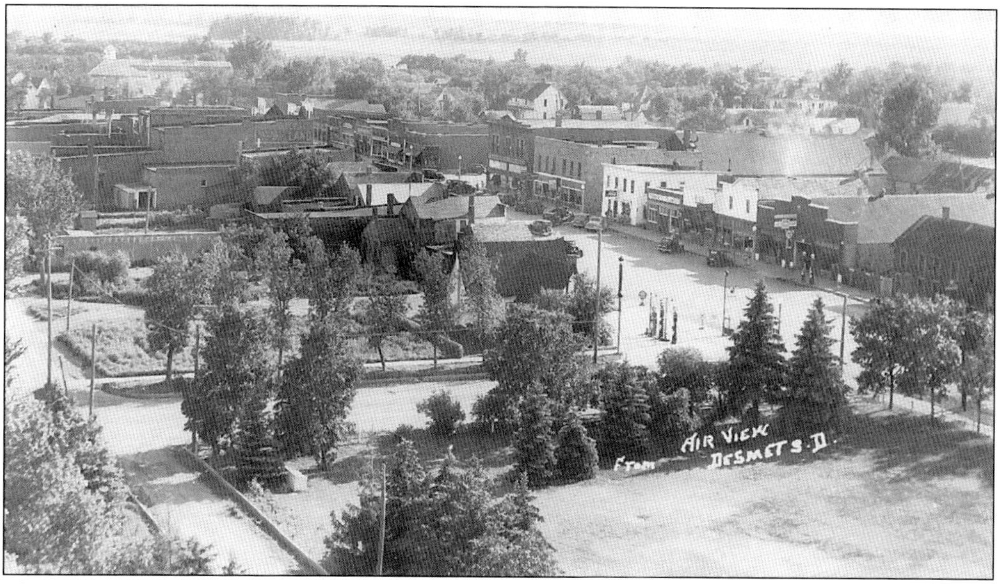

This scene, with a view looking from the north, gives a picture of how the little town came to be a growing city. Gas pumps and automobiles indicate that the horse-and-buggy era has been largely left behind.

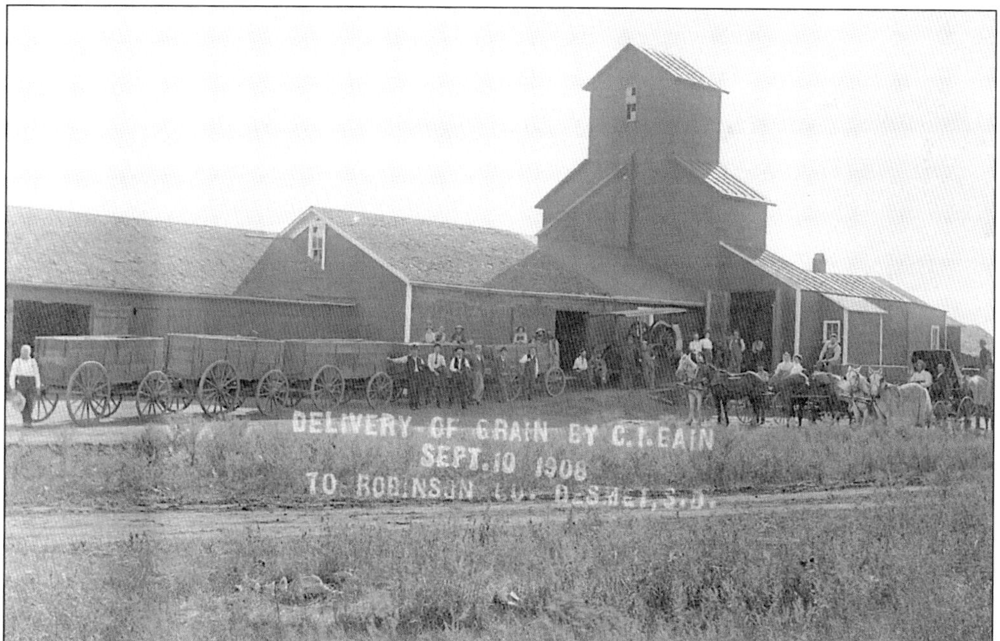

Apparently, whole families were involved in bringing grain to town, as there are women, men, and children in this 1908 postcard. Located at the corner of Calumet Avenue and First Street, Robinson Company was spread over quite a span of ground.

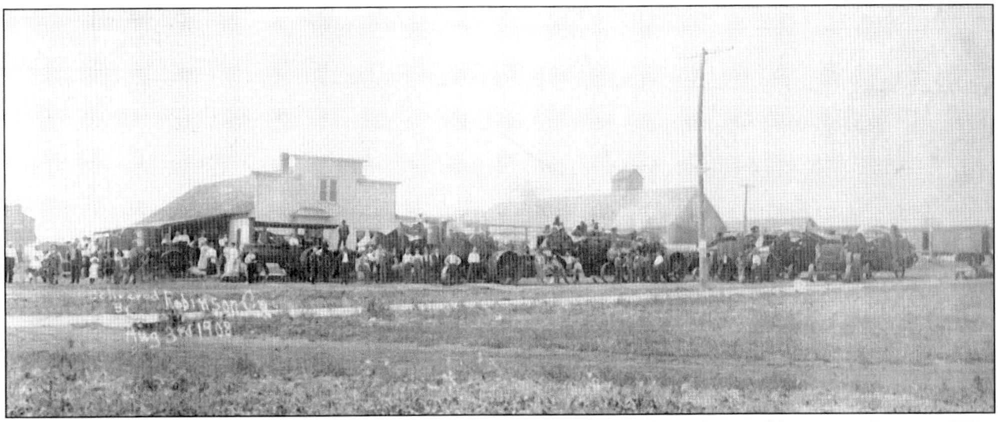

In 1908, the Robinson Lumberyard sold not only lumber but also a line of farm machinery. The whole family could check out the lineup. Thomas I. Robinson operated this business, with his brother William having a hardware store in De Smet and brother Elmer running businesses in Erwin.

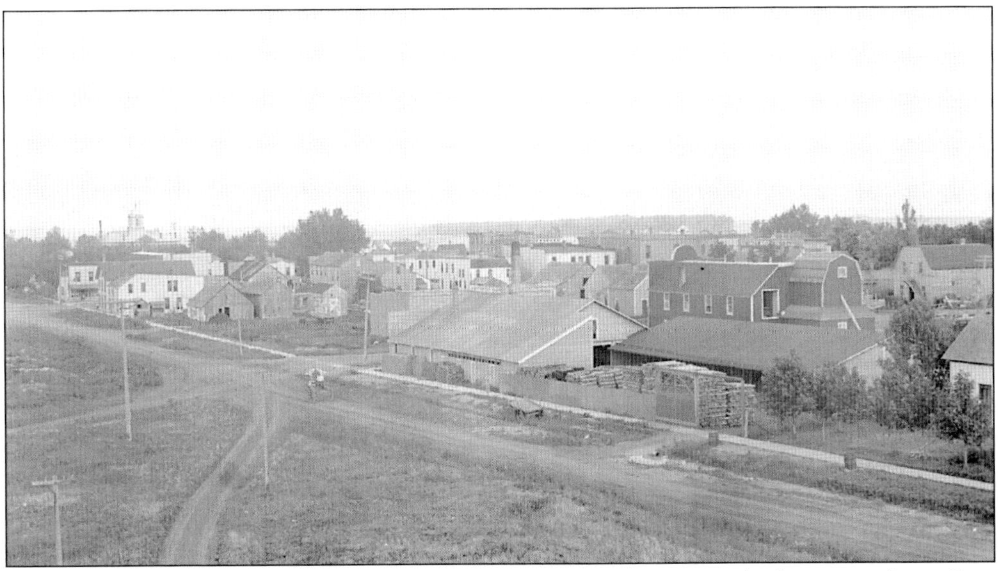

Another bird's-eye view of De Smet was captured in this 1909 view looking east down First Street. The dome of the stately Kingsbury County Courthouse soars into the sky. The houses and buildings seem to be snuggled up and cozy.

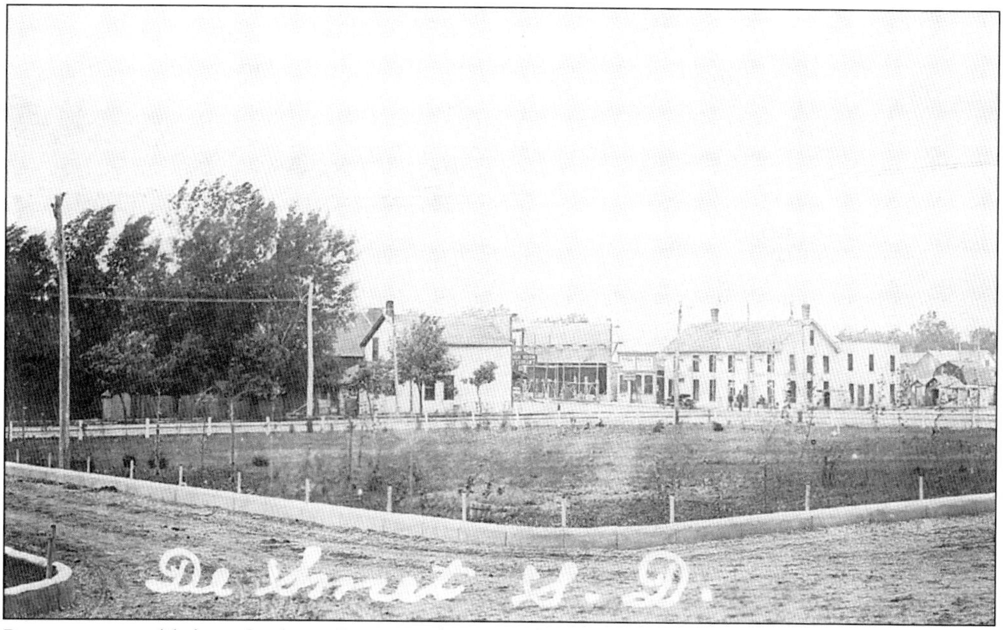

Passengers could disembark at the train depot and simply walk down Calumet Avenue to the Meade (later the Grand) Hotel to inquire about a room. The number of windows indicates an ample amount of rooms.

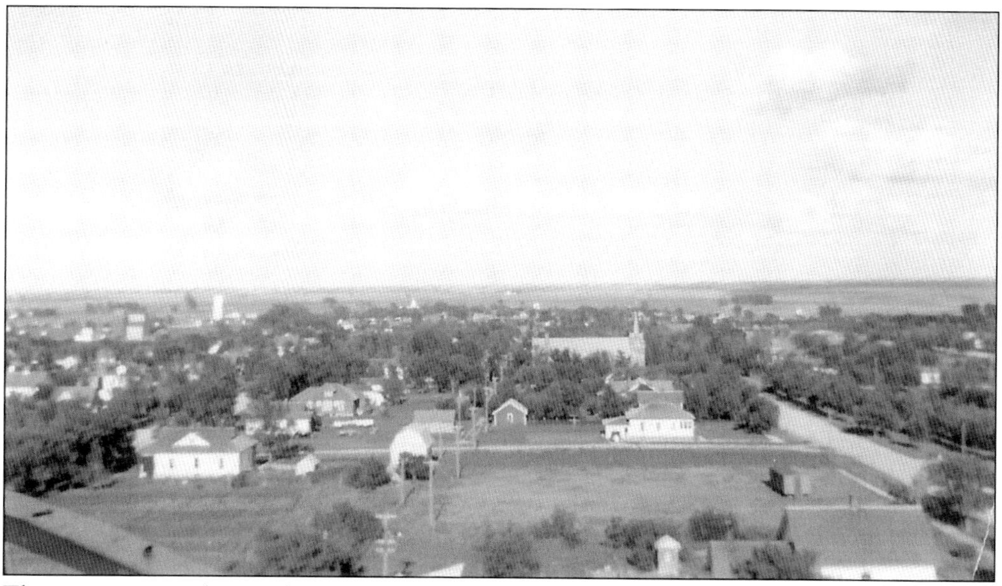
This picture turns the mind to the time of yesteryear, when houses were rather sparse in the west end of town. This picture was taken from the water tower, with a view looking east. The spire of the Catholic church is wending its way heavenward. The elevators stand tall, and a corner of Washington Park can be see on the right.

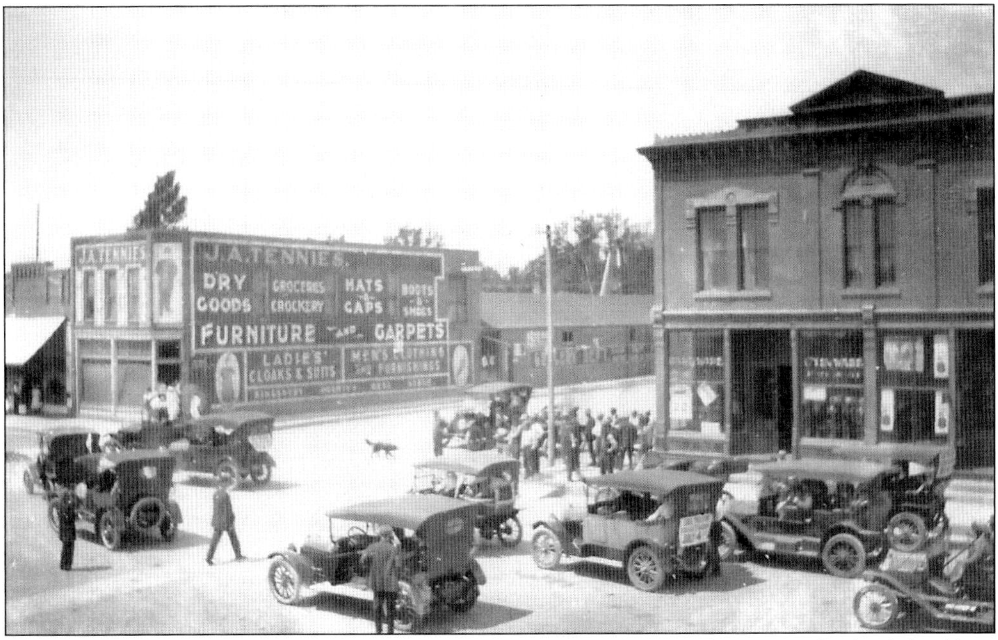

J.A. Tennies anchored the corner of Calumet Avenue and Second Street. The back building was the grocery department, according to the large lettering on its side. It appears as though the Tennies slogan could have been "if we don't have it, you don't need it." The sign on the back of the vehicle reads "Lake Preston Chautauqua July 4th."

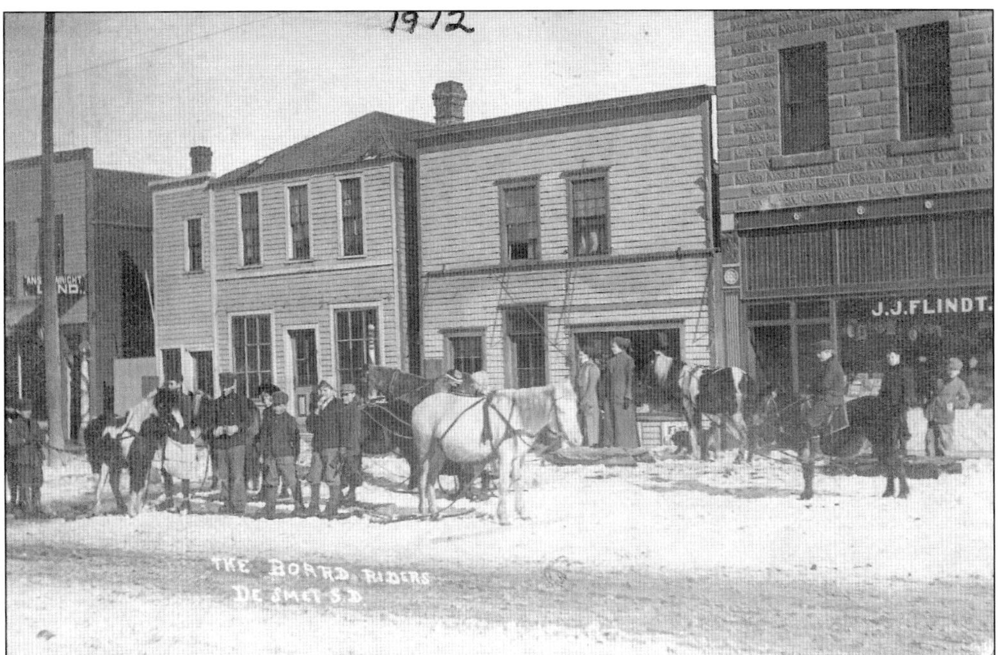

There could have been a feel of magic in winter 1912 as this group of boys with a sled, a board, and horses prepares to glide down the wide Calumet Avenue. The coat-clad ladies watch and listen, as they perhaps remember the yelling, laughing, and pure joy of this winter activity.

Three

A Firm Foundation

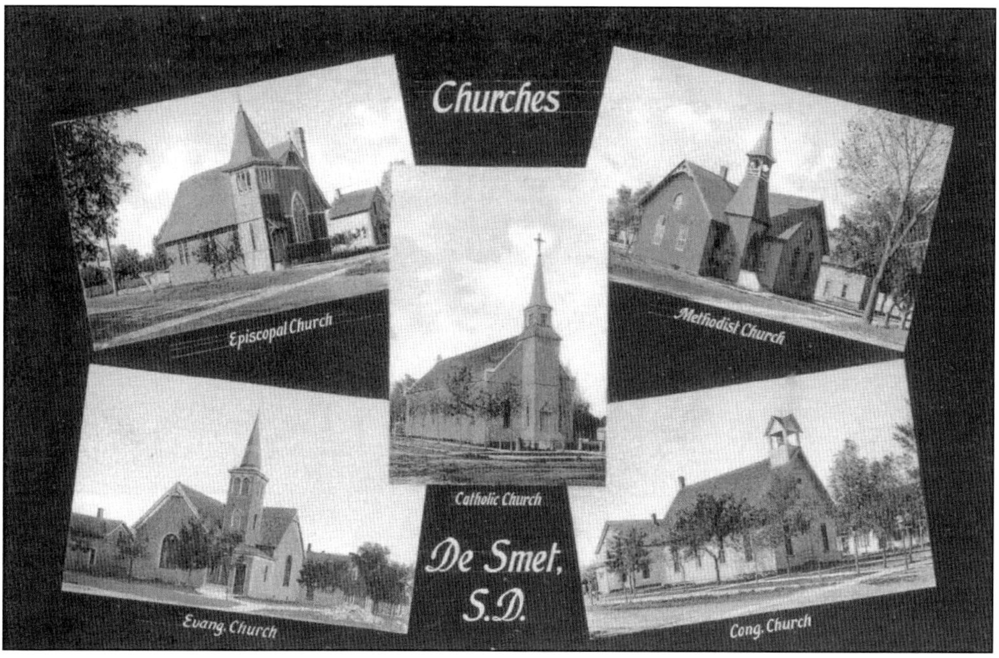

In 1880, most Protestants met for worship services in either the railroad depot or the public schoolhouse; however, throughout the years, the faith and dreams of De Smet residents were seen in the erecting of several main line churches in the community. The diversity and overall faith of its residents created a firm, strong foundation through which the small town absorbed the strength needed to endure.

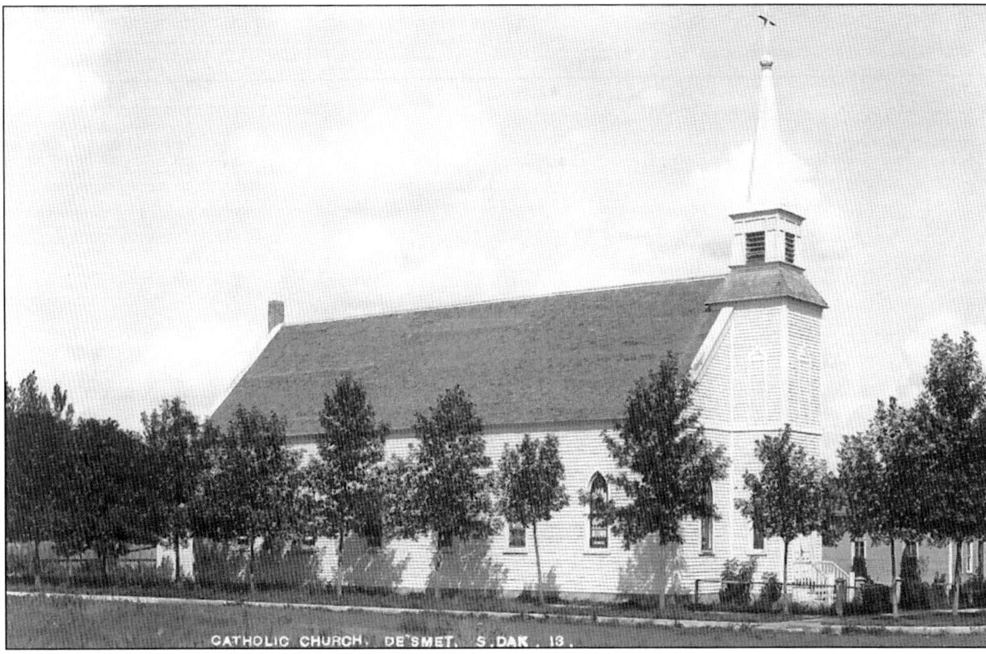

"Never give up!" was the solemn vow of the Catholic parishioners in this small community. In 1883, a tiny church was erected, only to be destroyed in a windstorm. In 1884, they built a more substantial building, the one shown in this photograph, only to have it completely destroyed by fire in 1918.

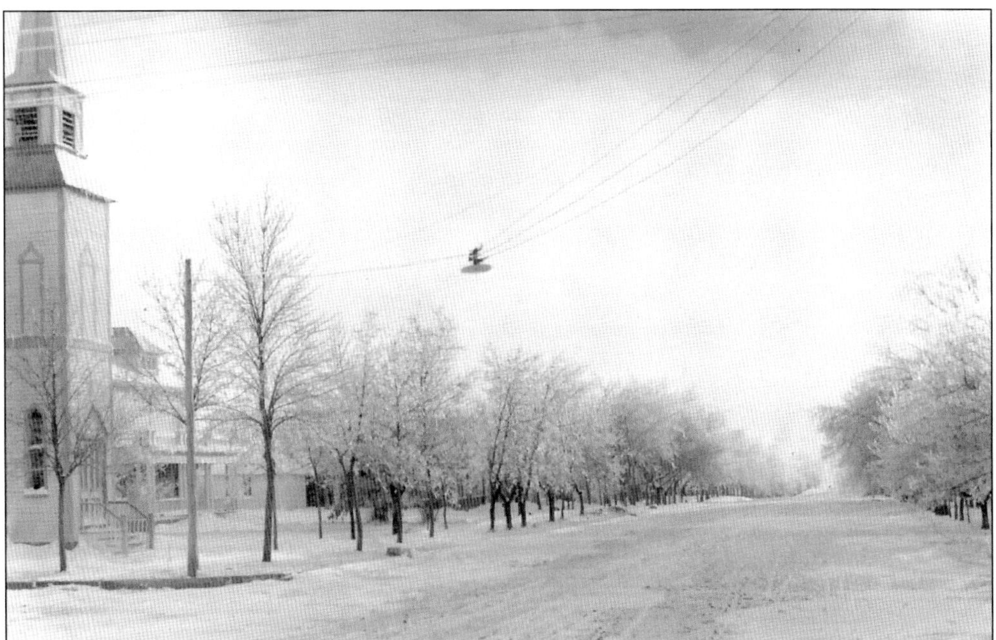

A flourishing Catholic membership built a rectory in 1908; it can be seen to the right of the church. Sold and moved out of De Smet, it became a private residence in Watertown, South Dakota. The rectory was home to several priests over its years of existence.

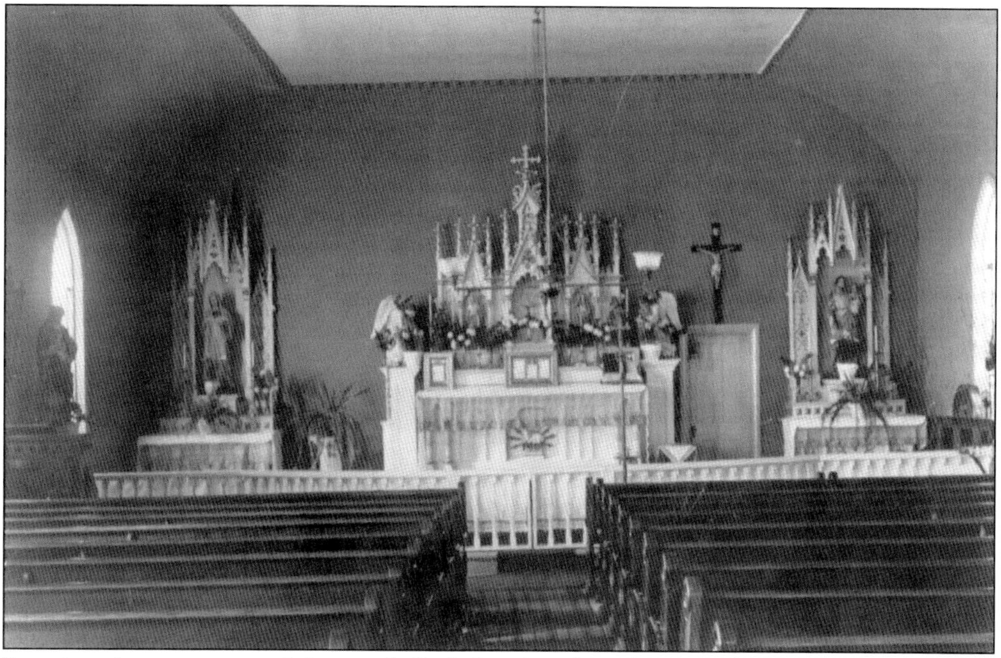

Entering the sanctuary of the small Catholic church and seeing the elegance of the altar appointments could only bring peace to the parishioners' hearts, so when it was destroyed by fire in 1918, their hearts could only grieve.

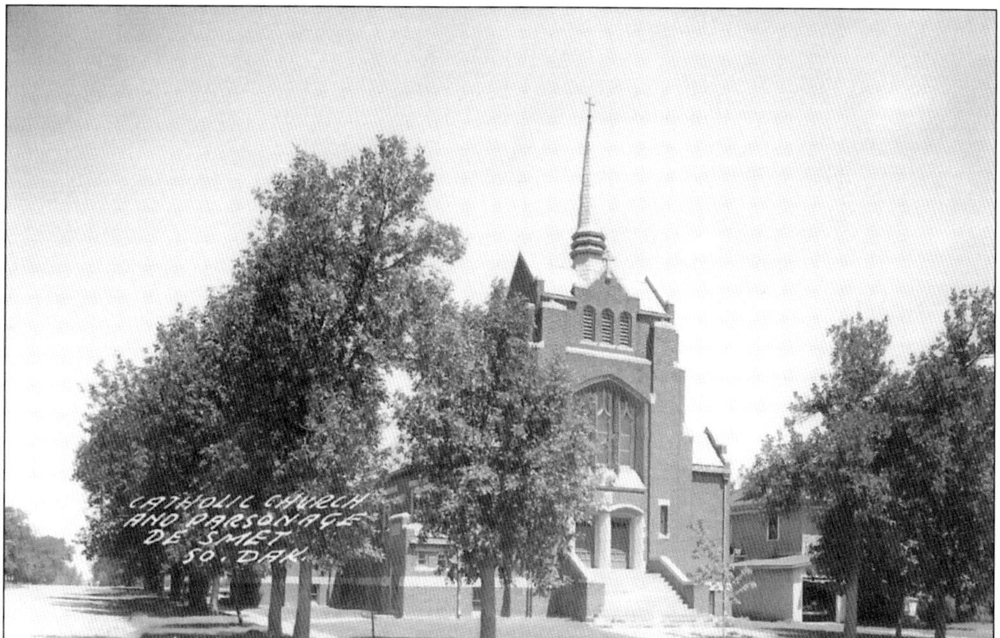

Just as a phoenix arises from its ashes, so to did this elegant Gothic-style structure. The corner stone was laid in 1920 for the present-day Catholic church. For some years, Mass was held and the sacraments distributed in the basement of the church. Work was finally completed on the interior of the church proper, and the first Mass was held upstairs in 1929—and continues to this day.

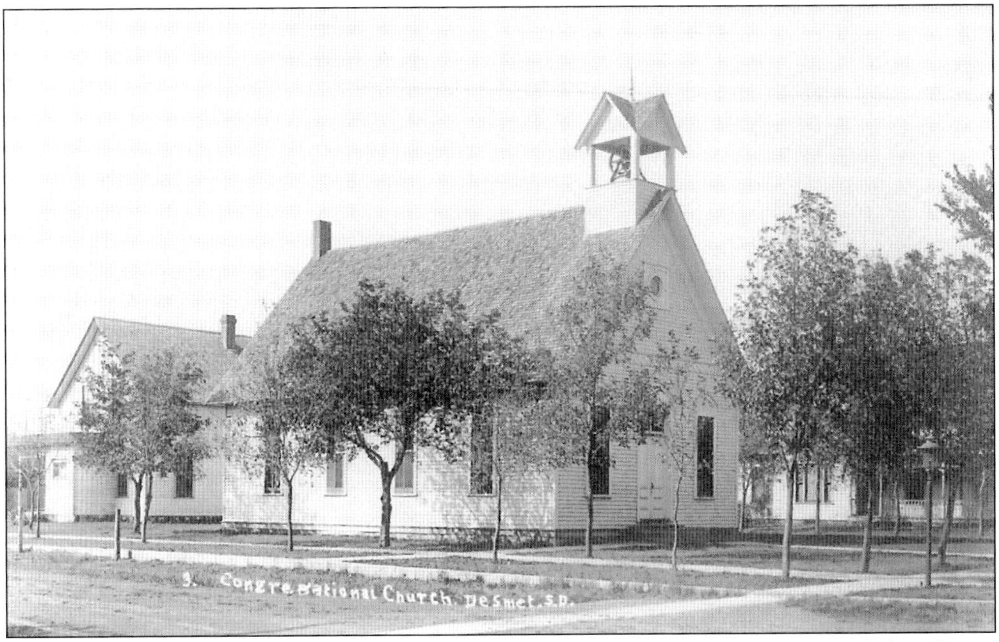

Known as the "Church that Pa [Charles Ingalls] helped build," the Congregational church was organized in 1880. The Rev. Edward Brown held the first service on August 30, 1882. In 1884, this was the first church bell to ring in Kingsbury County, and it continues to be rung today. The church was built on the corner of Second Street and Loftus Avenue.

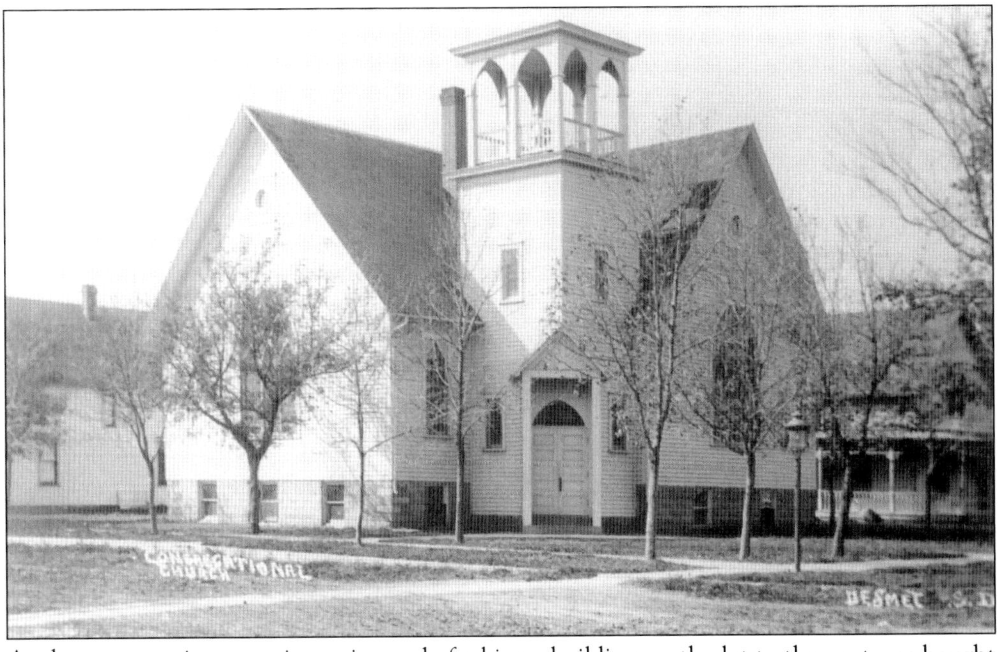

As the congregation grew, it was in need of a bigger building, so the lot to the west was bought and extensive remodeling was done in 1909. The Congregational members met here until 1967, when they sold the church to the Christian and Missionary Alliance. The large stained-glass window on the north side was a gift from the Drakola Congregational Church, near Oldham, South Dakota.

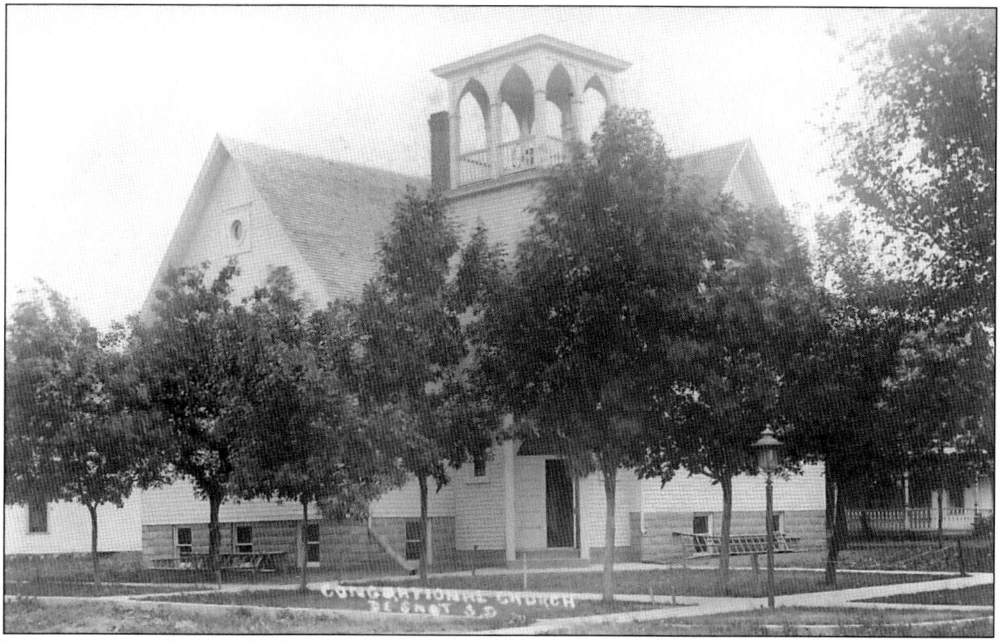

The trees are well established along the side and front of the Congregational church on Second Street and Loftus Avenue. They give a leafy background for the gas streetlight by the front sidewalk.

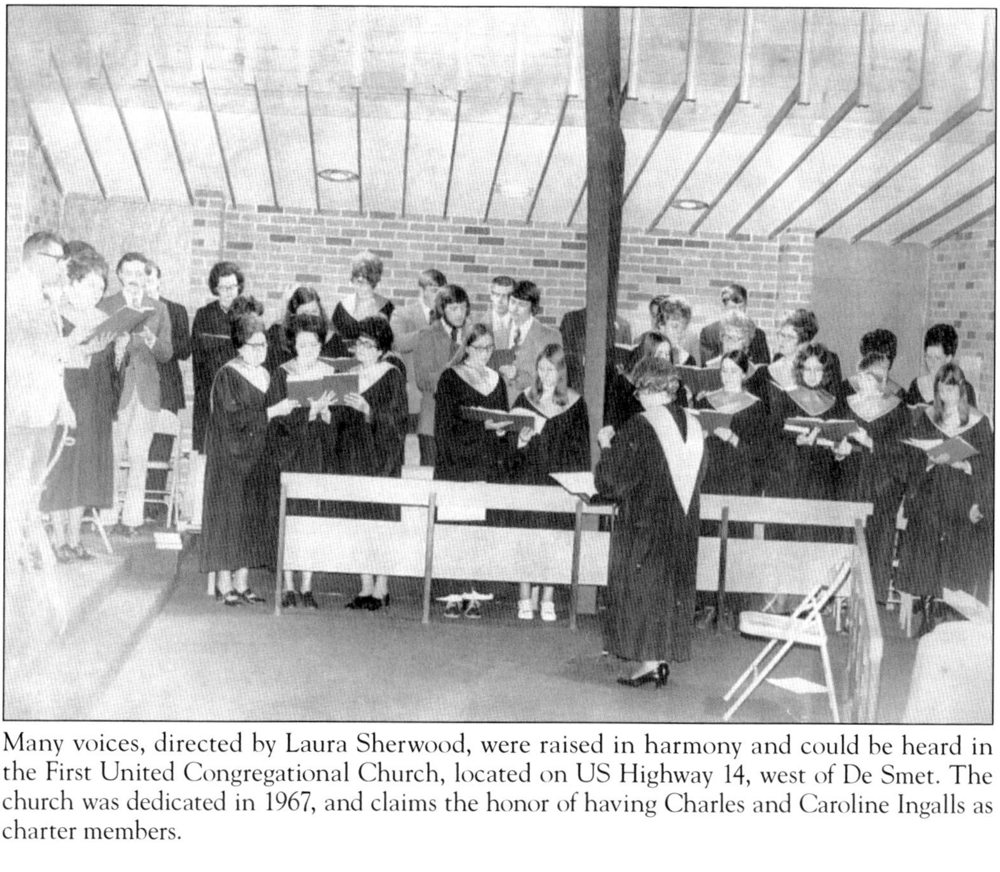

Many voices, directed by Laura Sherwood, were raised in harmony and could be heard in the First United Congregational Church, located on US Highway 14, west of De Smet. The church was dedicated in 1967, and claims the honor of having Charles and Caroline Ingalls as charter members.

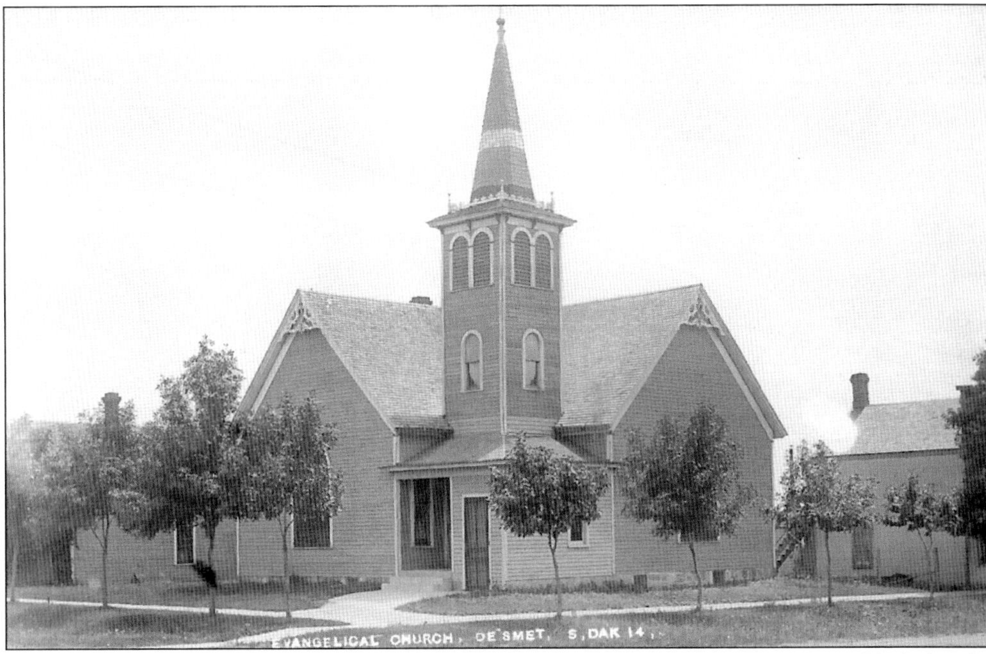

The growth and character of De Smet can be attributed to the residents' diversified beliefs. The regal structure of the Evangelical church still stands at the corner of Calumet Avenue and Third Street. Admittedly, the appearance today does not look the same. It is now home to the Masonic Lodge and Eastern Star. The houses appearing on the right and left of the building are no longer in existence.

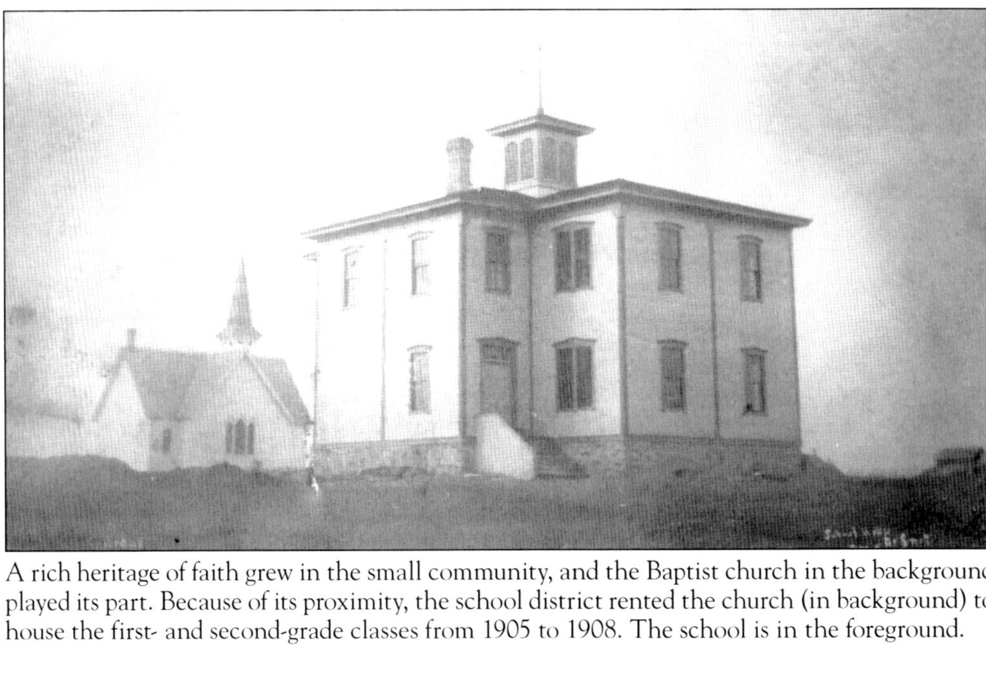

A rich heritage of faith grew in the small community, and the Baptist church in the background played its part. Because of its proximity, the school district rented the church (in background) to house the first- and second-grade classes from 1905 to 1908. The school is in the foreground.

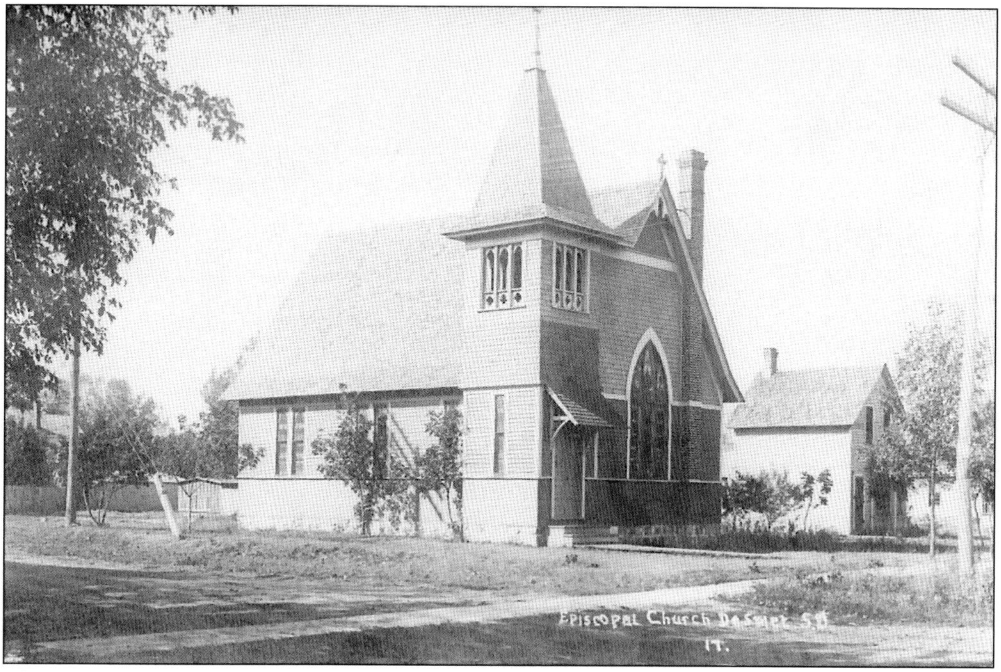

The faith and dreams of the settlers were realized when St. Stephen's Episcopal Church was erected on the corner of Second Street and South Dakota Highway 25. To the right of the church stands the former home of the Hinz family.

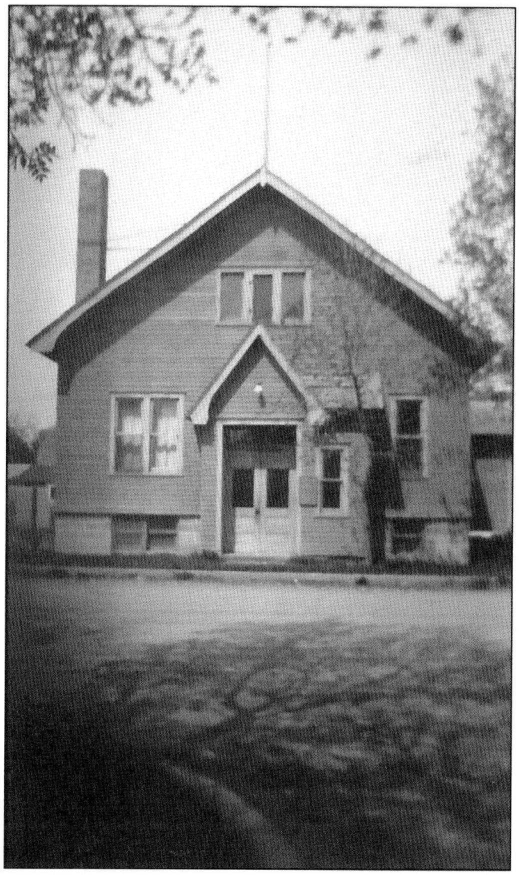

The guildhall was built later by the St. Stephen's Episcopal Church members as a fellowship hall. It not only sufficed for their group, but was used as a meeting hall for several community and social events.

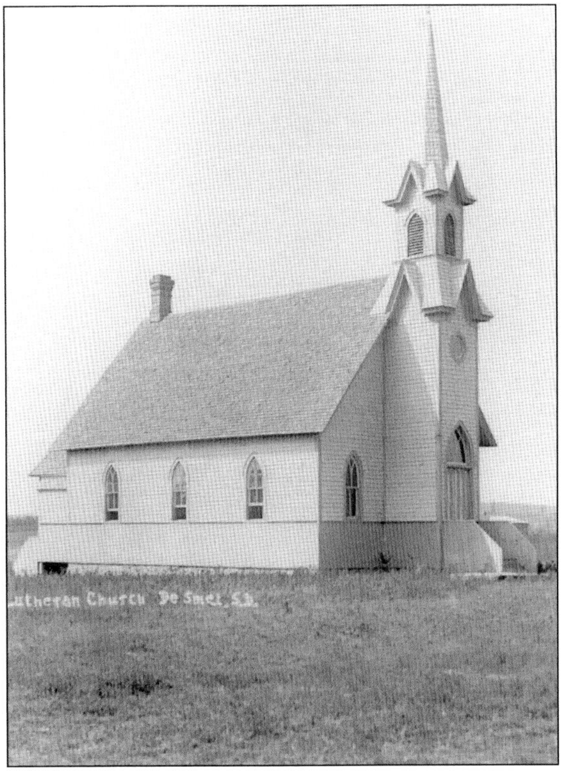

Many of the early settlers in the area were of Scandinavian and German descent. Even as they were erecting their sod houses or claim shanties, this group of settlers came up with the plan for the public preaching of the Word of God in the area. Today's American Lutheran Church is the combination of three such pioneer efforts—St. Paul (De Smet City), St. Petri (southeast De Smet), and St. Matthew (southwest De Smet).

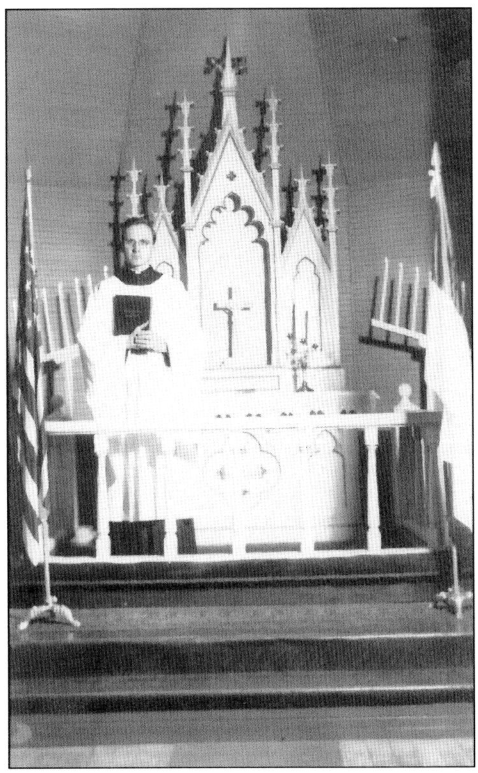

During Reverend Simonson's ministry, he worked unceasingly to encourage the building of a new church. He instilled into the hearts and minds of the members the goal of building it. The slogan became "Work, Pray, Give." In January 1945, the building committee began plans for the new church, and the present site was purchased. Native fieldstone was used in the random-rubble type of construction.

In 1947, as the walls crept higher and higher, a cornerstone was laid in the northeast corner. A copper box was imbedded in the cornerstone that included, among several items, a Bible, a Lutheran Hymnary, Luther's *Small Catechism*, a written church history, a list of church members, and the *De Smet News* for July 4–10.

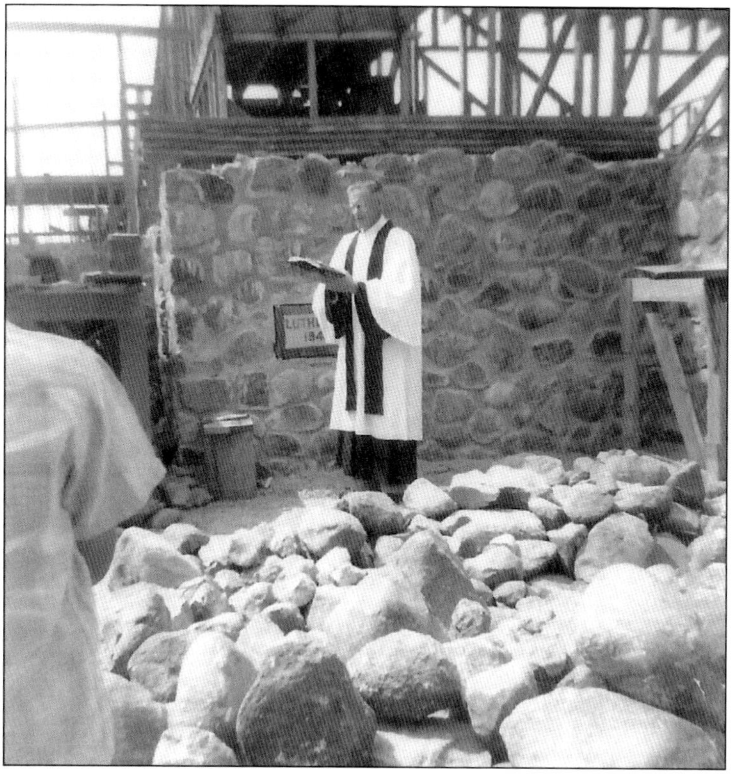

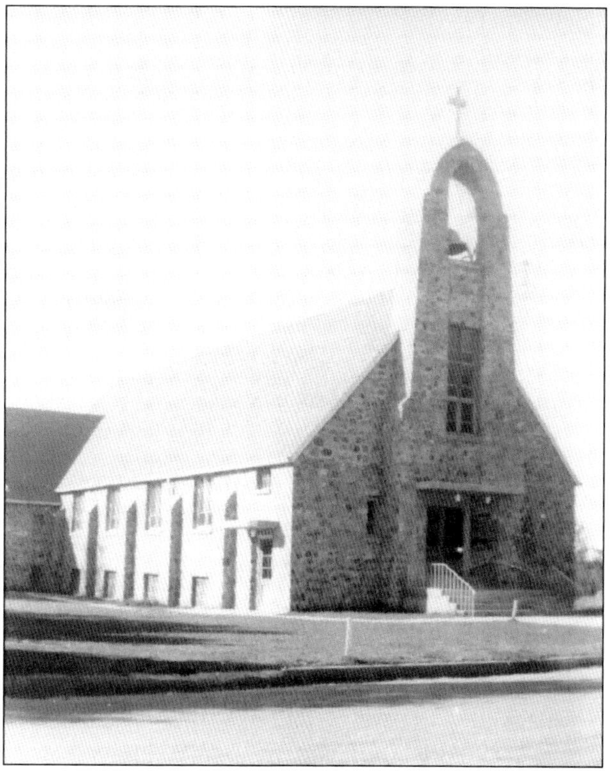

The doors of the newly built church opened to its faithful congregation in September 1949. Gone is the early settler's wood structure, and in its place stands a beautiful native fieldstone structure. The chiming of the bell that calls the congregation to worship is the original bell from the earlier St. Matthew congregation.

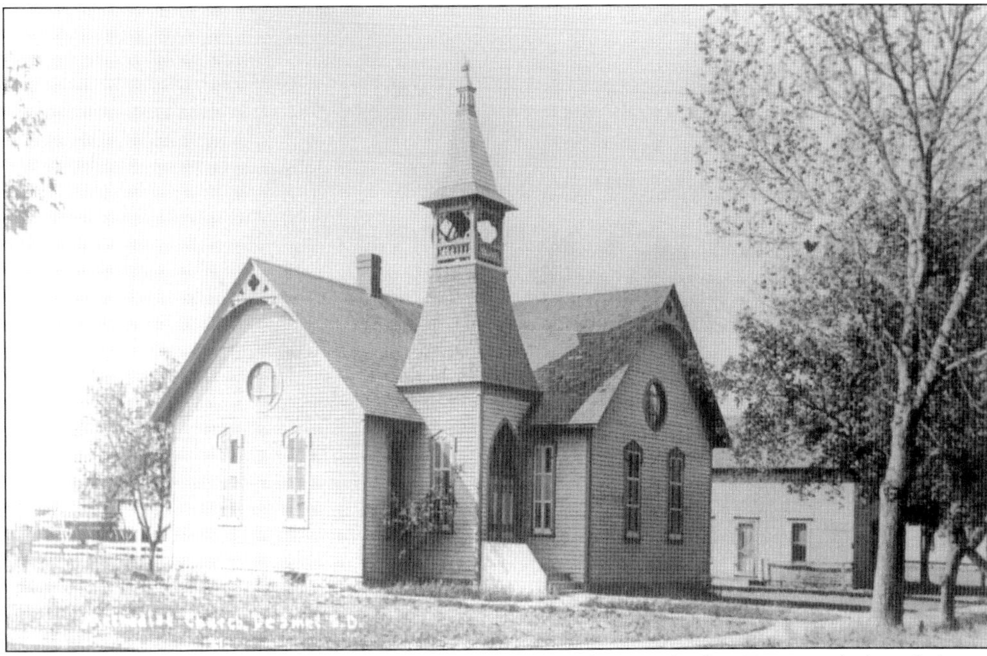

A profusion of ethnic backgrounds and beliefs led to the Methodist Episcopal church being formed in 1881. The church building was erected in 1885. It was located at the corner of Third Street and Loftus Avenue.

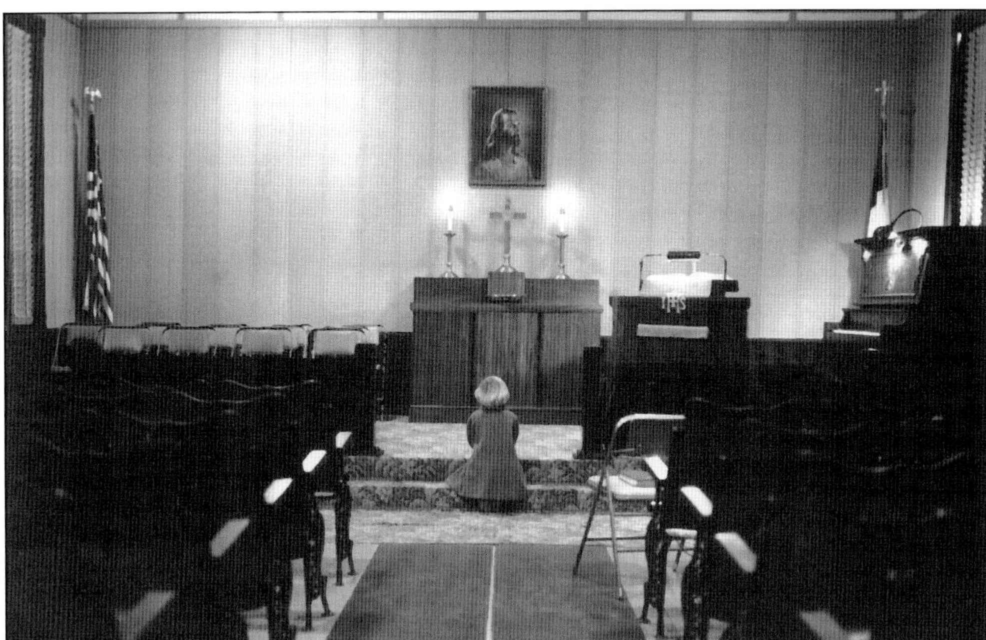

A picture of trust and comfort gleams in this photograph of one of Alice and Roy Brusse's daughters kneeling on the sanctuary steps of the Methodist church. The sounds of praise can be imagined from the chords Louise Ruskell played during services on the piano seen to the right. Theater seats, with men's hat holders under each seat, were in the main sanctuary.

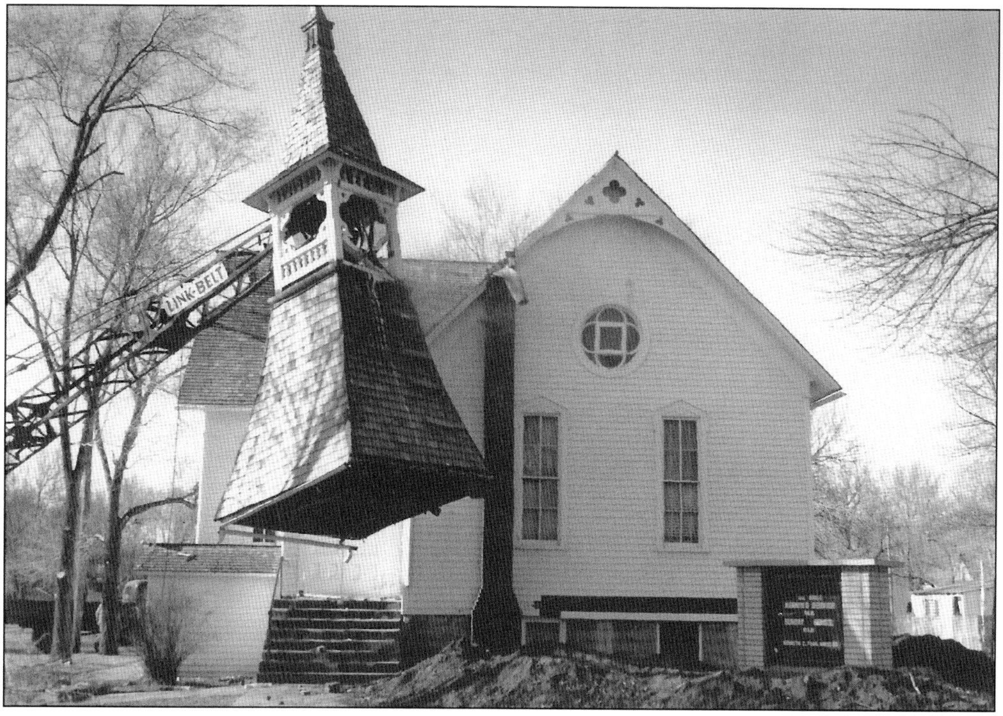

There were some smiles and some tears when the steeple was removed in 1965 for the Methodists to prepare to remodel their existing structure. The bell from the steeple now rests silently on top of the brick bulletin board seen at the right side of the photograph.

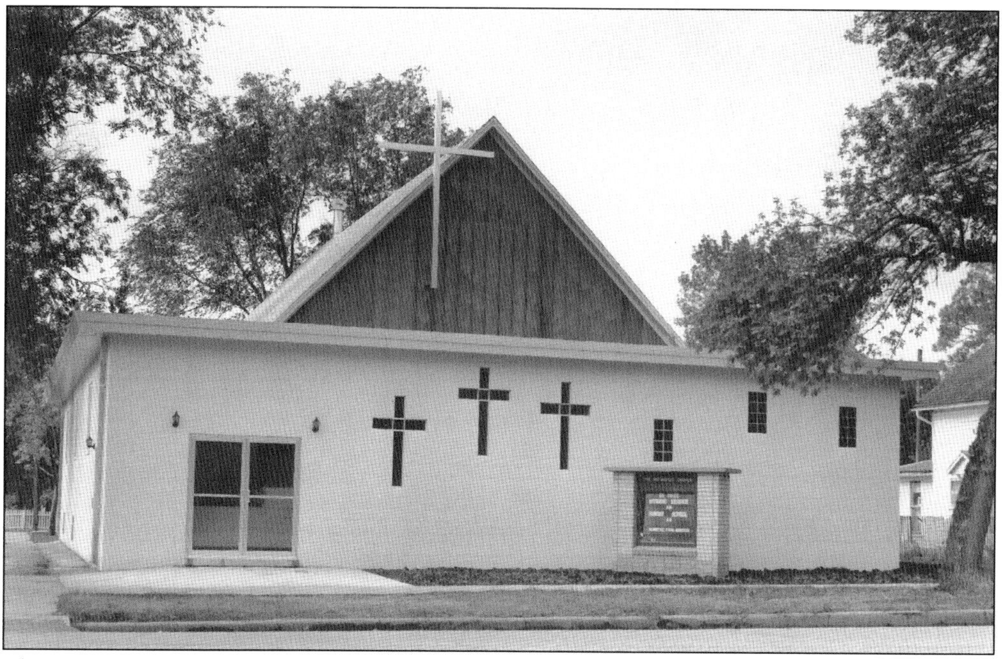

The incorporation of several denominations brought about the De Smet United Methodist Church as it is known today. This church is located at the corner of Third Street and Loftus Avenue, where it has always stood.

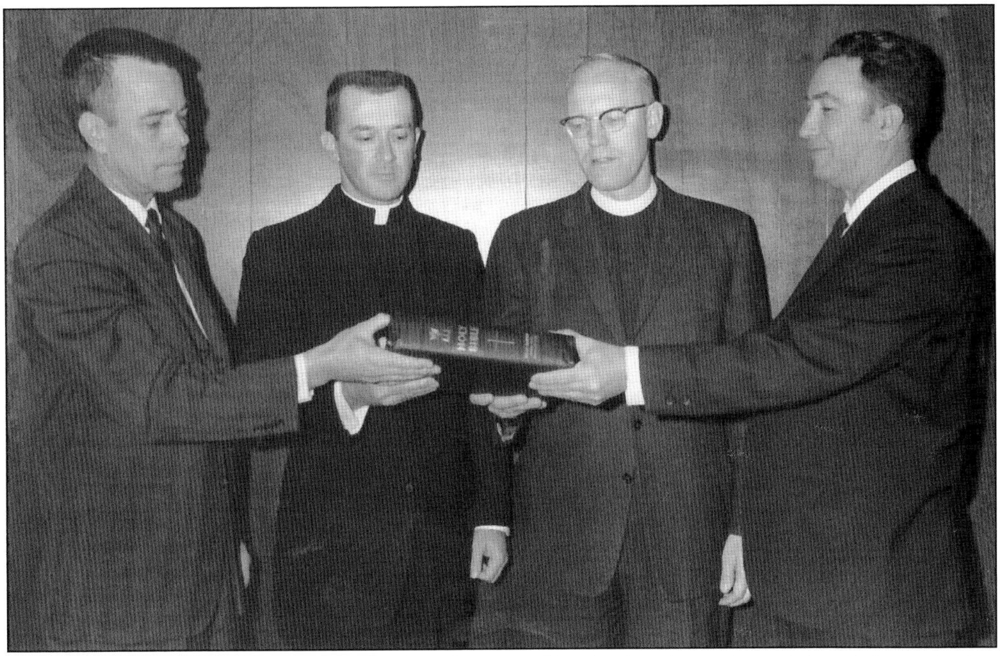

De Smet residents of the 1950s–1960s found spiritual leadership from the ministerial association that was formed by the ministers who are seen here from left to right: Rev. Robert Owen, United Church of Christ; Father Carleton Herman, St. Thomas Aquinas; Rev. LeRoy Stadem, American Lutheran; and Rev. Kenneth Farr, United Methodist.

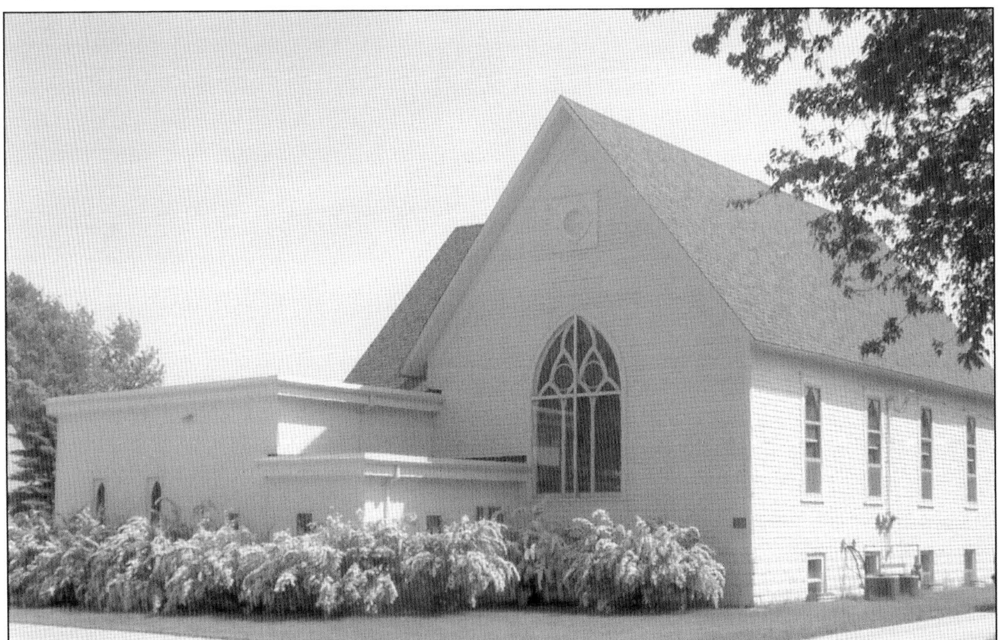

The De Smet Christian and Missionary Alliance Church originated with a group of interdenominational Christians seeking a place of worship. Prayers were answered when the former United Church of Christ church was offered for sale. The first service was held on June 11, 1967.

Four

READING, 'RITING, AND 'RITHMETIC

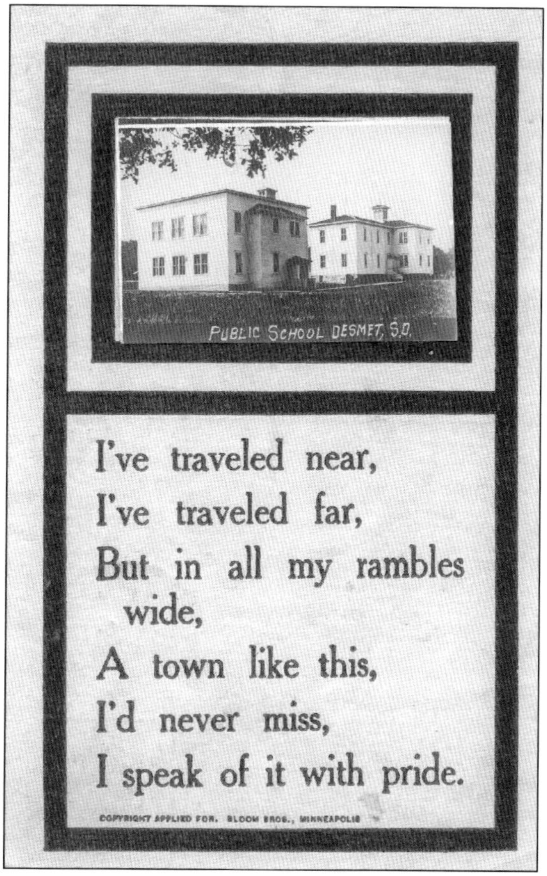

A common bond among the people of De Smet was their desire for education. With the typical settler's brand of energy and optimism, the first one-room schoolhouse was built. The ensuing years brought the construction of larger wooden buildings and, finally, a substantial brick building. Reading, writing, and arithmetic were elevated to the highest standards in the community.

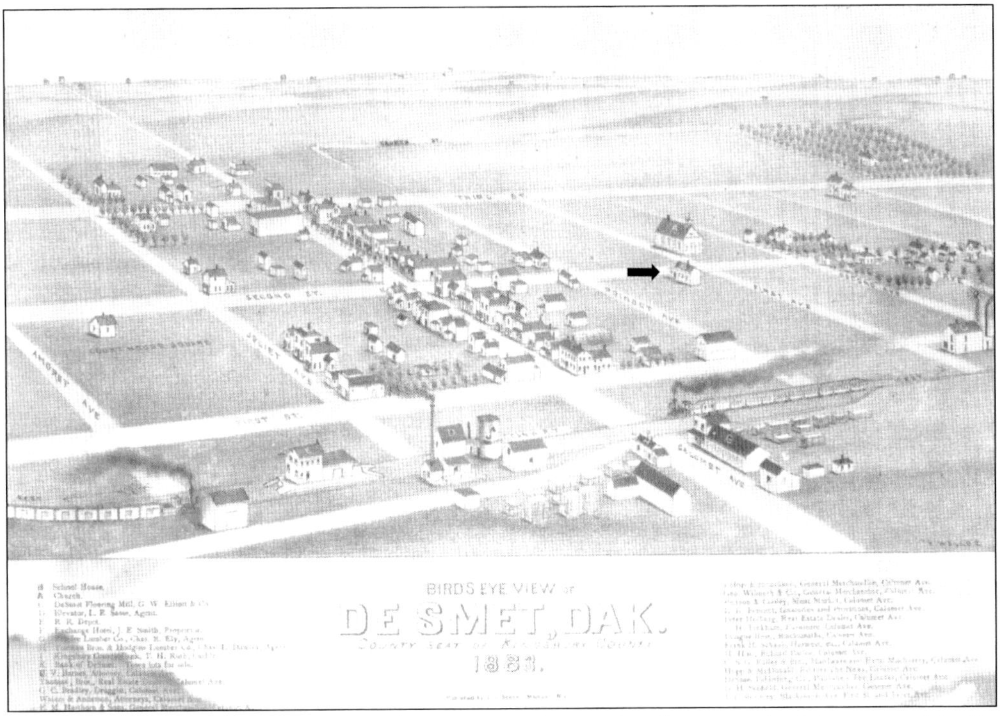

The one-room schoolhouse is a true American tradition. A solitary sentinel (see arrow) in De Smet, it stood on the corner of Second Street. In 1880, materials and labor for the schoolhouse were furnished by De Smet citizens, including C.H. Tinkham and A.N. Waters. It was later moved to Third Street and became a private home. Today, it can be seen on the premises of the Laura Ingalls Wilder Memorial Society.

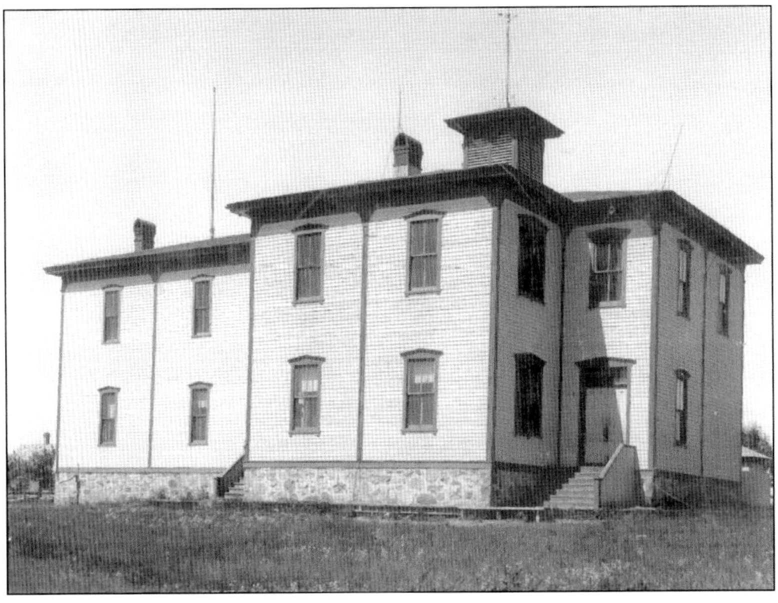

Few recall this two-story, wooden school building that stood majestically on Third Street. The first graded school was dedicated on New Year's Day 1885. As seen in this picture, it had an annex added to the south to provide two more classrooms.

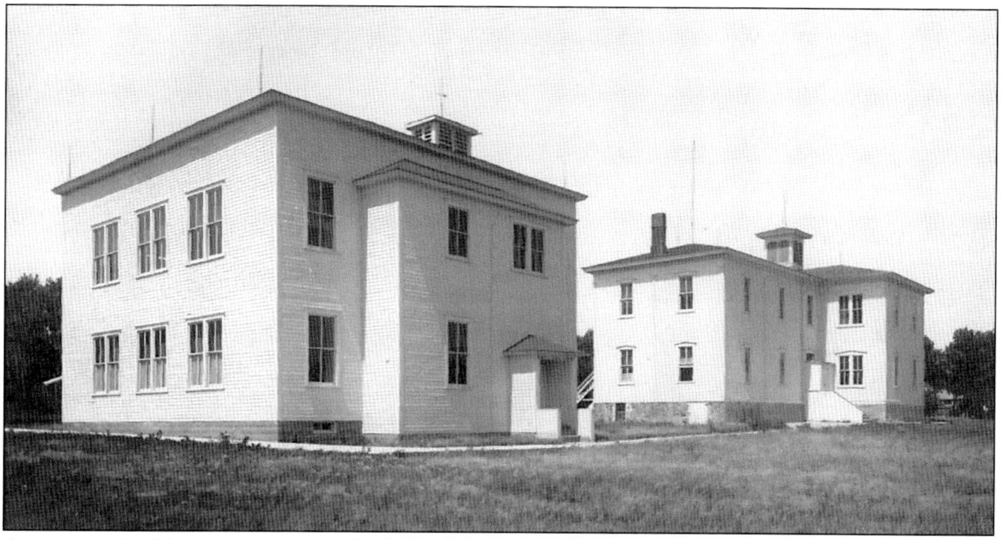

A separate building, standing to the left of the original school (furthest right), was constructed in 1908 for high school students. The grade school was moved to this building in 1922, when the new brick junior-senior high school building was erected.

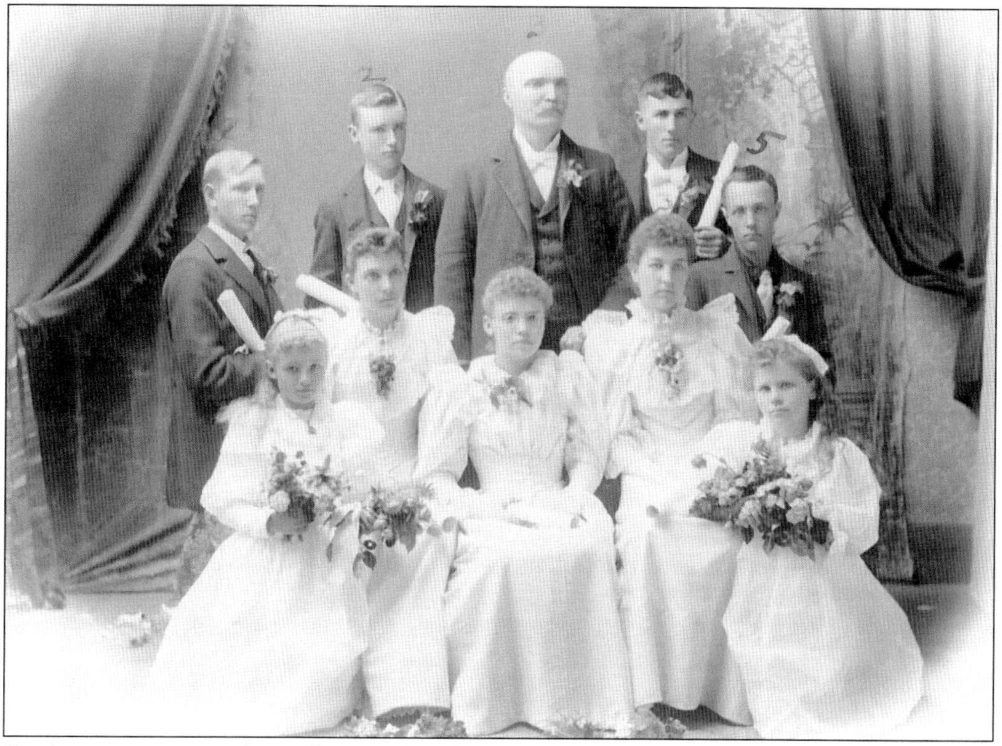

Graduating was not only a milestone, but almost a privilege, as many pioneers did not graduate from high school. Members of this graduating class had honors bestowed on them at the opera house on May 25, 1894. This photograph includes, from left to right, (first row) unidentified, Nellie Richardson (Tackaberry), Mattie Sleeper, unidentified, and Fanny Coulter; (second row) M. Whaley, ? Crothers, ? Farrel, L. Callahan, ? Sherman. Edna Robinson may be one of the unidentified ladies.

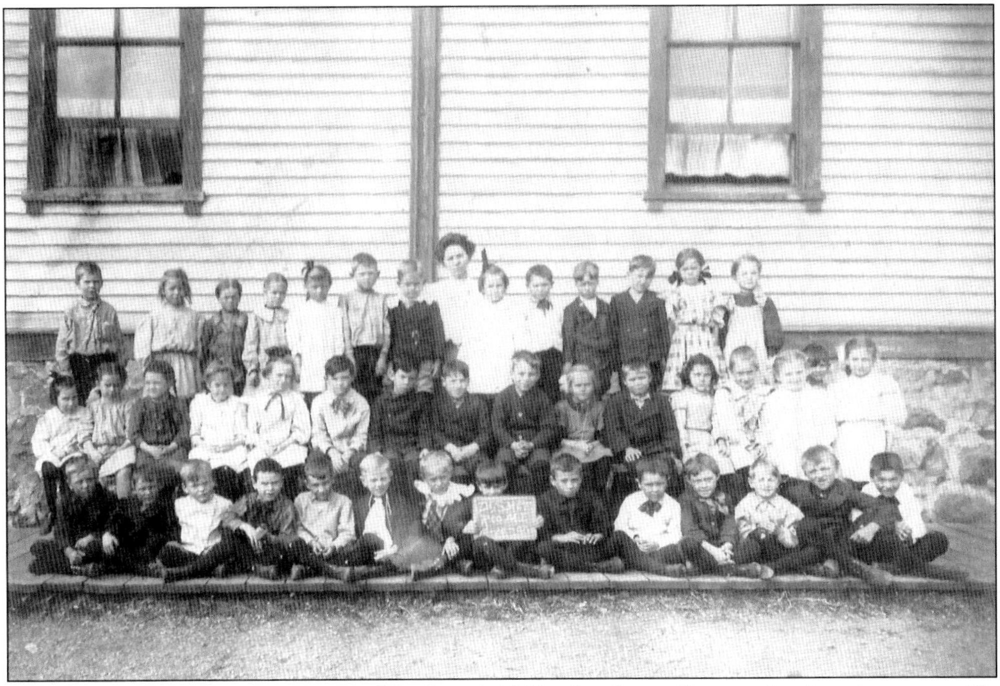

The pupils and teacher in Room I of De Smet's 1907 school proudly pose for this picture outside the wooden schoolhouse on Third Street. The room was kept cool in the warm months with an open window, curtains billowing in the wind.

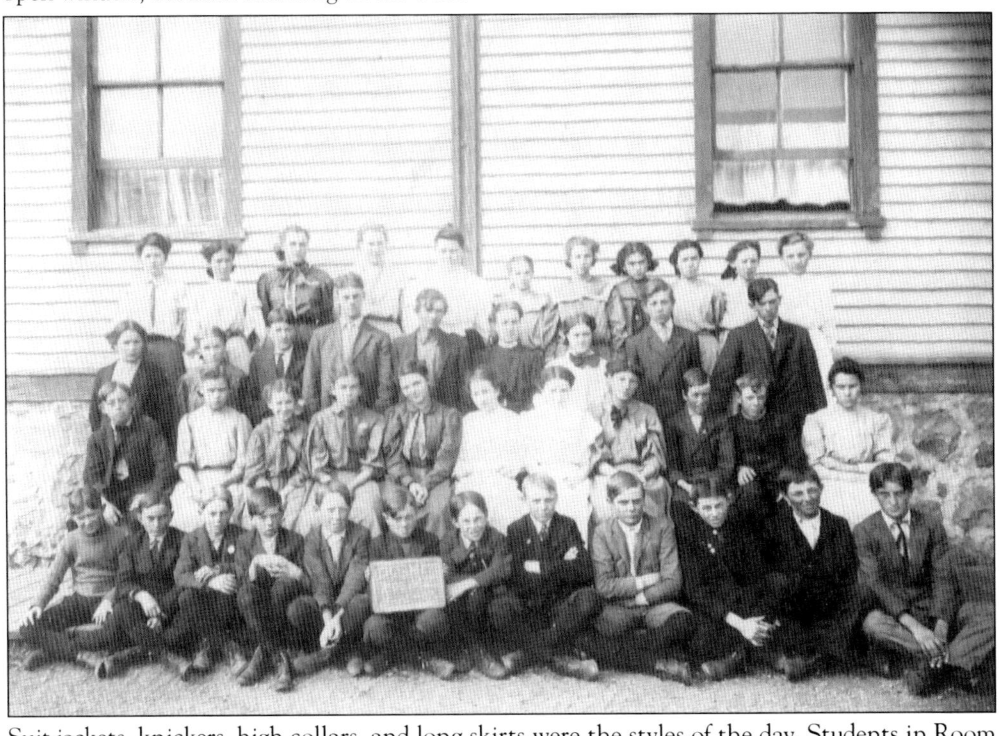

Suit jackets, knickers, high collars, and long skirts were the styles of the day. Students in Room V seemed to have dressed for the occasion of taking this picture on October 10, 1907.

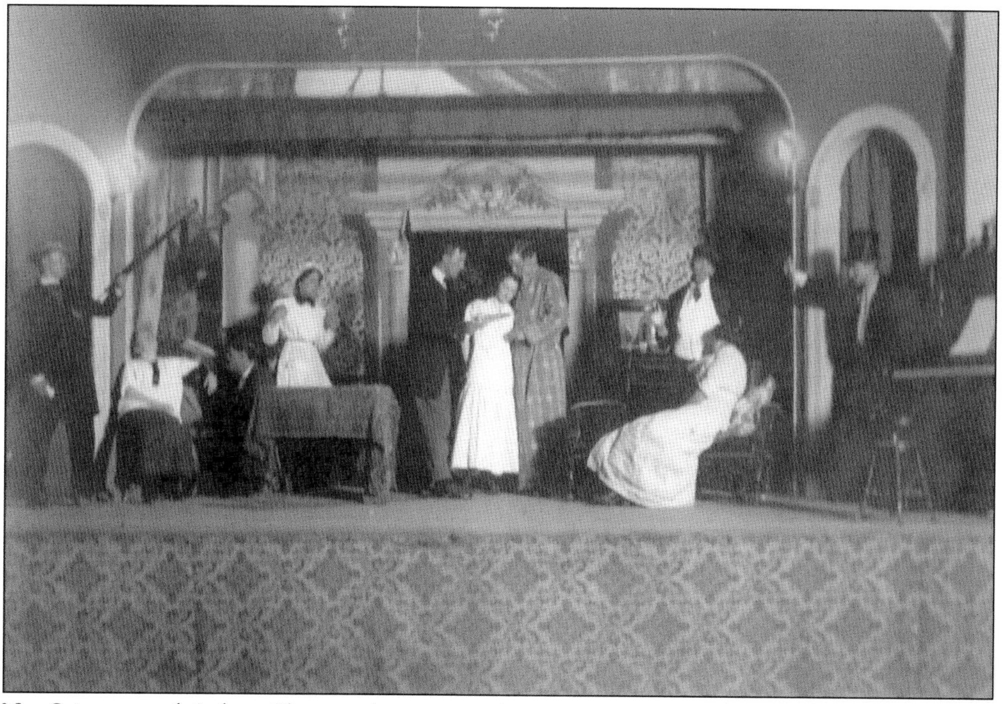

Nat Stimson and Aubrey Sherwood appear in the cast to present a class production performed in Couse Opera House by De Smet's class of 1912. Patrons could attend by ascending a set of steps on the north side of the Couse Building. Ward's Store and Bakery now occupy the Couse Building on the corner of Calumet Avenue and Second Street.

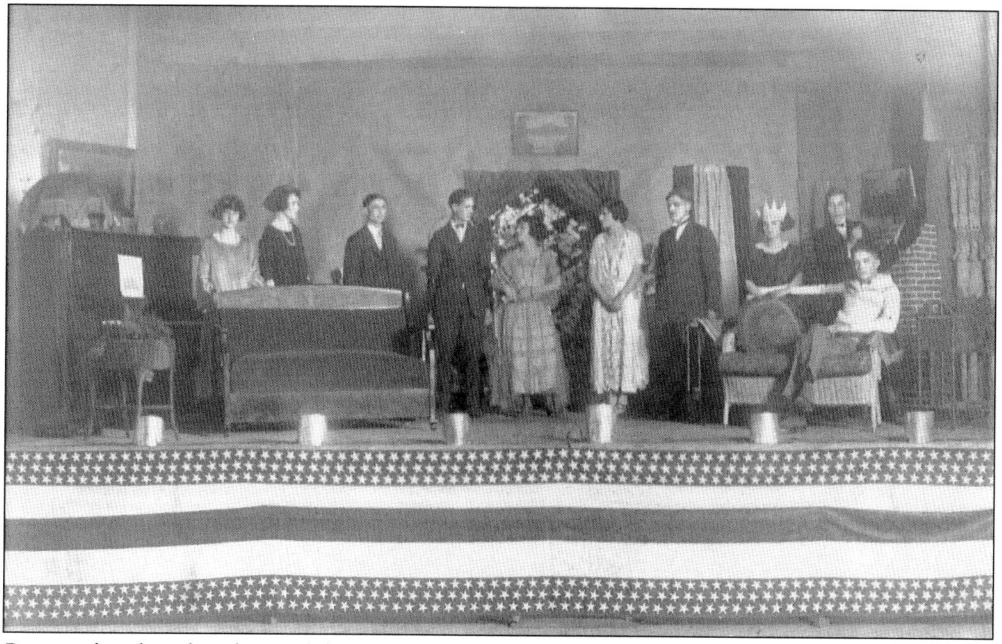

Seemingly relaxed in front of the tin can footlights, this cast appeared in a 1925 production at the opera house. This show was directed by none other than Laura (Engebretson) Sherwood, the wife of Aubrey Sherwood.

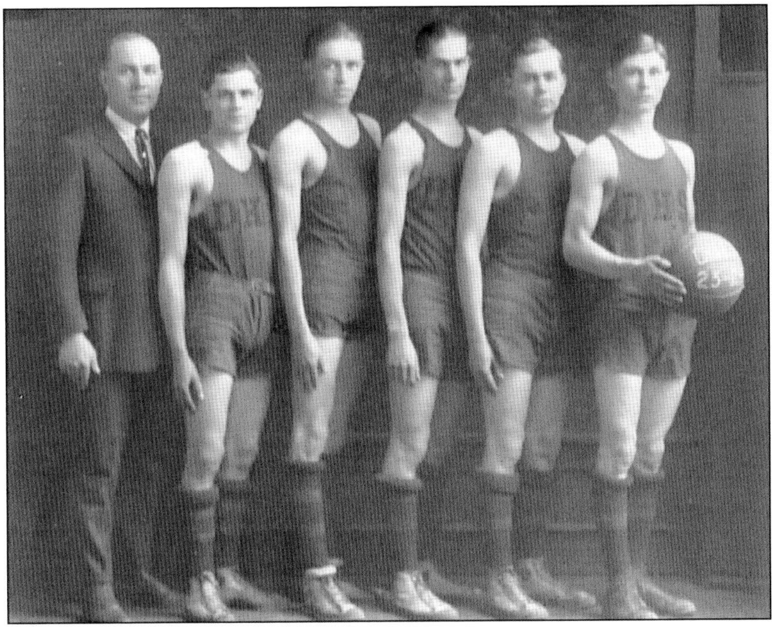

This photograph of the 1923–1924 De Smet team includes, from left to right, Coach Itzen, Fay Smity, Kermit Buchele, Fay Munger, Ray Ely, and Oscar Myre. "DHS" appears on the shirts, and the basketball has "DHS 23–24" written on it.

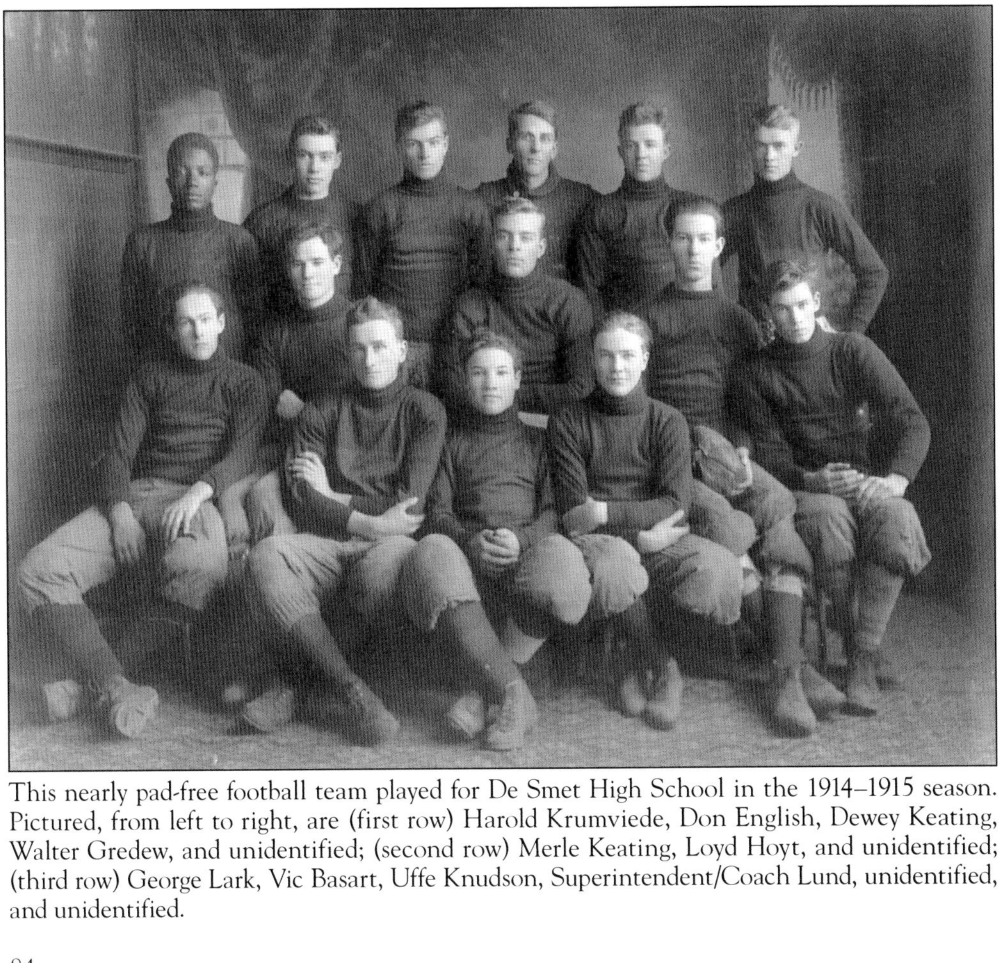

This nearly pad-free football team played for De Smet High School in the 1914–1915 season. Pictured, from left to right, are (first row) Harold Krumviede, Don English, Dewey Keating, Walter Gredew, and unidentified; (second row) Merle Keating, Loyd Hoyt, and unidentified; (third row) George Lark, Vic Basart, Uffe Knudson, Superintendent/Coach Lund, unidentified, and unidentified.

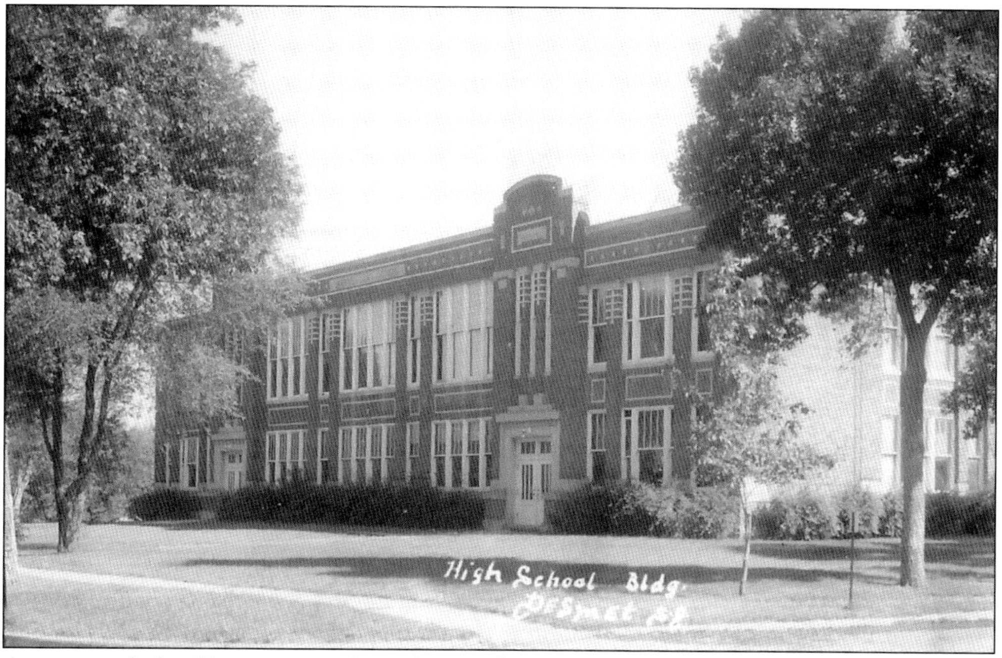

A new era of school history was taking place in the 1920s, when the public school moved from an old wooden building to a modern brick one. This brick structure was built in 1922 for the junior and senior high school students. It was razed in 1997 and replaced with an even more modern building in 1998.

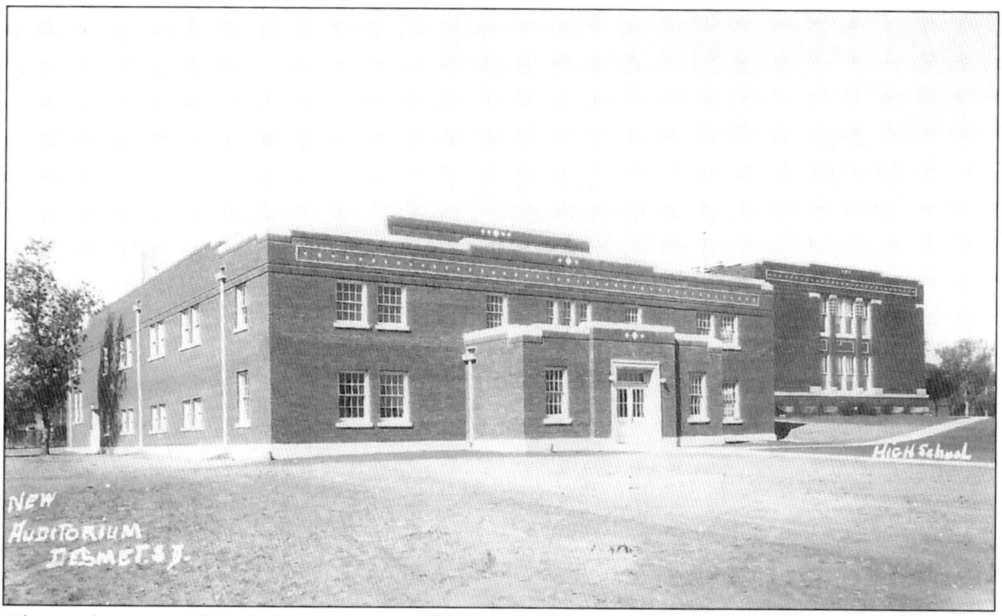

Cheers, boos, and hand-clapping can still be heard in the 1938–1939 WPA-built auditorium. The City of De Smet contributed $7,000 and had the use of three rooms; $18,000 was raised through bond sales, and the federal government contributed the rest. The National Guard used the auditorium for $75 a month. The first graduation exercise was held in the new auditorium in May 1939.

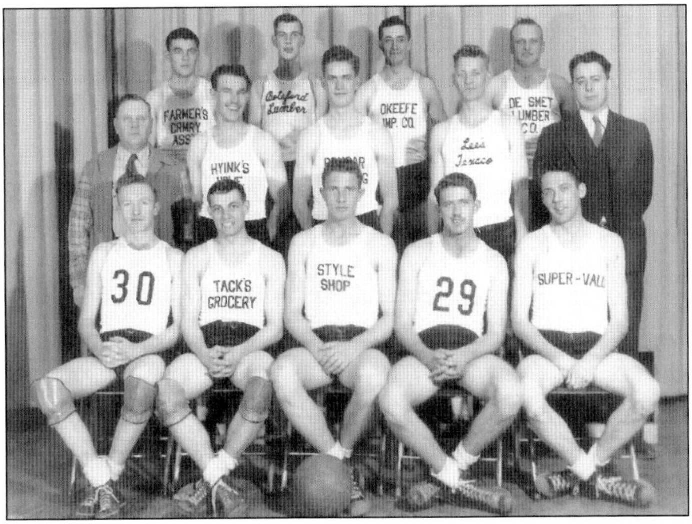

The businesses stitched on the 1946–1947 jerseys bring memories to some. Those pictured here are, from left to right, (first row) Bob Klinkel, Dick Coughlin, John Swenson, Bob Melstad, and Jim Melstad; (second row) assistant coach Charles Lindsey, Bob Cavanaugh, Glen Madsen, Norman Madsen, and coach Pat Hartnett; (third row) Jim Coughlin, "Tex" Myers, Bill Coughlin, and Barney Mahoney.

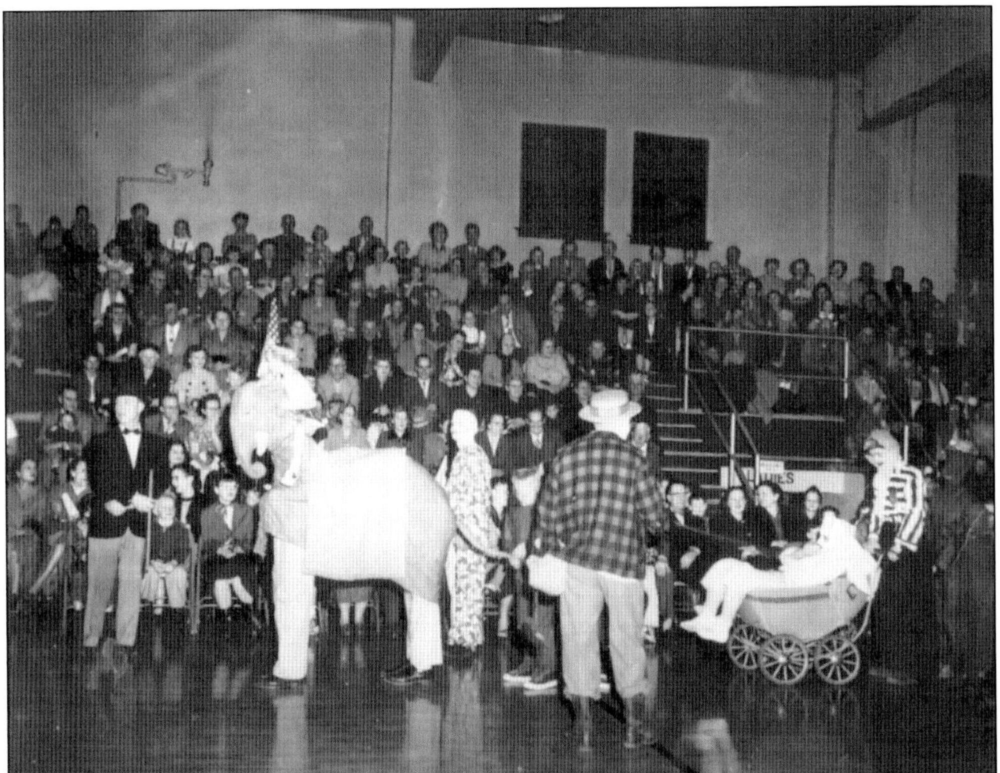

In 1957, crowds roared with laughter as the "trainer" (unidentified) put the "elephant" (Donald Schultz and Alan Wellman, respectively) through its paces. Nancy Schultz is riding on the shoulders of the "elephant." These carnivals were yearly events sponsored by the PTA and always brought a great time to the school year.

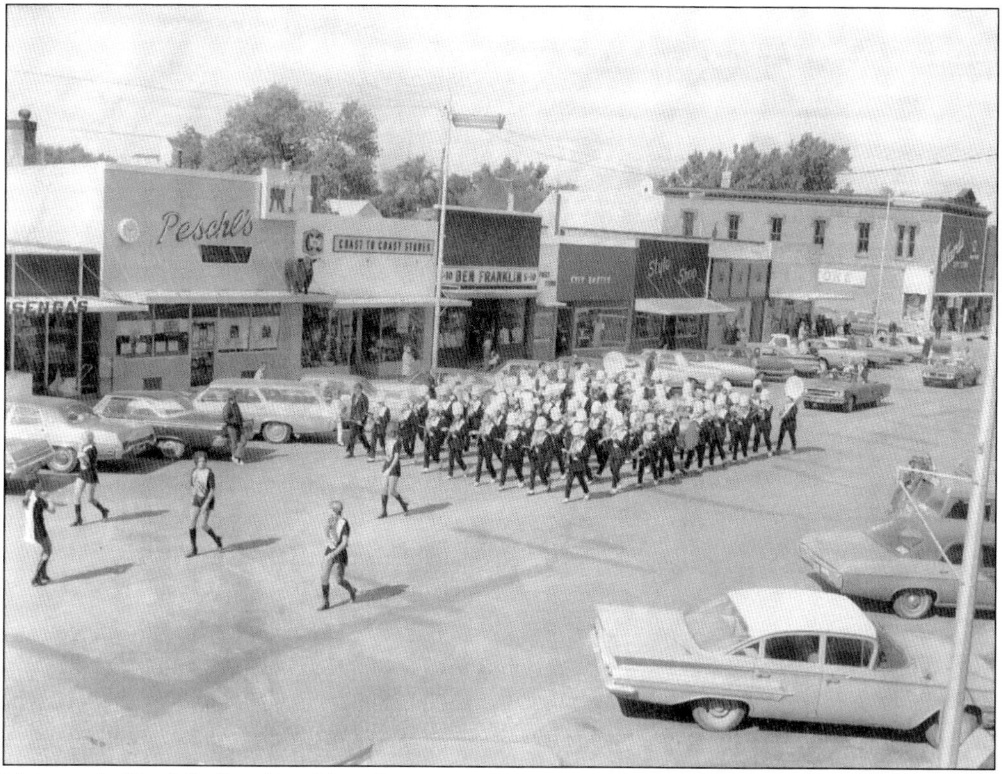

Huisenga's, Peschl's, Ben Franklin, City Bakery, Style Shop, Buchele Drug Store, and Ward's Store all line the street as the De Smet High School Band leads the 1972 homecoming parade with the homecoming king and queen, Marvin McCune and Bergie Belzer, and their court immediately behind.

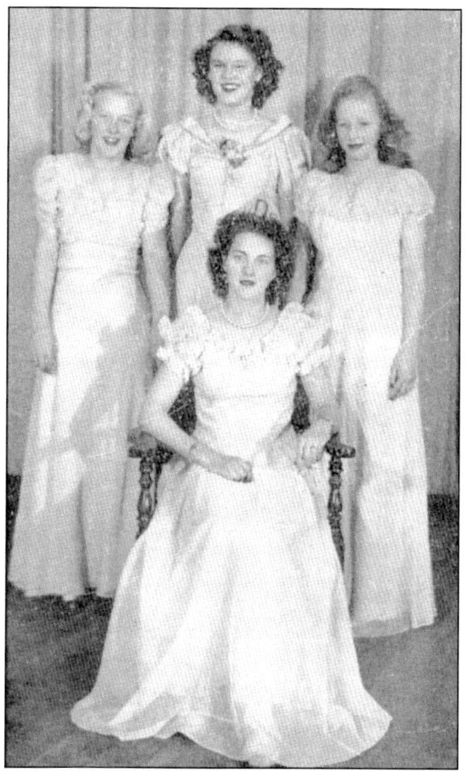

Queen Pearl Smith (Coughlin) reigns as the first homecoming queen for De Smet High School. The year was 1946; attendants are, from left to right, Stacia Larson, Marcine Brandner and Annie Smith. Pearl says she had to rush up to the high school office and make her own crown and the letter *D* to put in the center out of construction paper; she fastened it all with a paper clip.

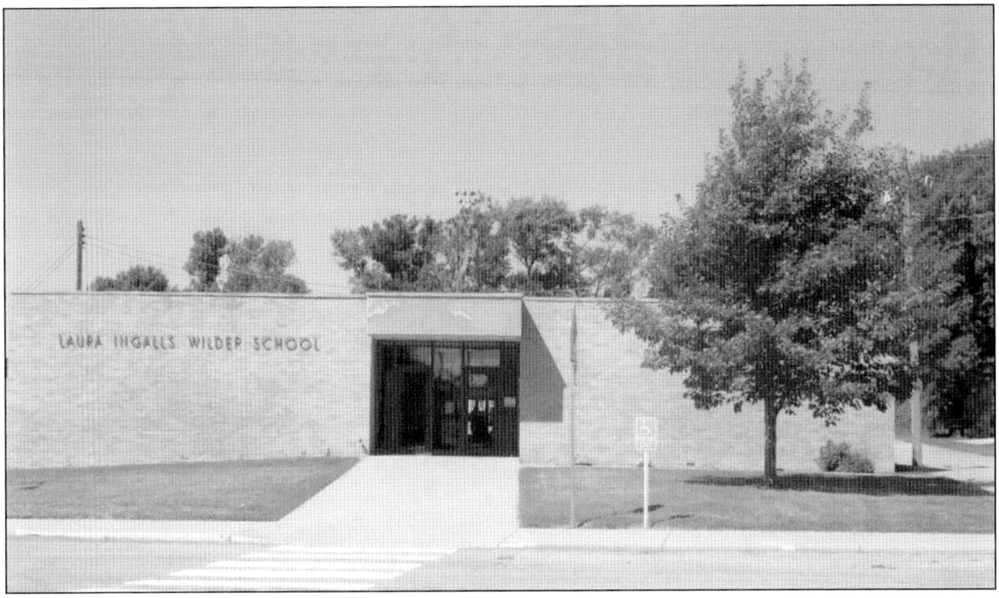

The Laura Ingalls Wilder Elementary School became a dream come true on March 12, 1963. An agreement with the City of De Smet allowed the school district to acquire the present armory and extend its classroom availability. This was an improvement over using rented rooms in the American Lutheran Church. The building houses kindergarten through fifth grade.

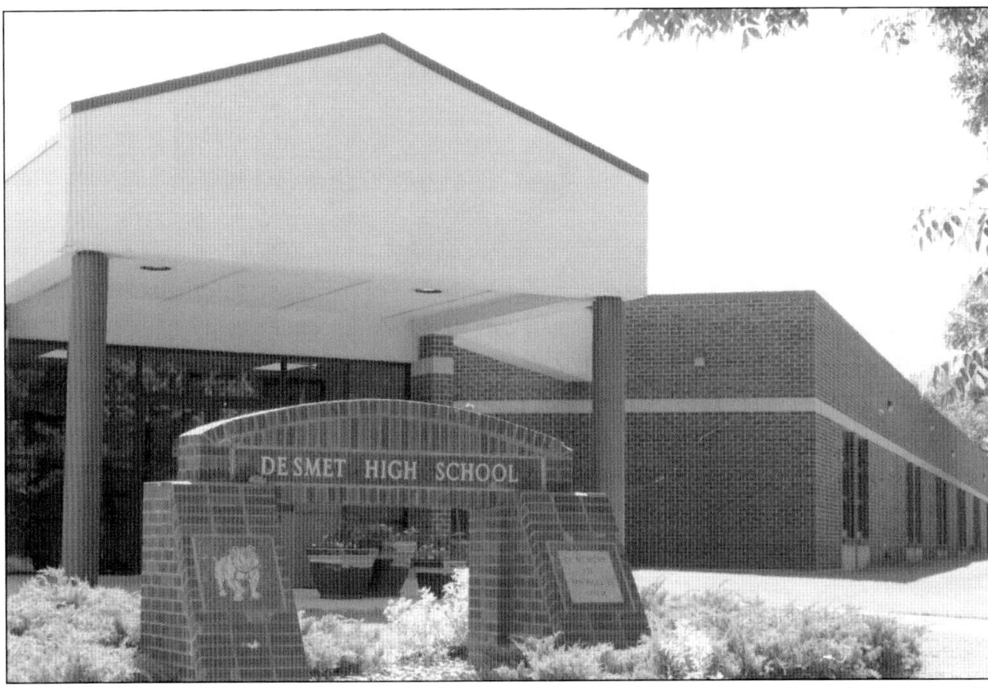

The residents of the De Smet area were always seeking to improve the quality of education for their children and to give them the best setting possible to acquire knowledge. The "grand old lady" of 1922 was demolished, and from its dust arose this new building in 1998. This school building now houses grades 6 through 12.

Five

THAT'S ENTERTAINMENT

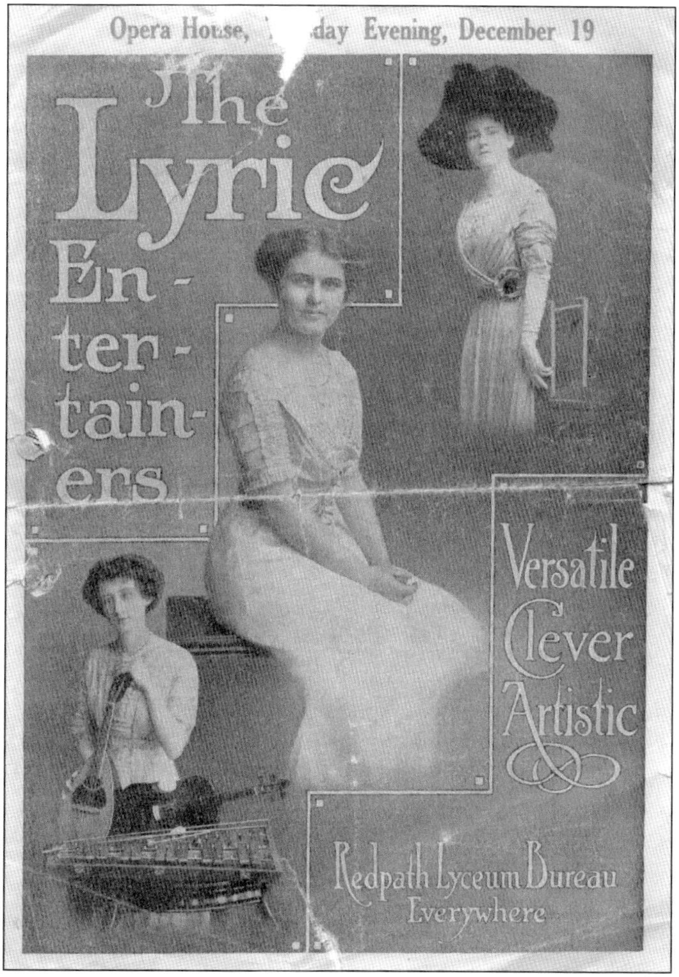

Picnics, Chautauquas, boating, and community gatherings were welcome affairs. Baseball teams played their way into the hearts of De Smet's people. Any tavern big enough to have a dance lured in customers with the sounds of the latest tunes. Basketball filled the break between baseball and football seasons. All this, and more, was part of the entertainment of the era.

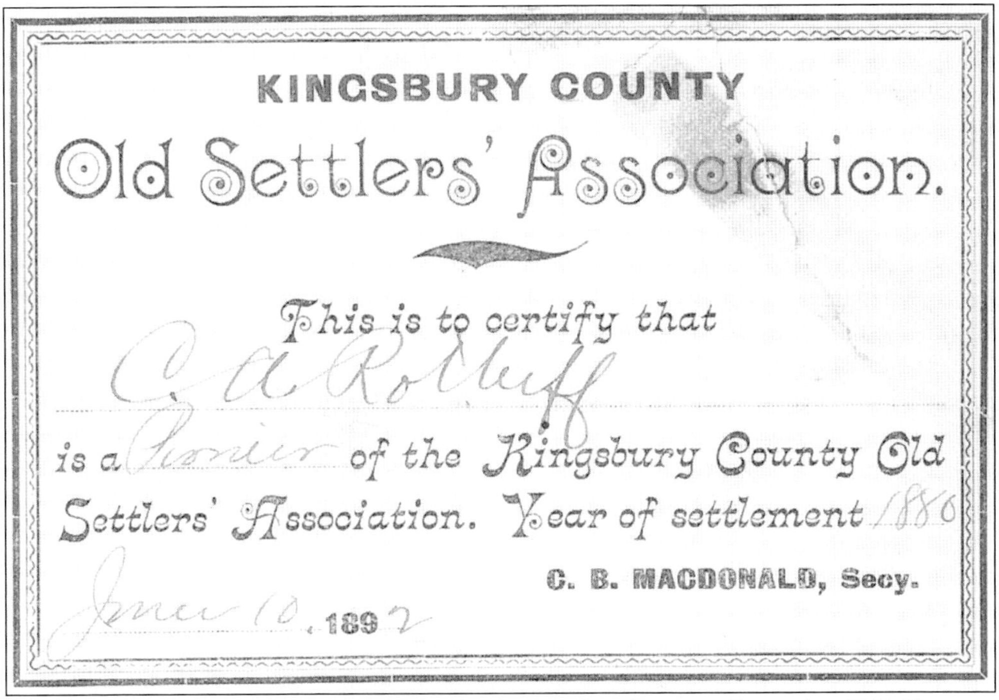

KINGSBURY COUNTY

Old Settlers' Association.

This is to certify that

C. A. Roluff

is a Pioneer of the Kingsbury County Old Settlers' Association. Year of settlement 1880

C. B. MACDONALD, Secy.

June 10, 1892

The longest continuous celebration in eastern South Dakota began in Esmond in 1888. For want of a better name, it was advertised as "Old Settlers' Reunion." It was an immediate success. On June 10, 1890, De Smet joined the celebration. Folks from all points of the compass converged on the small town. In the minds of many current De Smet citizens, June 10 is remembered as a gala event.

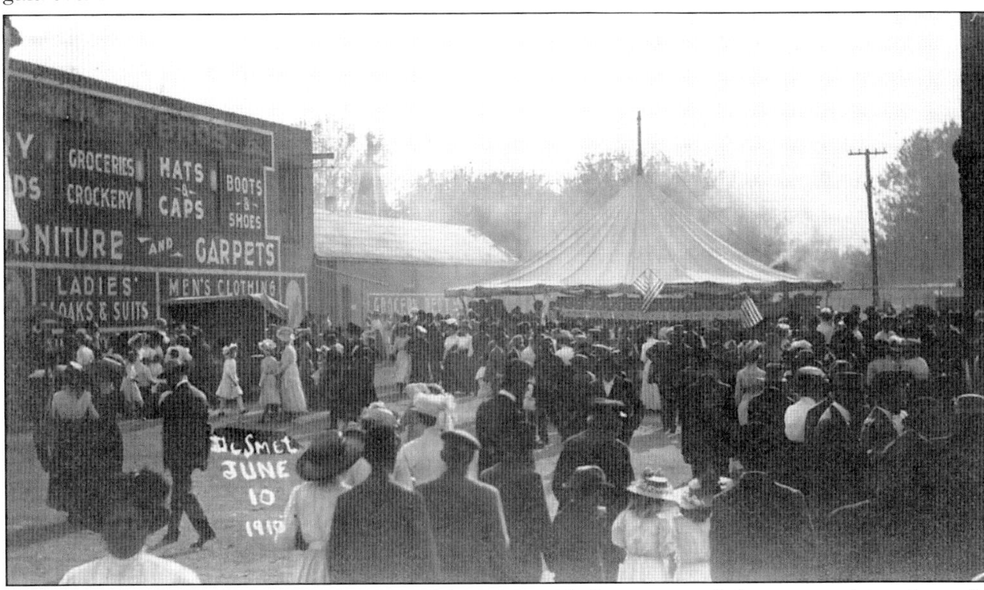

Excitement for the Old Settlers Day Celebration and the magic of the carnival has brought crowds of hundreds to De Smet since 1890, as seen in this June 10, 1910, photograph. The wooden windmill standing aloft to the right may have been one reason De Smet proclaimed, "We have ample water."

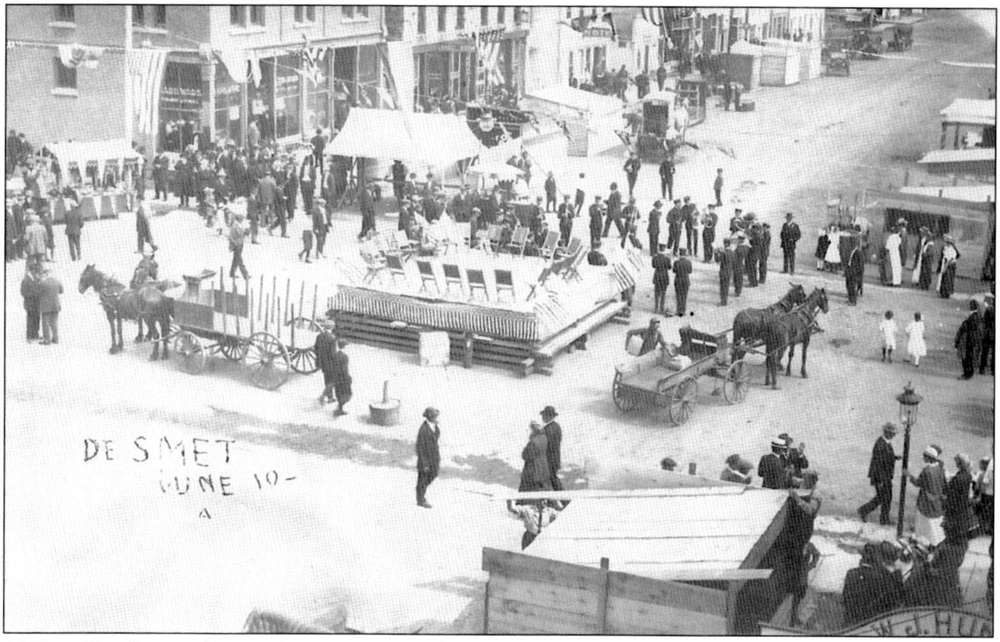

Miller's Hardware, the pool room, and the hotel are in good positions on the west side of Calumet Avenue to witness all that is happening in De Smet on a June 10 around 1910.

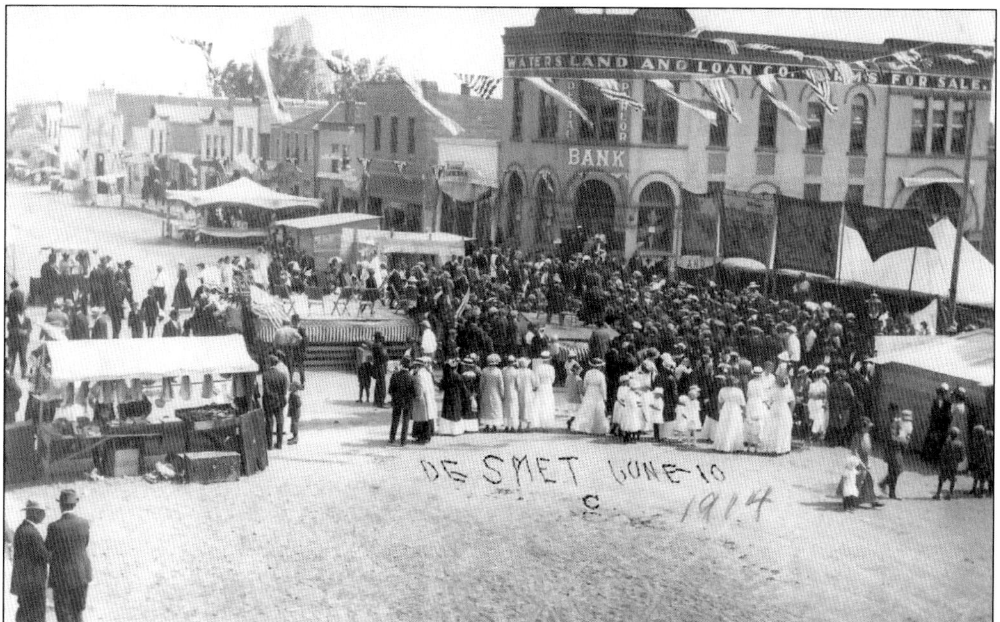

Waters Land and Loan building captures a large part of the northeast corner of Calumet Avenue and Second Street. However, all eyes seem to be turned to what is happening on the small stage nearly in the middle of the crowd. Painted ponies on the merry-go-round gallop in a circle of fun and laughter.

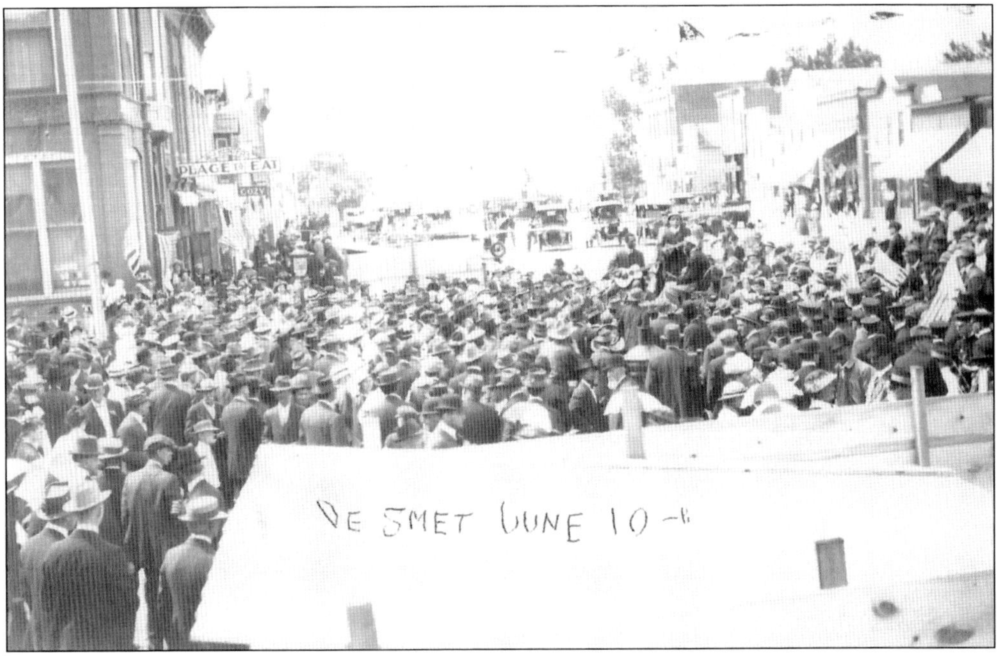

Large crowds gathered to celebrate Old Settlers Day on a June 10 in the early 1900s. The occasion meant bringing out "your best duds" and joining the festivities. W.J. Hunter, owner of Place to Eat, was probably grinning ear-to-ear in anticipation of serving many of the groups.

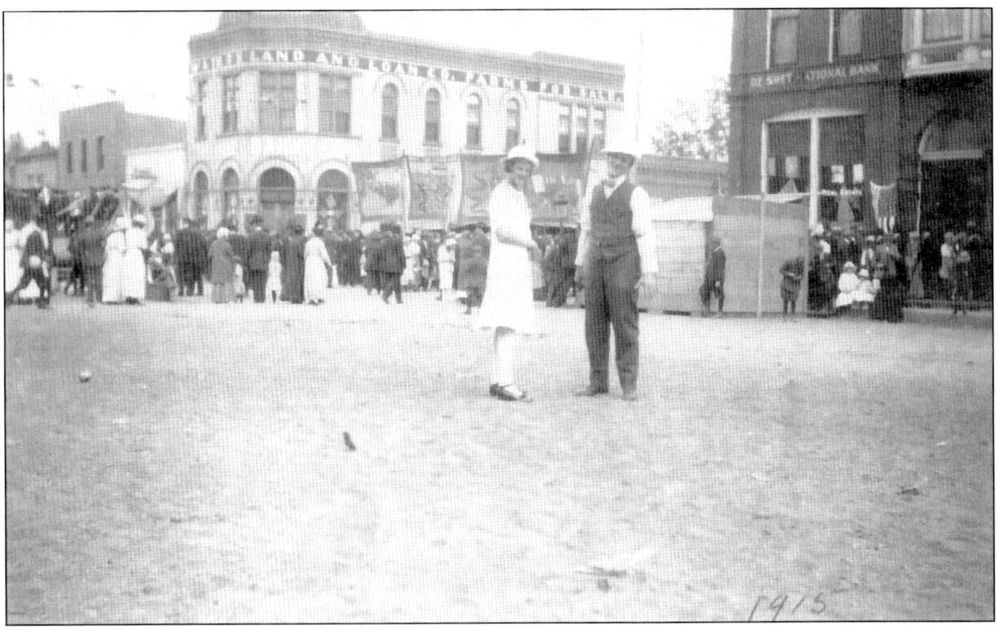

In 1915, F.L. and Ellen Brewer are all decked out for the June 10 celebration. The De Smet National Bank stands on the southeast corner of Calumet Avenue and Second Street. The sideshow banners can be seen stretching between the bank and the Waters' Land and Loan.

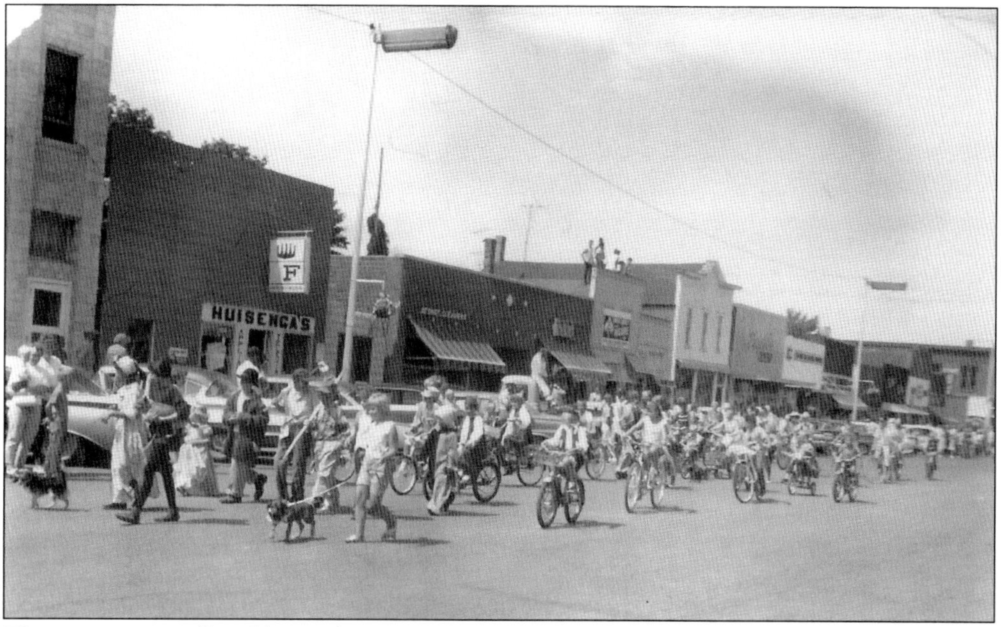

This picture is a collectible as it has Huisenga's Appliance in the background. Huisenga's history speaks of "taking on the Frigidaire line" in 1950. Owners moved the business farther north in 1968; therefore, the image can be dated to between 1950 and 1968. The parade appears to consist of children, bicycles, and dogs. Folks on top of Wika-Jensen Insurance have a bird's-eye view.

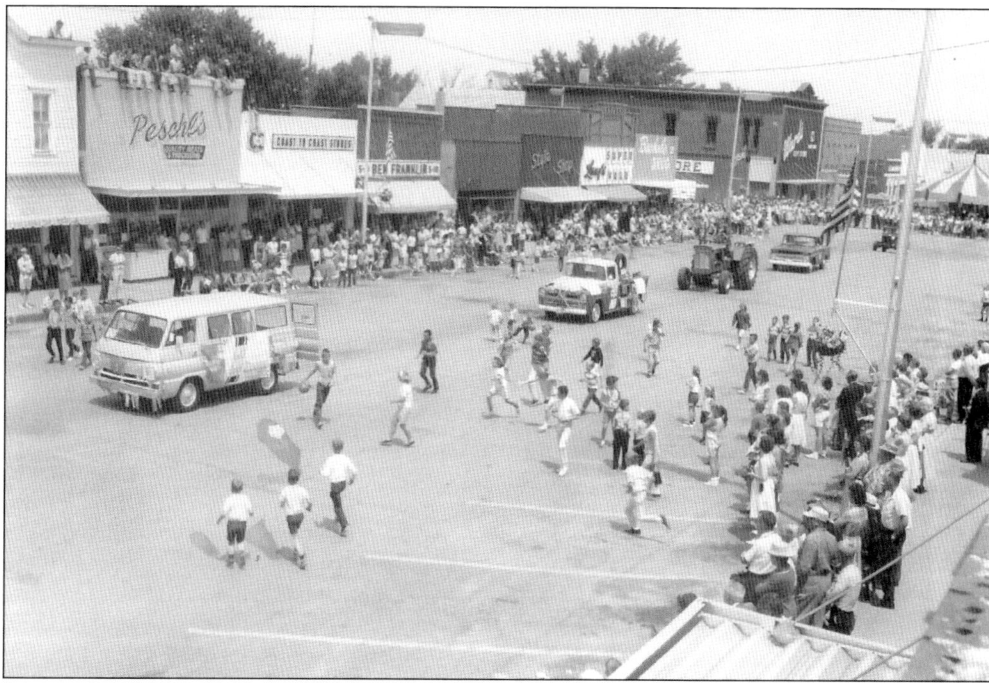

A few kids, a parade, some dogs, and crazy characters led to the wildest day that De Smet had ever seen when it held its first Circus Day event. Merchants dressed as clowns put on a real celebration. People for miles around attended the event. The top of Peschl's building gave a perfect overview of all that was happening.

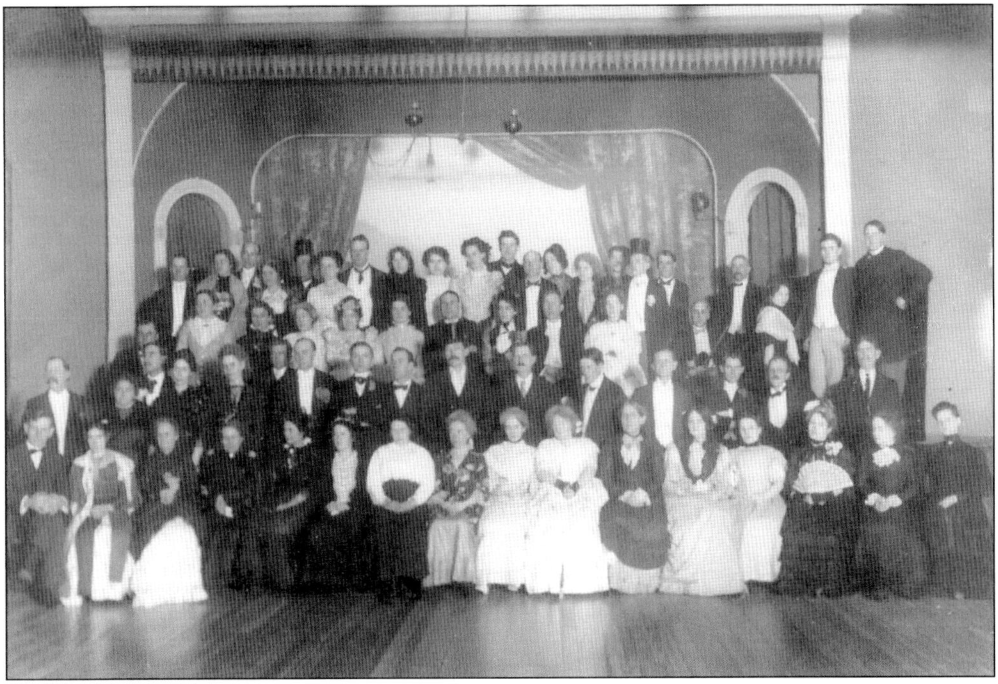

An opportunity to escape into another world came in the form of the play *The Cloud Chasers*, which was presented at Couse Opera House. According to this photograph, a large cast was needed to produce and perform the play.

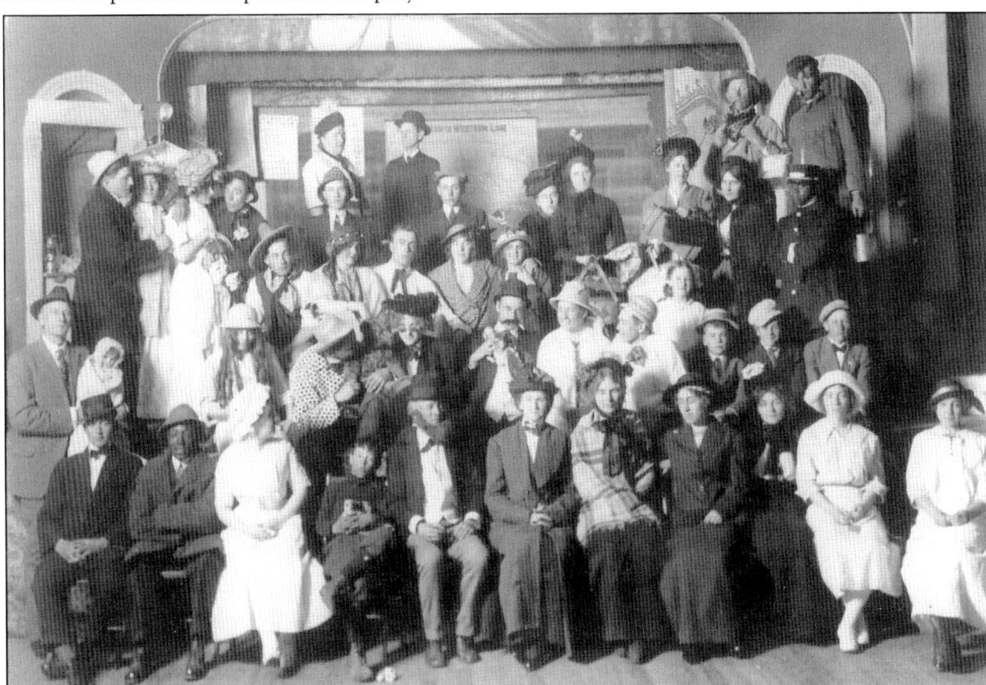

These performers put forth their best to make this play a success at the Couse Opera House. Some—maybe all—appear as though they remained in costume to have this photograph taken.

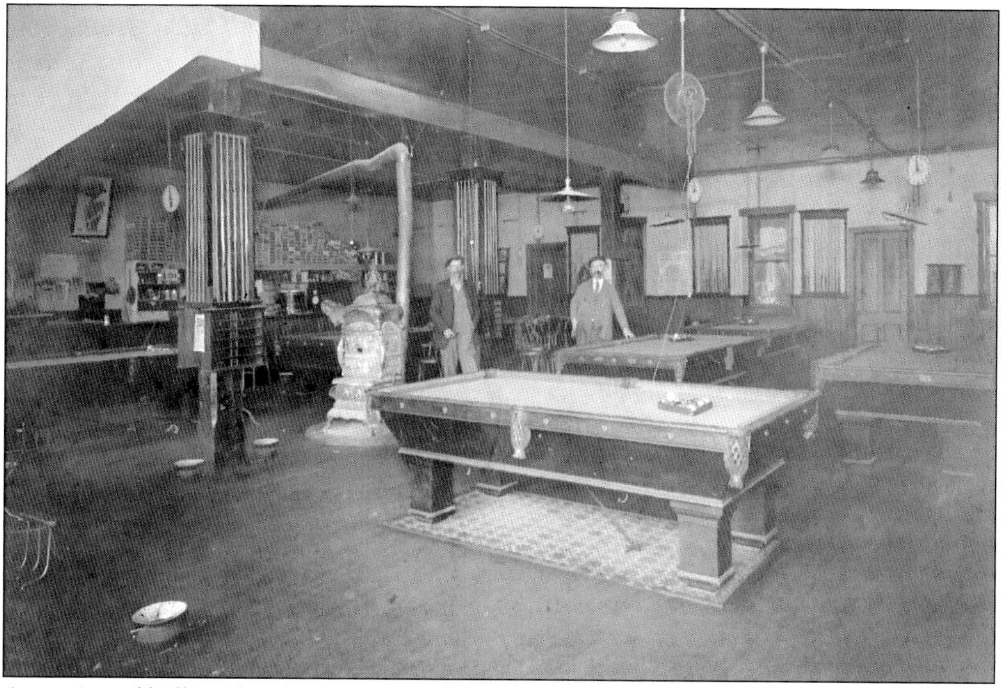

A town's pool hall can be a lively crossroads where friends meet to exchange news and shoot some pool over a cool libation. Fred Floto stands to the right in this 1921 photograph of his pool hall, located where the present-day Dugout is on Calumet Avenue. Floto's establishment was heated by the ornate coal stove to the left of the unidentified man.

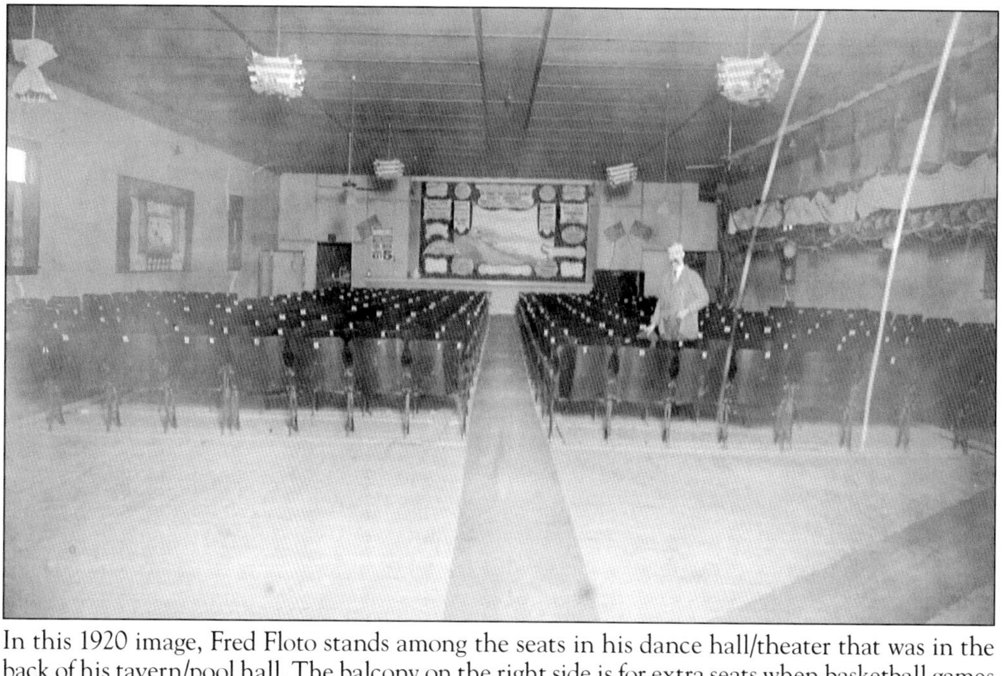

In this 1920 image, Fred Floto stands among the seats in his dance hall/theater that was in the back of his tavern/pool hall. The balcony on the right side is for extra seats when basketball games would be played here. Today, after some alteration, this section of the Dugout is still maintained for dances and other social events.

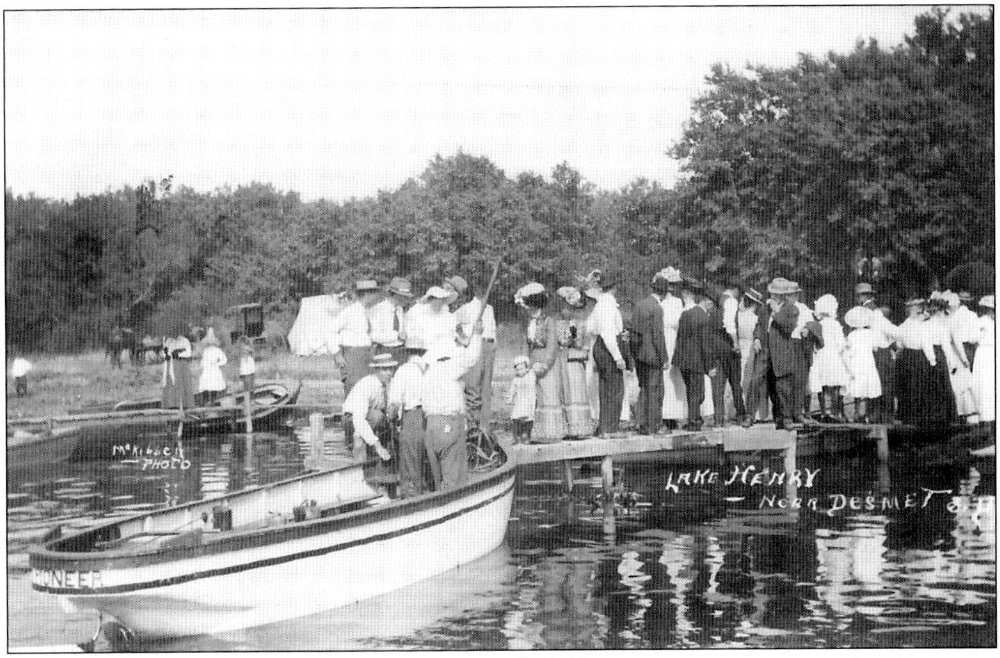

A McKibben photograph shows ladies, gents, and children waiting to step into the *Pioneer* on Lake Henry. Lake Henry was named for an Army surveyor and is one of the Twin Lakes, Lake Thompson being the other. The large grove seen in the back of this picture would have been perfect for a picnic, or, as the tent indicates, camping.

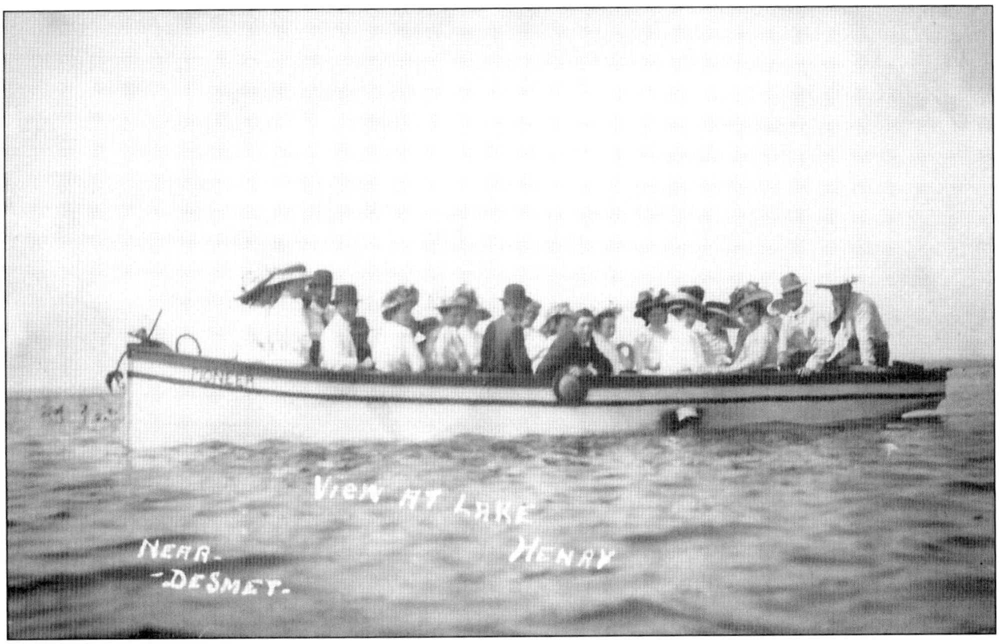

Lake-goers are afloat in a boat built by George Pirlet and Jim Patterson. Cruising on Lake Henry on a summer afternoon brings sweet memories of the rides they offered in their gas-powered boat. The *Pioneer* could accommodate 28 people, and it appears from looking at the above photograph that they would have to have made more than one outing on some afternoons.

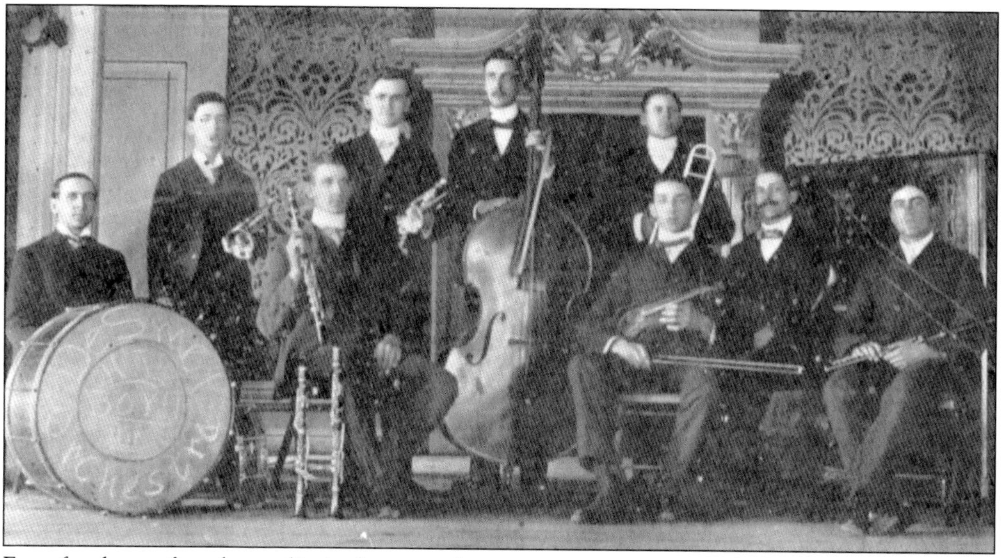

Even for those of modest or limited means, there was entertainment to be had in the small town. The De Smet Concert Orchestra appears to be set to go in the Couse Opera House. Unfortunately, the names of the participants are unavailable.

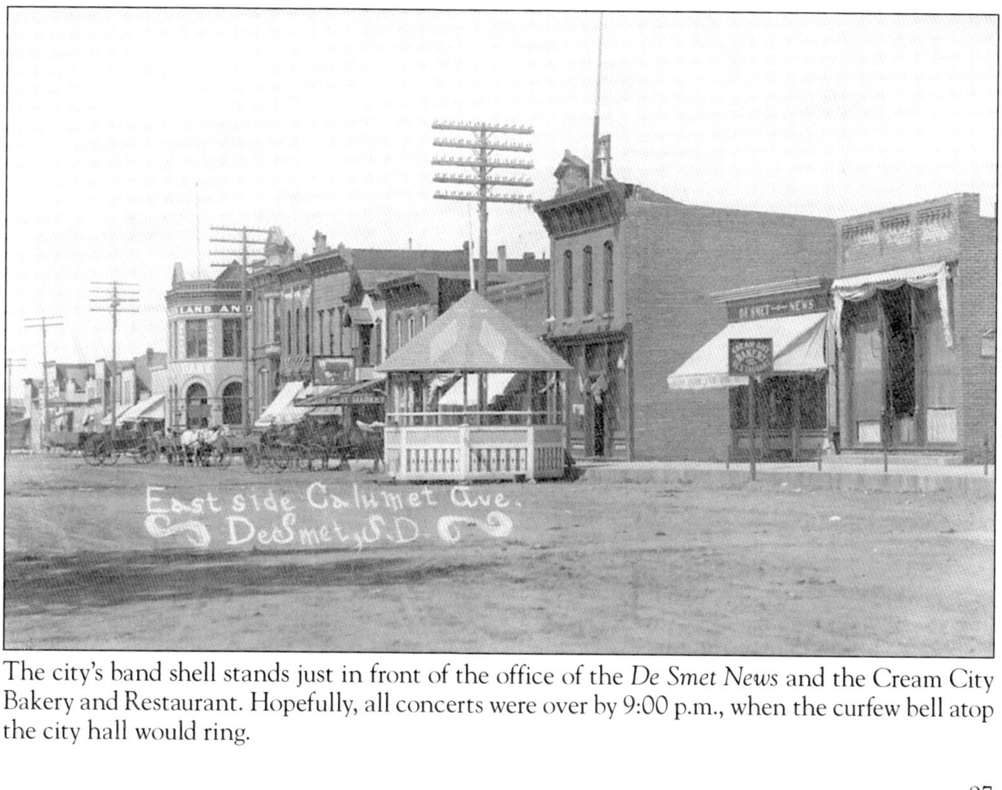

The city's band shell stands just in front of the office of the *De Smet News* and the Cream City Bakery and Restaurant. Hopefully, all concerts were over by 9:00 p.m., when the curfew bell atop the city hall would ring.

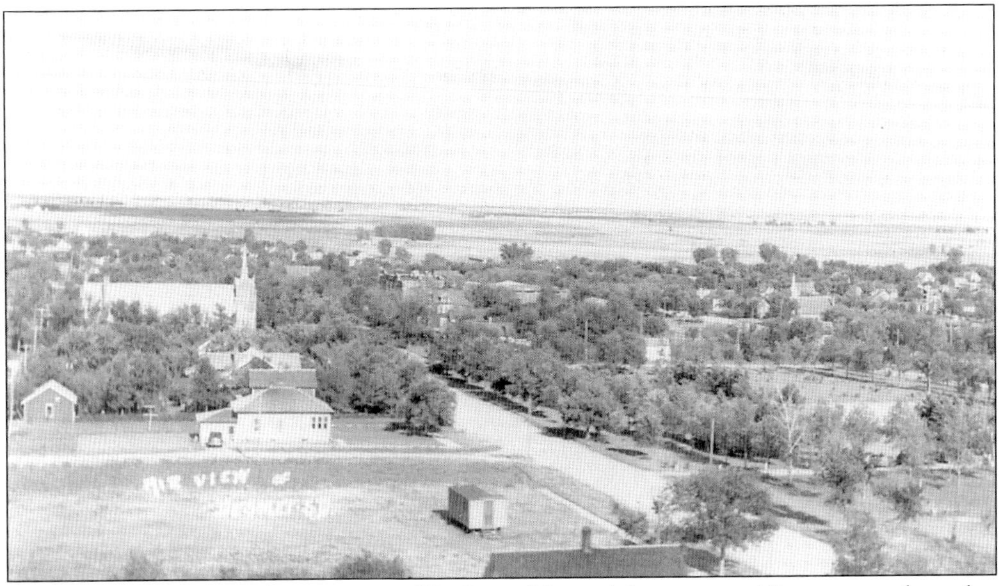

Washington Park lies in the west part of De Smet. The park became a public property through a bank failure in 1929. Already existing, several trees made it an ideal city park. In 1930, driveways were added—one running north-south (seen in the picture, just at bottom edge; it no longer exists); the other, east-west, continues today to divide the park area from the athletic complex.

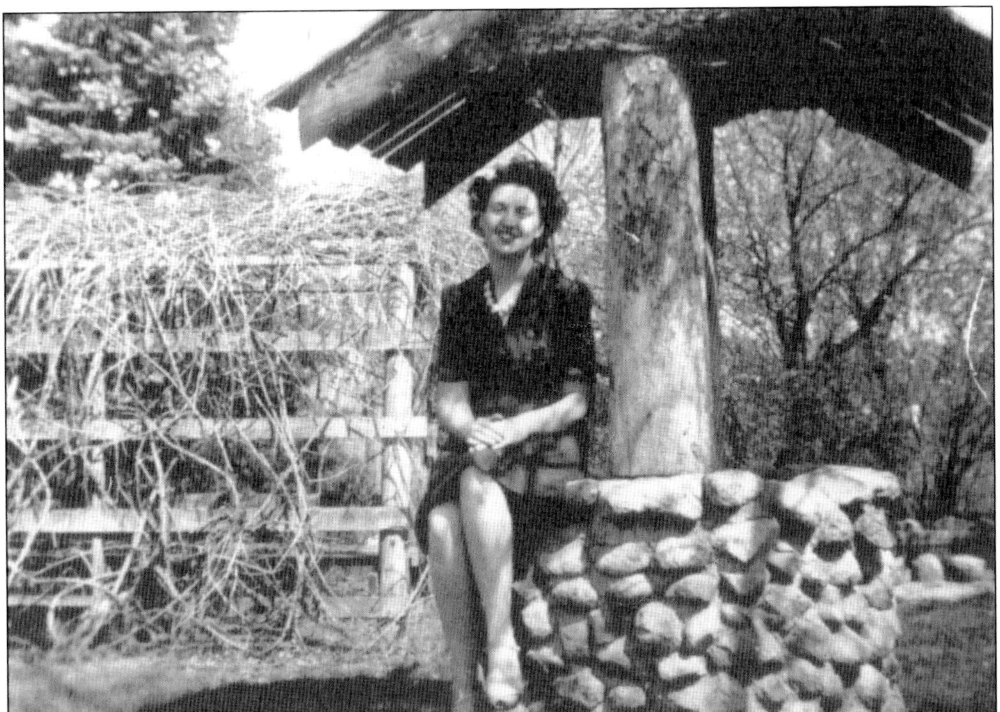

This c. 1940 image shows Dorothy (McAdaragh) Smith sitting on the wishing well in Washington Park. Long-gone now, the grape arbor would have been beautiful come spring and summer. To the delight of youngsters, the pond, just to the right corner, was filled with goldfish.

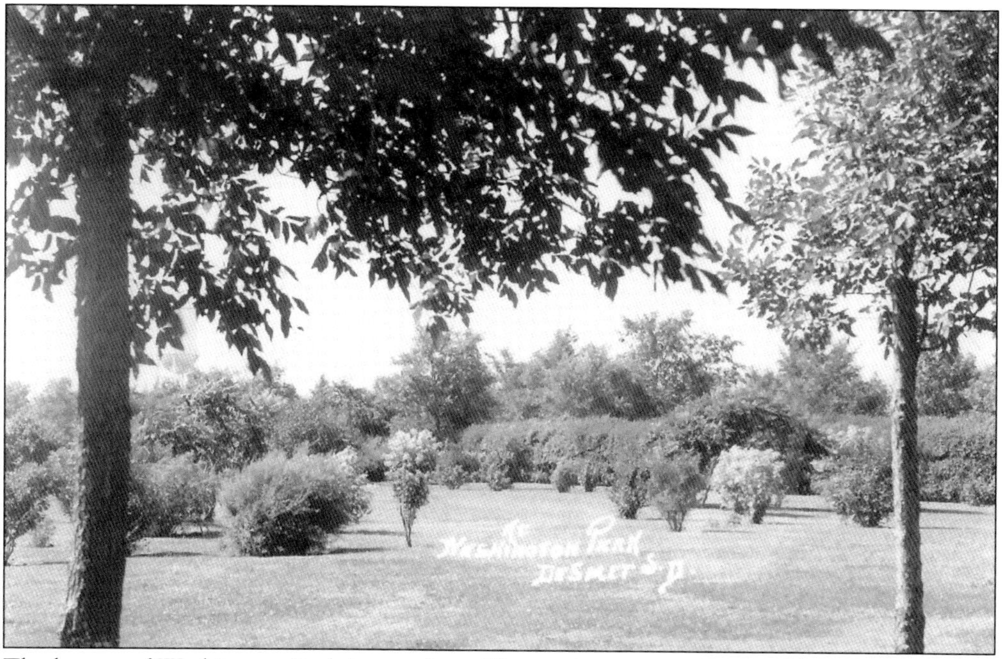

The beauty of Washington Park is seen here. The city's water tower is visible to the top left of the picture. The park continues to be an attraction for many people and organizations. Family and class reunions are often held within its shady confines.

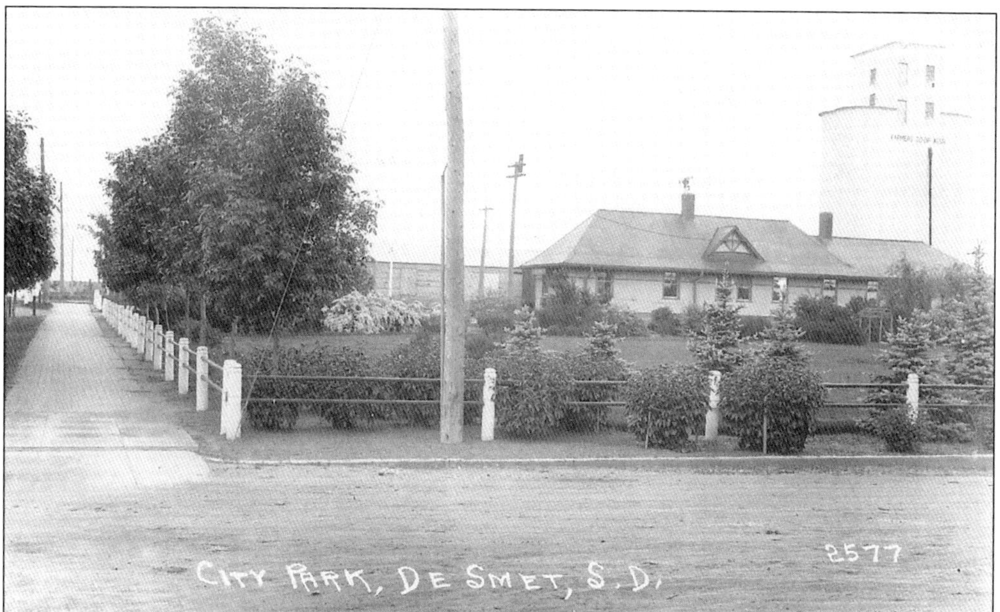

Shown here is the first park in De Smet. Still known as the Railroad Park, it no longer sports the fence; however, the brick walk to the left remains. The many voices of children could be heard in play in days gone by; now, the voices of those living in apartment houses or private homes can be heard. The Farmers Co-op (later Sexauer) elevator was razed 2009.

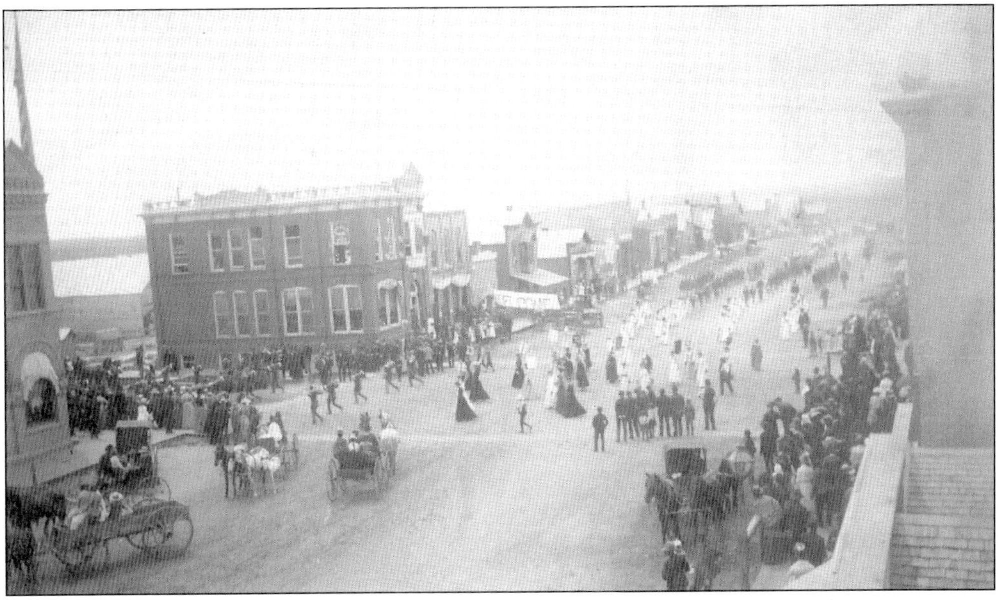

The June 10, 1920, *De Smet News* reports that 42 Esmond young ladies costumed as representing the states and 24 Merchant's Carnival young ladies with banners, all under command of Laura Remington, formed part of the parade that marched down Calumet Avenue and Second Street to the grandstand near the courthouse square.

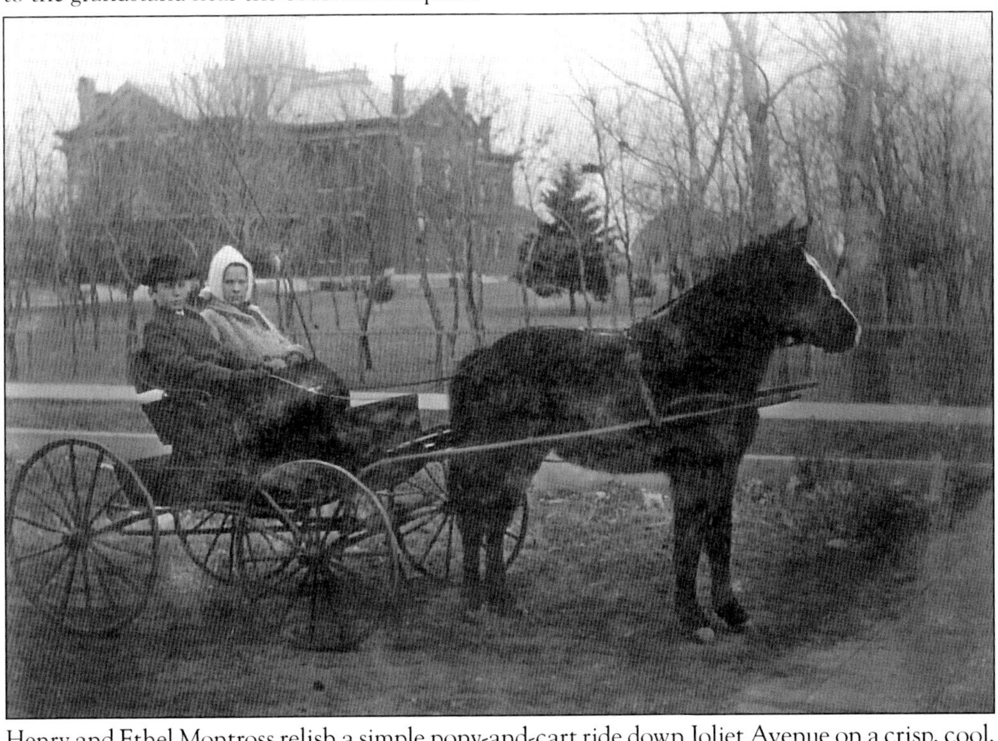

Henry and Ethel Montross relish a simple pony-and-cart ride down Joliet Avenue on a crisp, cool, autumn day. In 1920, the county board decided to make a park out of the courthouse grounds because of the large expanse of lawn, trees, bushes, and gravel walks. It would be assumed this picture was after 1920, as the walk appears to be cement.

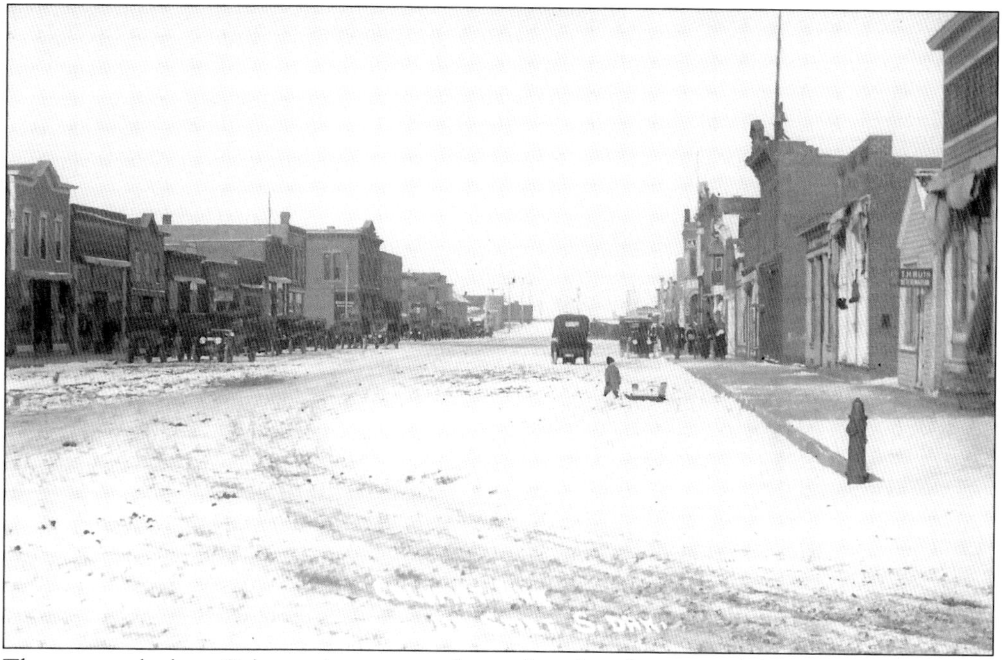

The snowpack along Calumet Avenue was the perfect place for young children to pull their sleds in 1916.

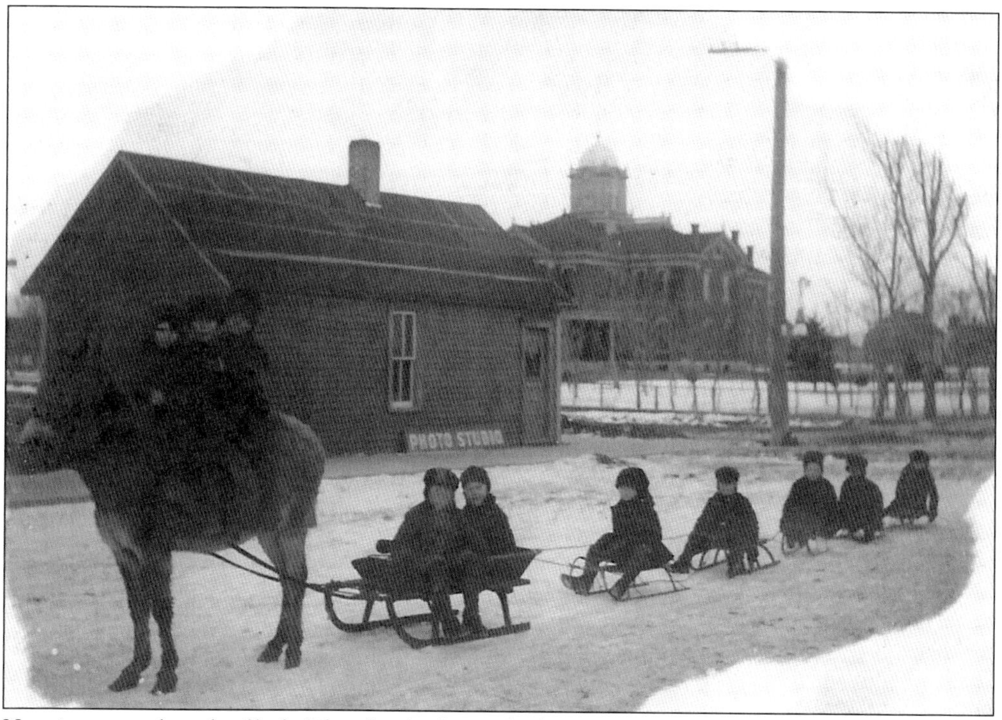

Here is a smart bunch of kids: They let the horse do the work. Ten young children linked together by rope and sled made for winter fun down snowy Second Street. This image was taken before 1920, as there is no cement walk in front of the courthouse fence.

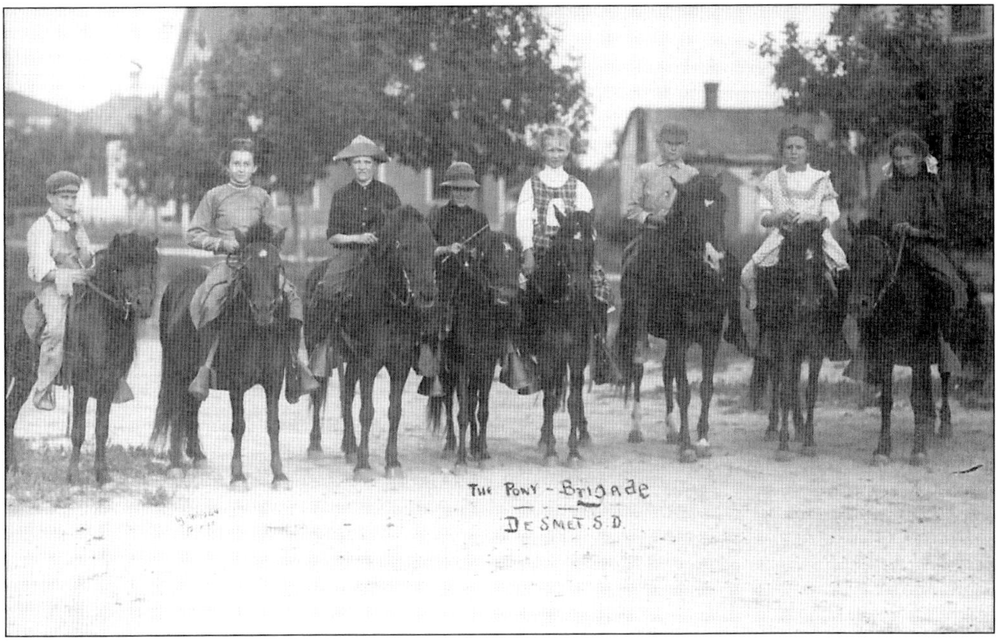

Several postcards depicting De Smet's history show pony brigades. The first young lady to the right in this image is Florence Zahler (Munger).

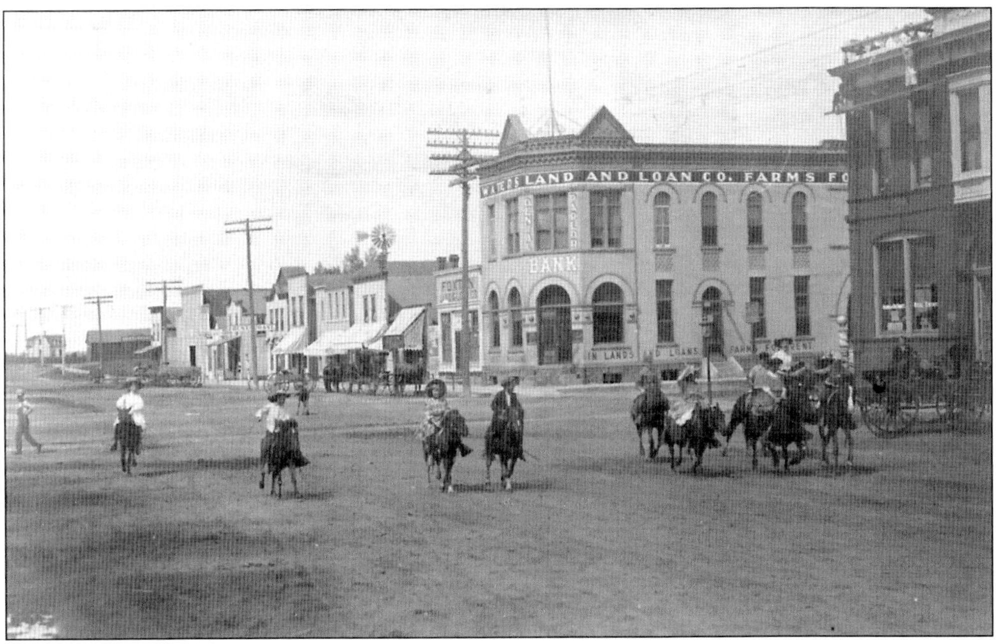

The wide Calumet Avenue gave ample room for the pony brigade to make a run for it, and these playmates appear to take advantage of the opportunity. They have even caught the attention of the gentleman standing on the scaffolding near the top of the bank building.

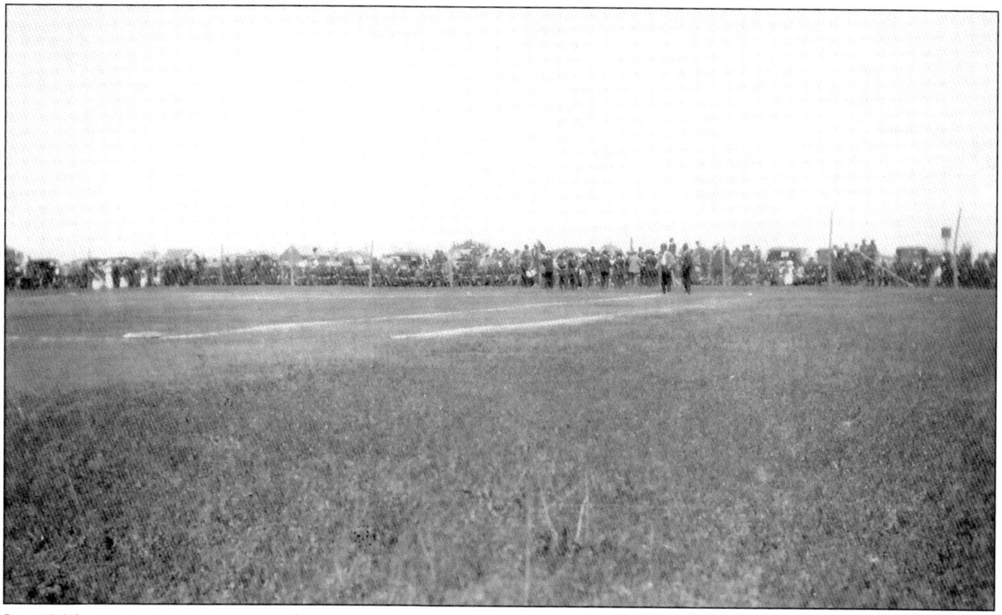

In 1903, six acres were purchased in east De Smet by an athletic association. In 1920, the city bought the site as a ballpark (4-H grounds) and erected a concrete grandstand, high board fence, and a woven wire fence.

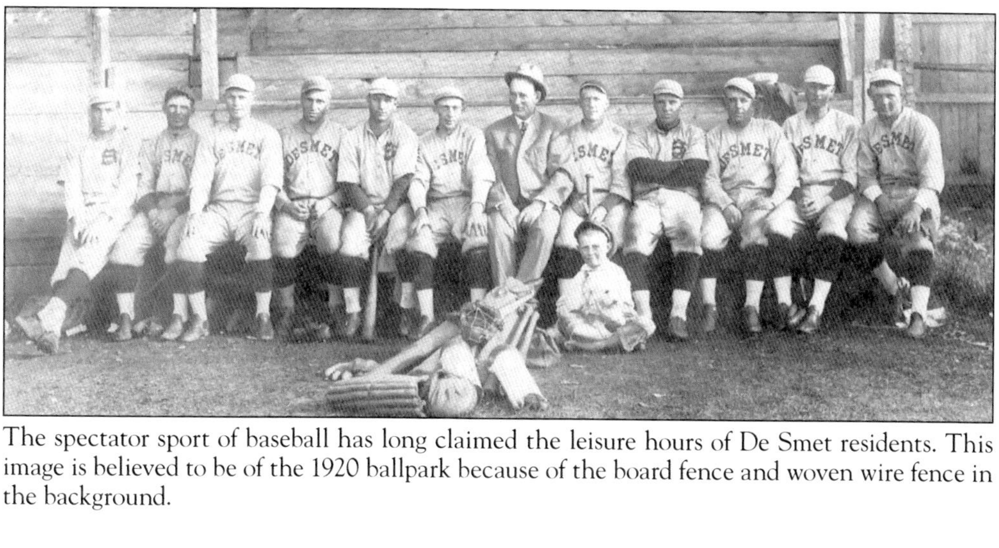

The spectator sport of baseball has long claimed the leisure hours of De Smet residents. This image is believed to be of the 1920 ballpark because of the board fence and woven wire fence in the background.

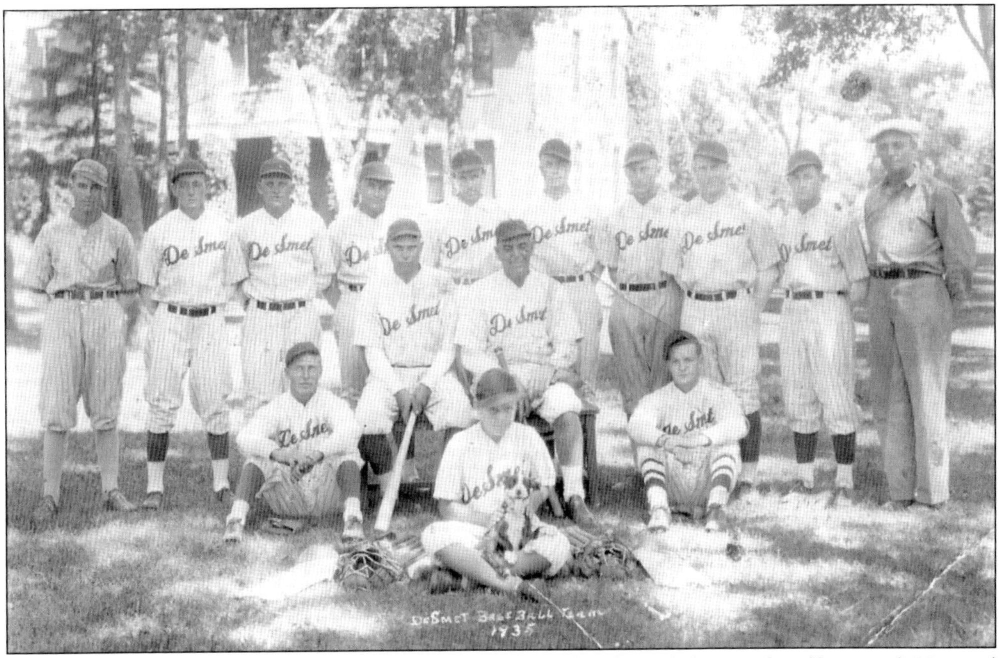

This picture of one of De Smet's baseball teams includes, from left to right, (first row) Howard Schultz, batboy Frankie Hargrove, and Vincent Antle, (second row) Harold Hargrove and Claude Phinney; (third row) DeVere "Nuke" Meyers, Charles Warner, Ross "Hi" Minier, Ben Valder, Russ Hunter, Ray Anderson, Roy Johnson, Francis Geisen, Lester Rodney, and umpire Herman Grothe.

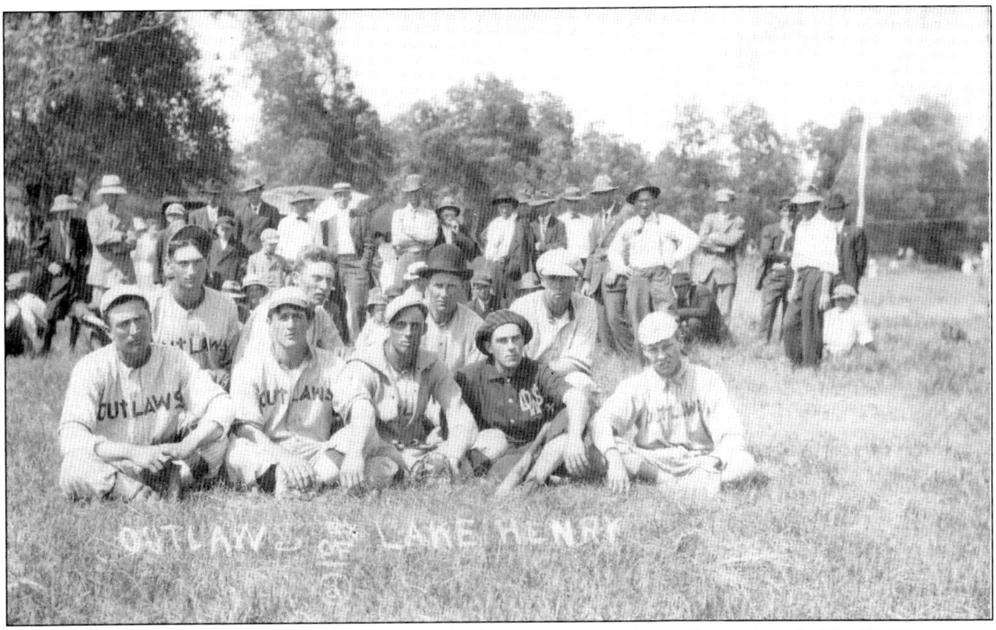

This c. 1920s image shows the Lake Henry Outlaws, a team to be reckoned with. Phyllis Taschner, daughter of Olai Johnson, identified those pictured as, from left to right, (first row) Henry Forsburg, Emmett McKittrick, Herman Grothe, Vern Washburn, and Roy Johnson; (second row) Owen Grothe, Olai Johnson, ? Steenson, and Paul Dahl. Not pictured is Elmer Forsburg.

Six

Aches and Pains

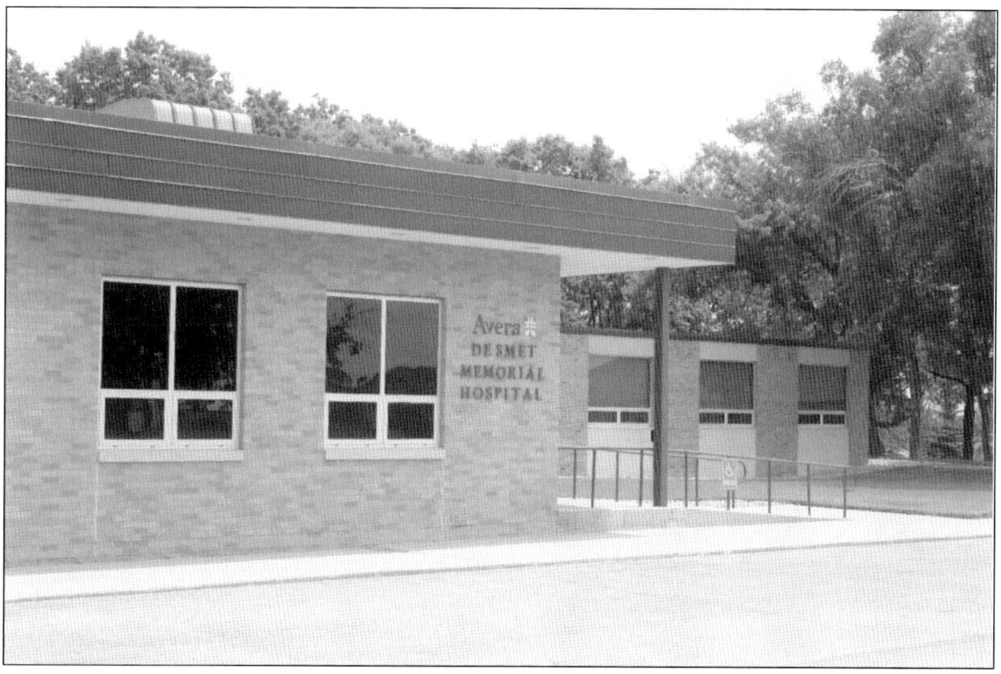

Operations on kitchen tables and babies born in sod shanties and homes was the fate of the families who made up this settlement. When a country doctor arrived and hung out his shingle in De Smet, he found he had competition from home remedies and patent medicines. What the doctors, dentists, chiropractors, and veterinarians in those early days lacked in skill, they often made up in compassion. Picture here is the Avera De Smet Memorial Hospital.

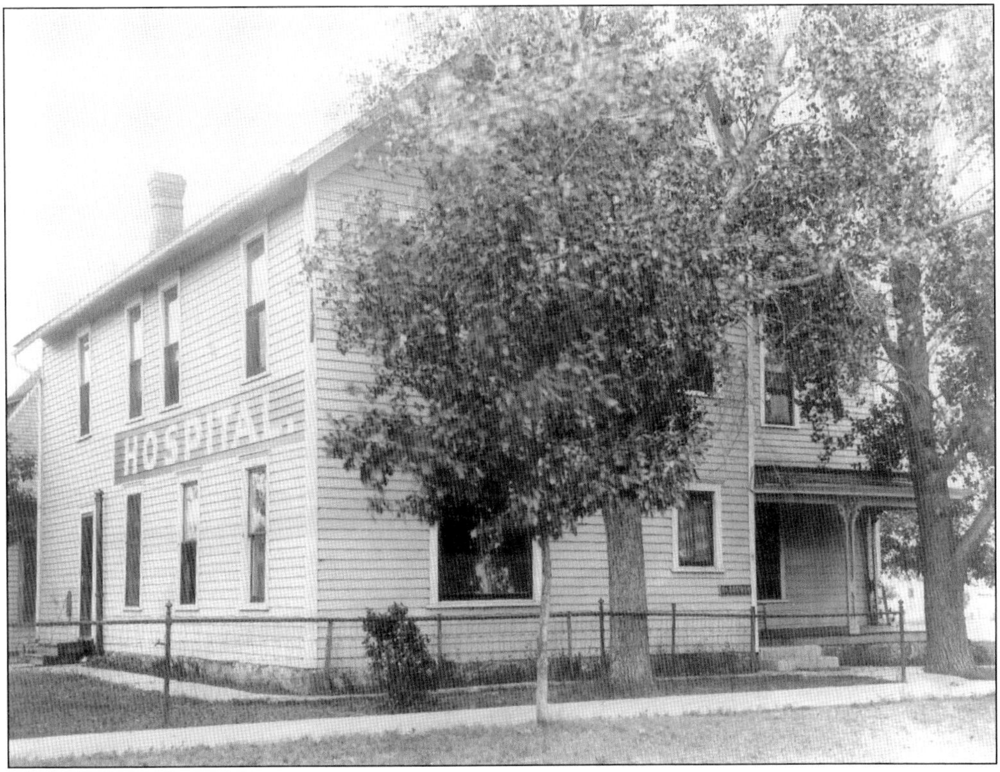

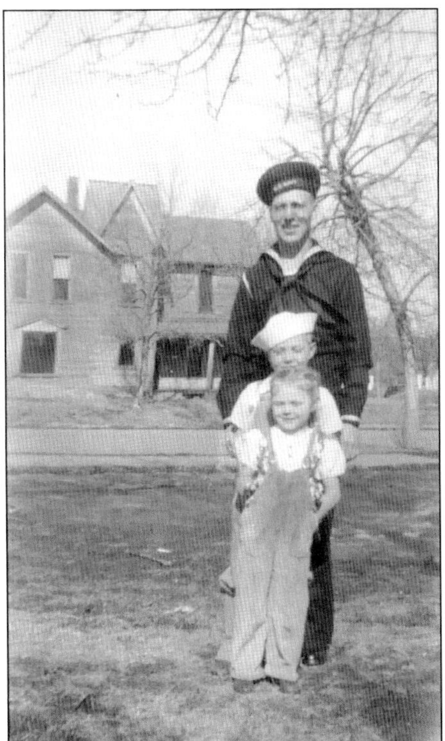

Kingsbury County Hospital opened for business on April 8, 1910. The large home was leased from Elizabeth Sasse, and Louise Knapp was hired as superintendent. Doctors Bostrom, Haberman, Dyar, Davies, and Jamieson were among some of the early physicians and surgeons. The building is located on Joliet Avenue and Third Street.

The background of this picture shows how the hospital seen in the previous image slowly became the Bee Hive Apartments. Long known as the Bee Hive, it derived its name from the many families that moved in and out of the building. This 1944 picture shows Howard Schultz on leave from the Navy with his two children, Donald and Sharon. The apartment complex remains on Joliet Avenue and Third Street.

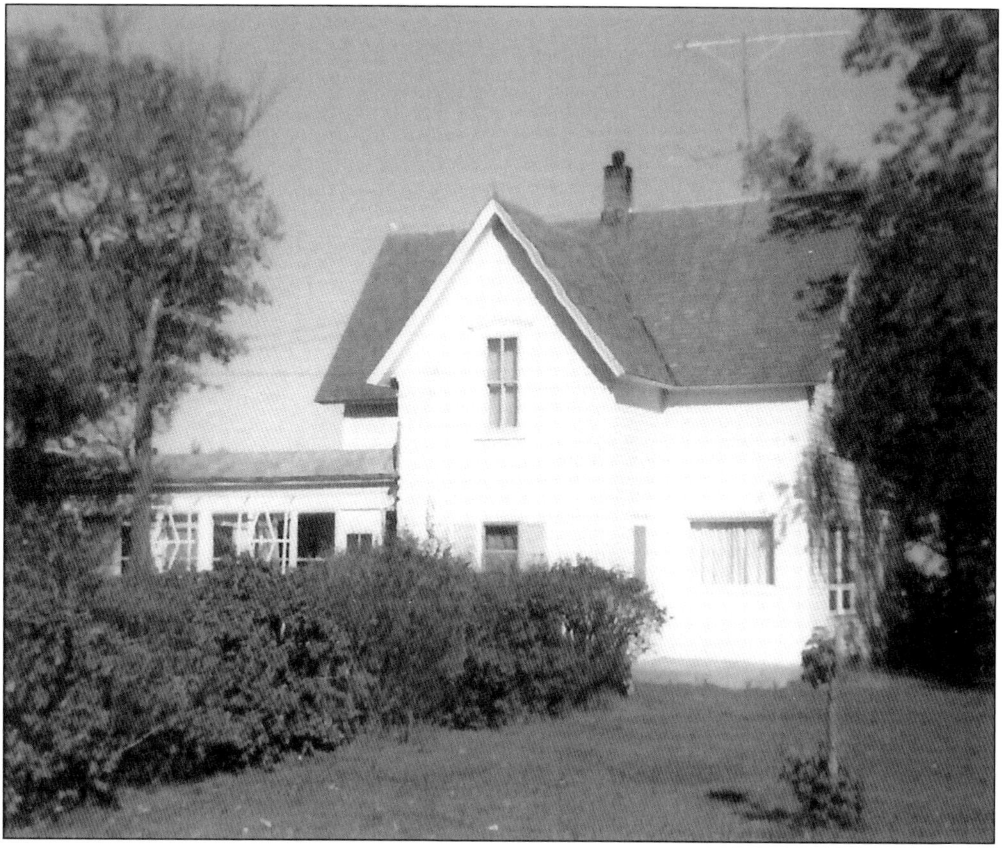

Pictured here as the home of Boyd and Delores (Anderson) Pratt, Anderson Nursing and Maternity Home was created in the late 1920s and operated through 1930. This was Axel Anderson's home, and it was operated by Wallace (Mrs. Axel) Anderson, a nurse who had been with the Kingsbury County Hospital. Maternity, appendectomy, and tonsillectomy cases were often done on Sunday afternoons by local physicians. The site of this building is north of De Smet, on South Dakota Highway 25. The house was razed in 2003.

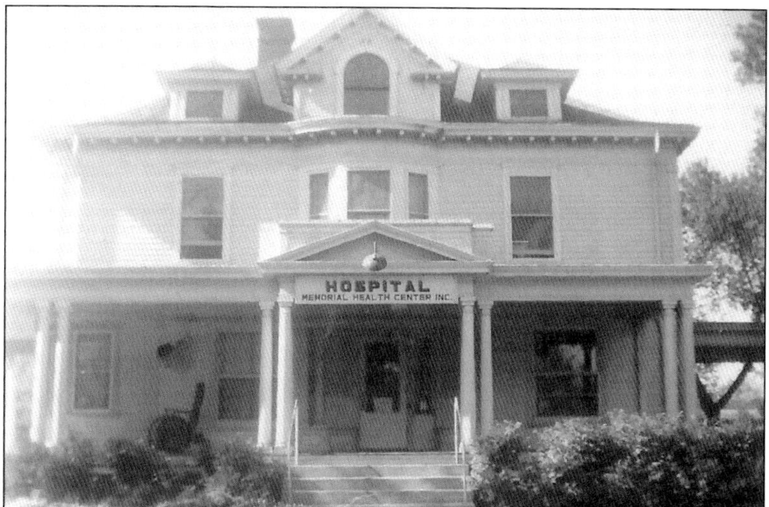

The stately home of A.N. Waters overlooks Second Street just a bit east of Sherwood Avenue. It became Memorial Hospital when it was purchased in 1947, and was ready for use by 1949. It has been reclaimed as a private residence.

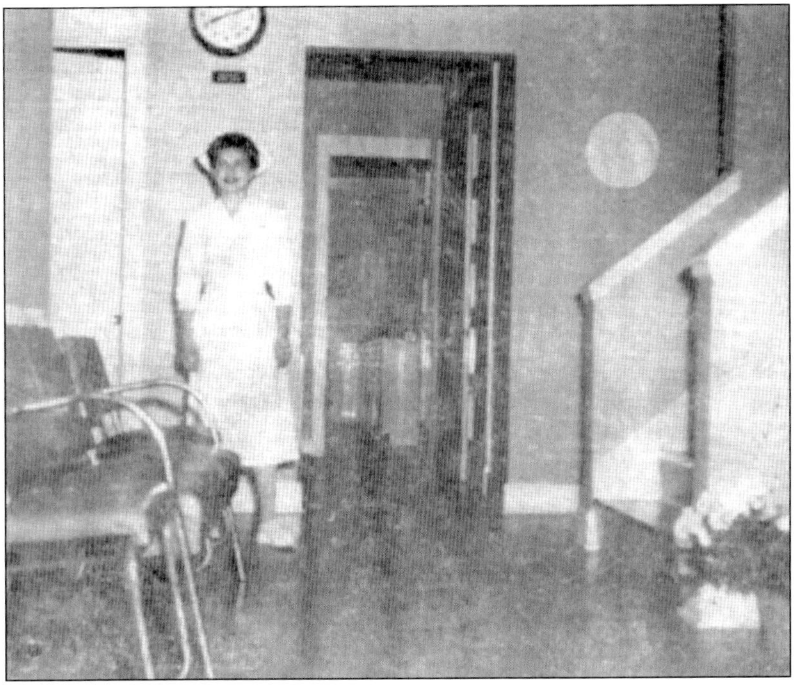

The world of early medical practice in De Smet often collided with the dire need for money, of which the City of De Smet did not have an abundance. But De Smet undertook to cure this malady by purchasing the A.N. Waters home and remodeling it as a hospital. Pictured is Ruth Zeller, a nurse.

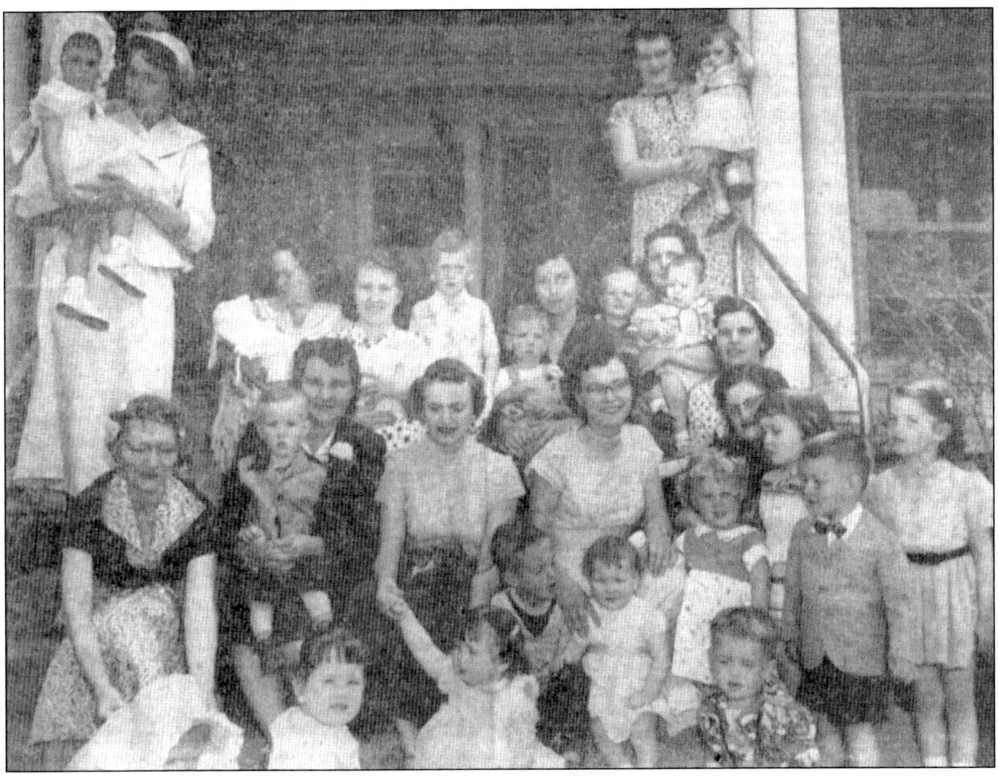

In 1950, it was reported that 72 babies had been born since the hospital opened a year before. It was a grand celebration when the mothers and babies returned to the Memorial Hospital for a one-year celebration.

A Tschetter family album produced this picture of Dr. Paul Tschetter and his son, Richard. Posed on the steps of their brick home, located on Fourth Street, they make a handsome pair. Dr. Paul practiced medicine in De Smet from 1930 to 1945. The home remains a private residence.

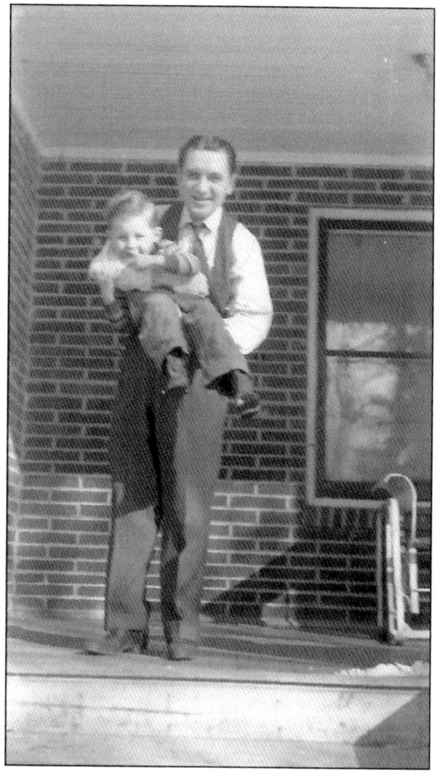

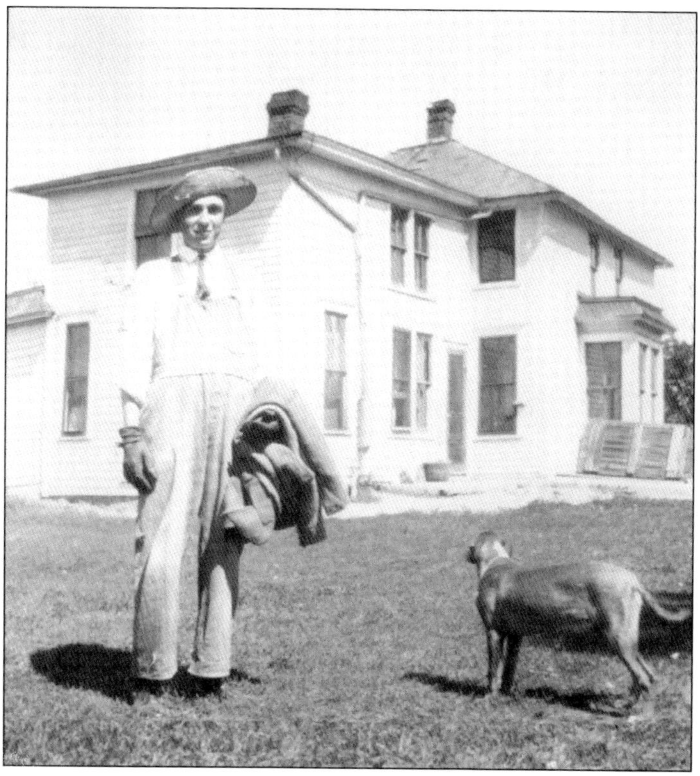

Veterinarian ? Betke stands in the yard of Harold Fritzel's farm, located on US Highway 14 and Prairie Avenue in De Smet. The house has been remodeled, but part of it still stands as a private residence.

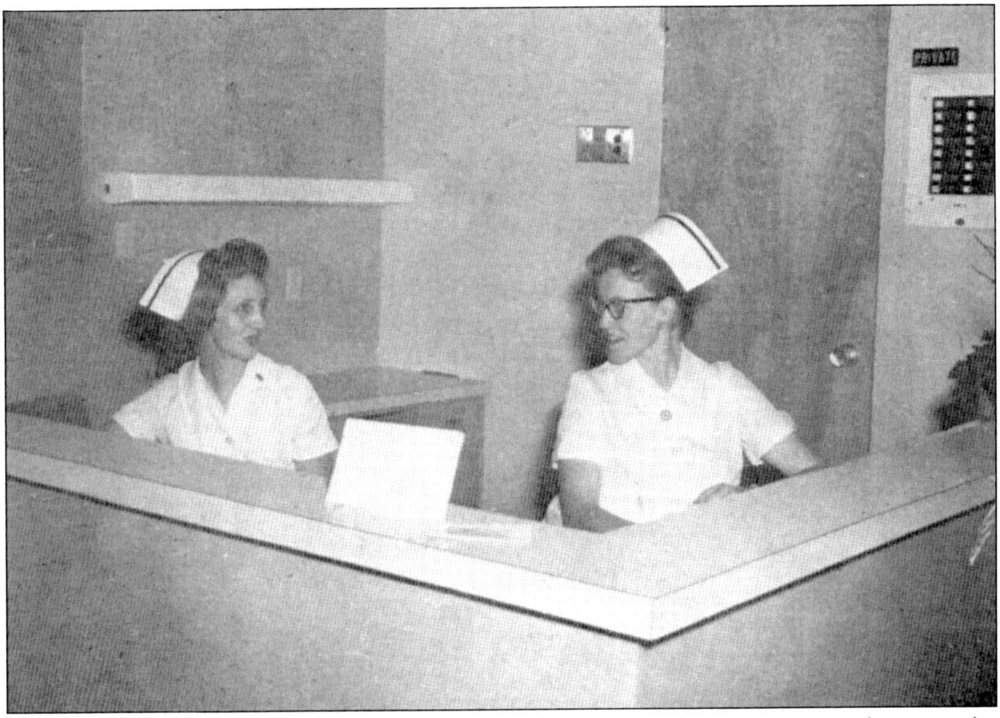

Mildred Warne (left), superintendent of nurses, and Judy (Nelson) Johnson are shown at the nurses' station of the newly built De Smet Memorial Hospital on Prairie Avenue.

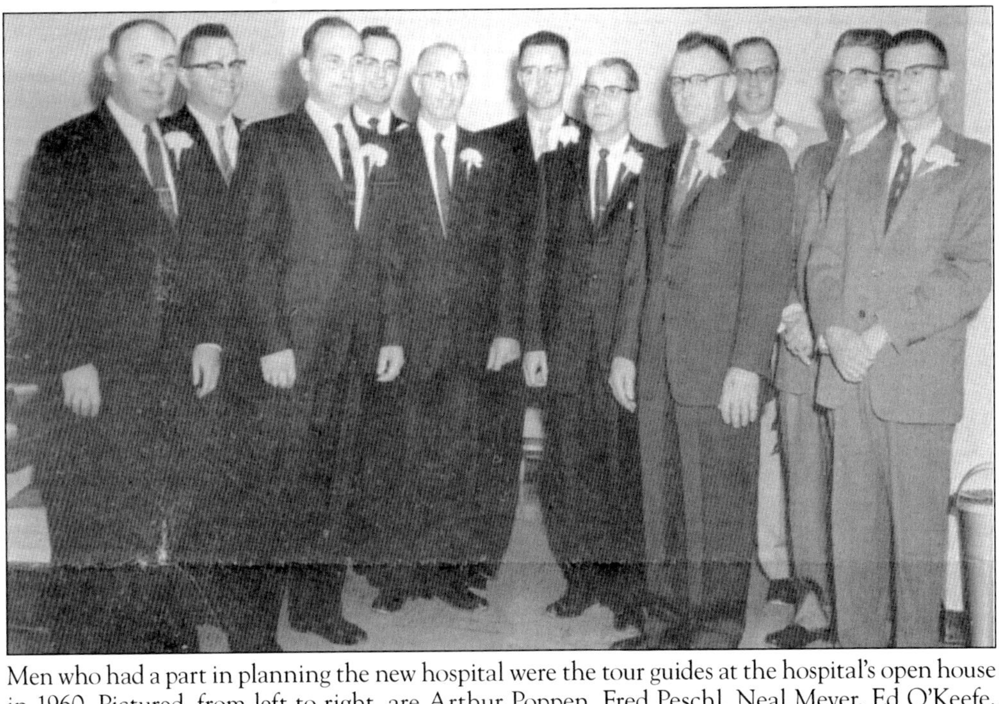

Men who had a part in planning the new hospital were the tour guides at the hospital's open house in 1960. Pictured, from left to right, are Arthur Poppen, Fred Peschl, Neal Meyer, Ed O'Keefe, G.S. Barnes, Floyd Abrahamson, George Kreiger, Maurice Wika, Marvin Ketelsen, Lawrence McKibben, and Gerhard Magnuson.

The new operating room equipment is being inspected in 1960 by, from left to right, Dr. Robert Bell, chairman of hospital board; Maurice Wika; and Dr. William Hanson.

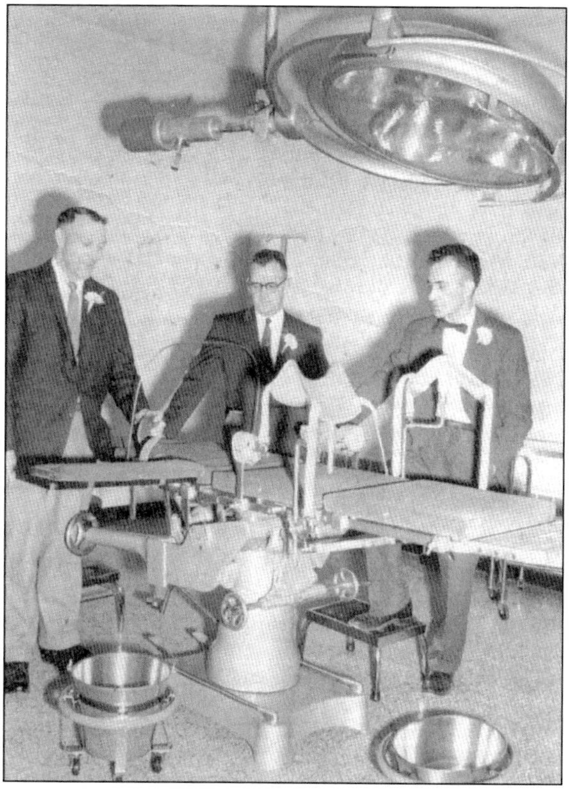

Taking part in the open house for the newly built hospital are, from left to right, (first row) Vera Abrahamson, Alice Williamson, and Marge Jensen; (second row) Myrtle Barnes, Evelyn Krieger, Eva McKibben, Adeline Springer, Norma Wika, and Audrey Meyers.

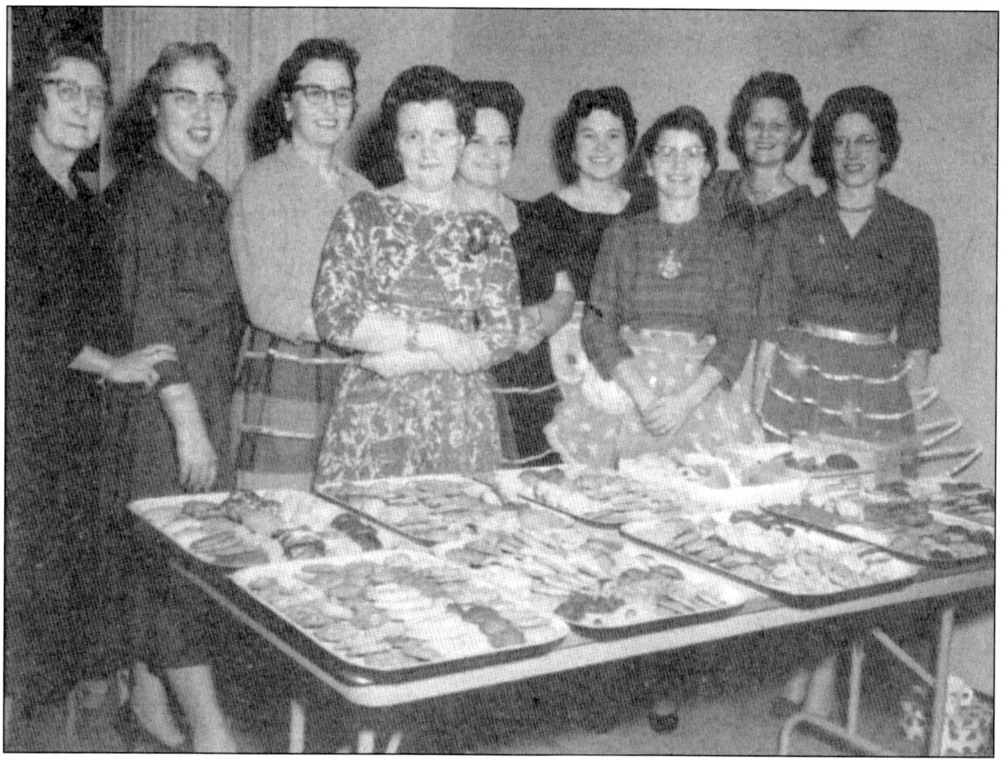

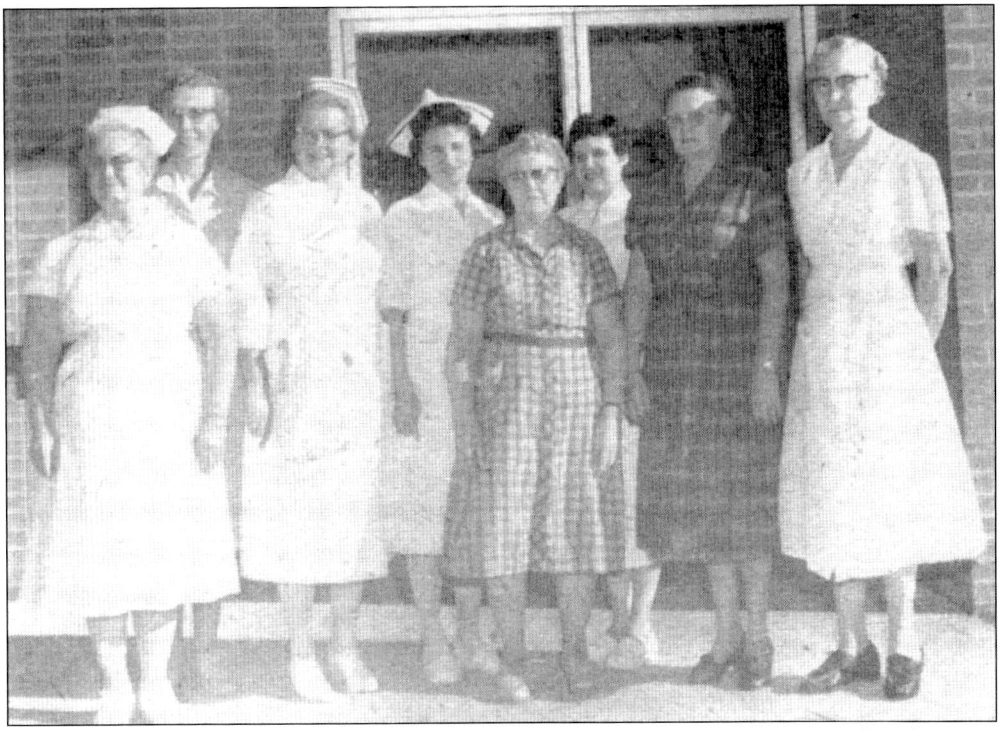

Some of the staff of the 1960 De Smet Hospital include, from left to right, Harriett Albrecht, LPN; Lorene Washburn, cook; ? Stensland, RN; Ruth Zeller, RN; Inez McAdaragh, laundry worker; ? Gilbertson, NA; Etta Penney, custodian; and Emma Serfling, cook.

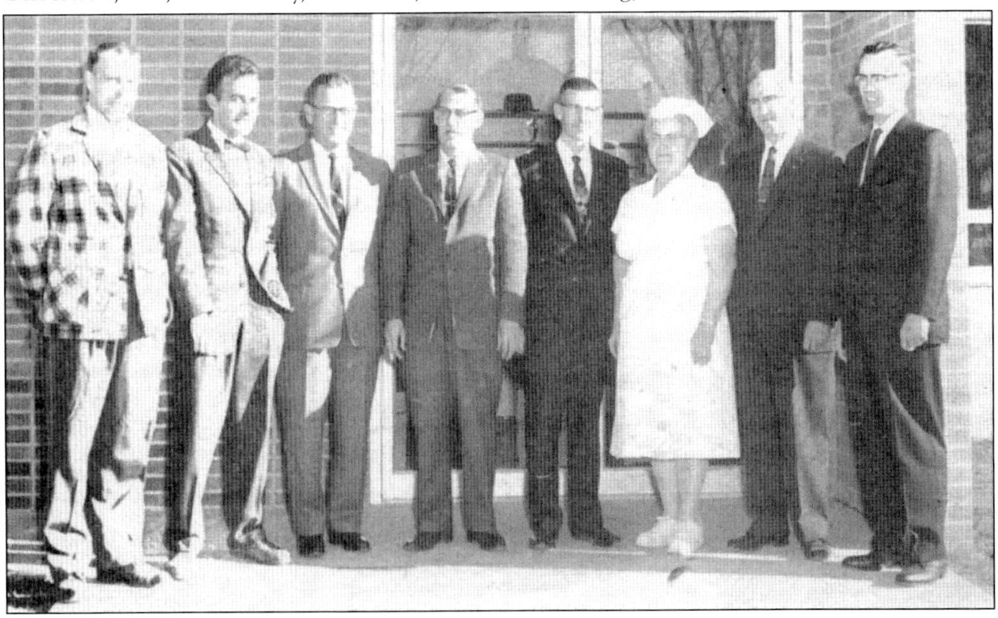

Posed for the camera at the entrance to the new hospital are, from left to right, Dr. Robert Bell; Dr. William Hanson; Maurice Wika, chairman of the hospital board; George Krieger, vice chairman; Gerhard Magnuson, secretary-treasurer; Harriett Albrecht, administrator; G.S. Barnes, mayor; and Edward O'Keefe, board member.

Seven

The Old Neighborhood

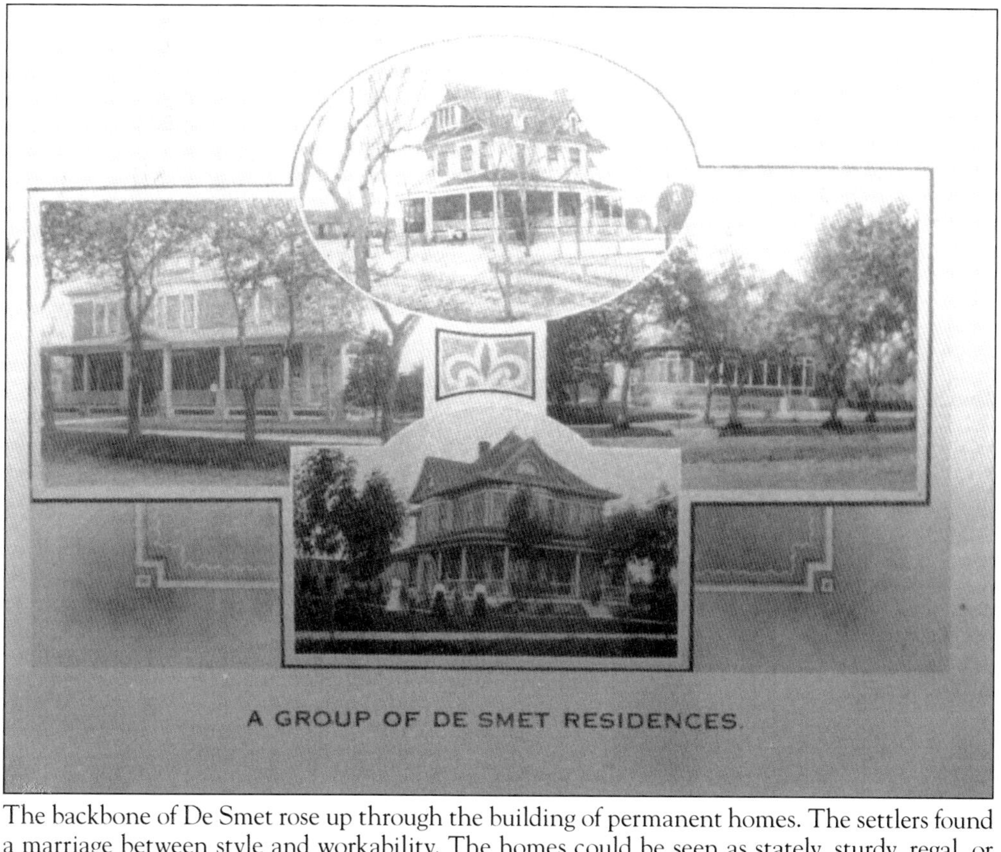

The backbone of De Smet rose up through the building of permanent homes. The settlers found a marriage between style and workability. The homes could be seen as stately, sturdy, regal, or rough, but each was always a home. The leaders of the small town's society were emerging through the structure of their stately homes, but a middle class was also developing at the same time.

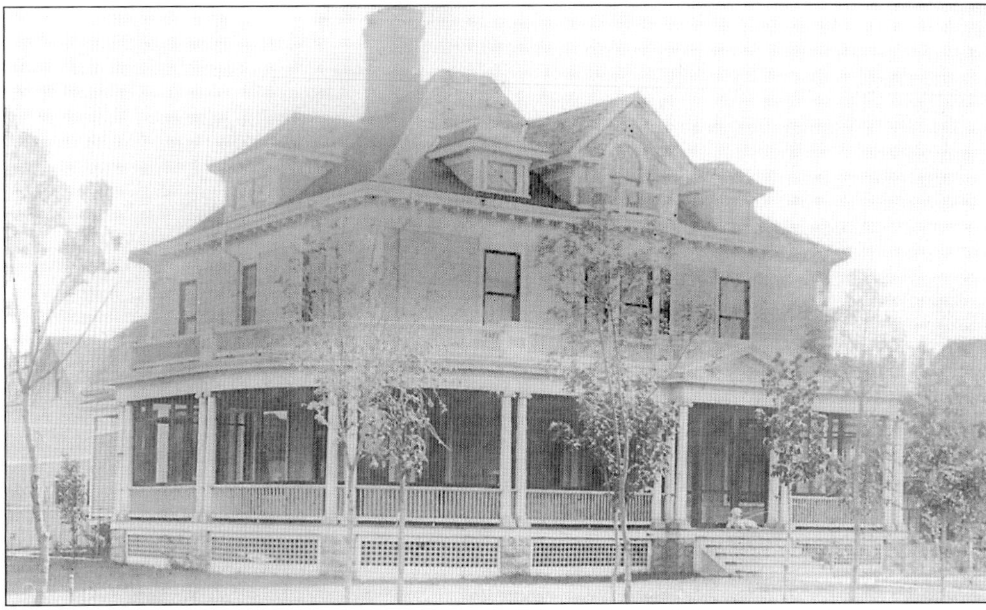

The opulence of the A.N. Waters residence presided over Second Street. It spoke of the success that Waters achieved in his land business. In 1947, the house was purchased and used as the Memorial Medical Center. In 2014, it continues to stand in all its majesty as a private residence of Dr. Clint, a veterinarian, and Jan Hof.

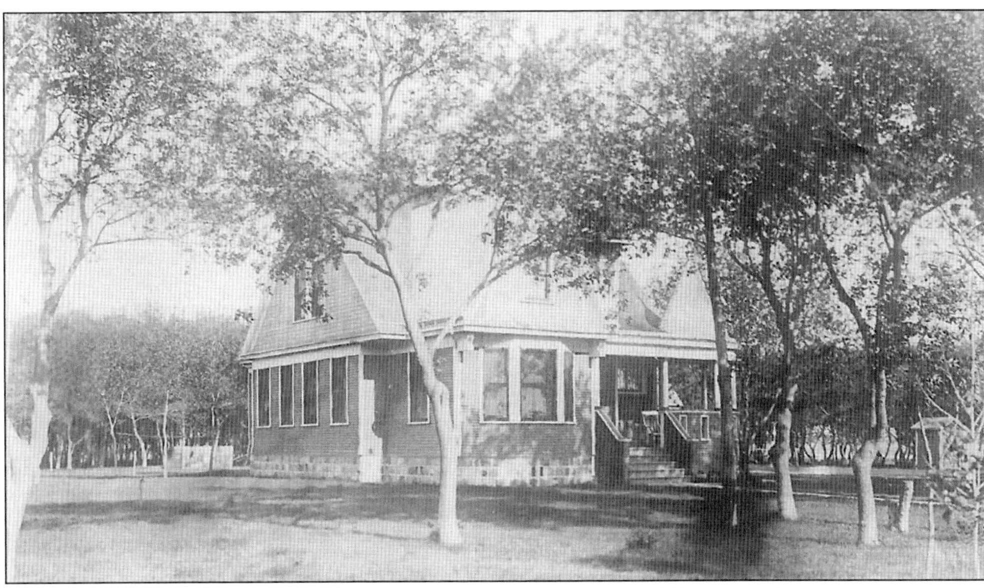

The home of E.S. Johnson was erected on South Dakota Highway 25, south of De Smet. Artistically crafted, the home sat among a cluster of trees. The house continues to stand in the same location as the private residence of attorney Gregg Gass and his wife, Glenda.

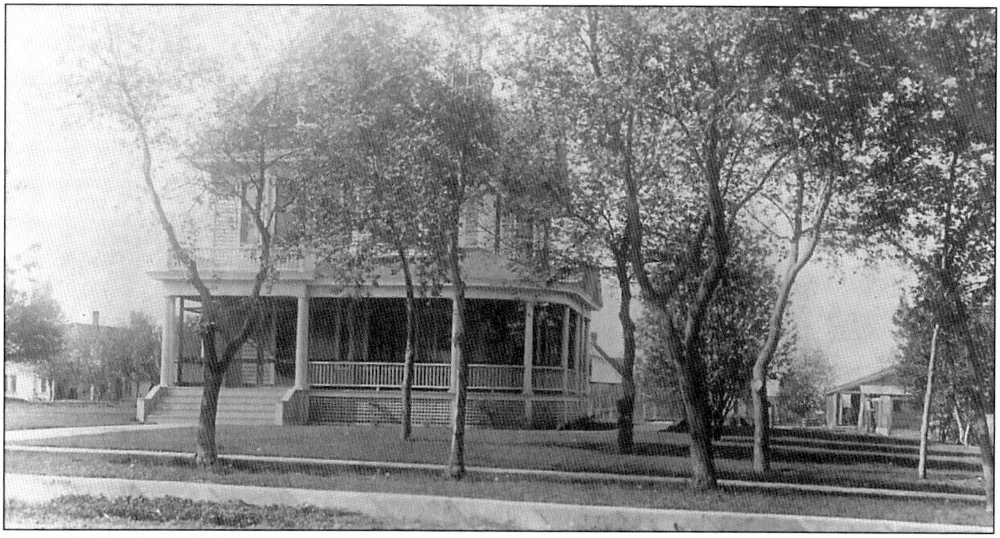

L.T. Altfillisch built this home, which still stands today at the corner of Second Street and Ingalls Avenue. At one time, it was home to the Glenn and Rose Van Tassel family; it is now the home of Randal and Myrna Knadle.

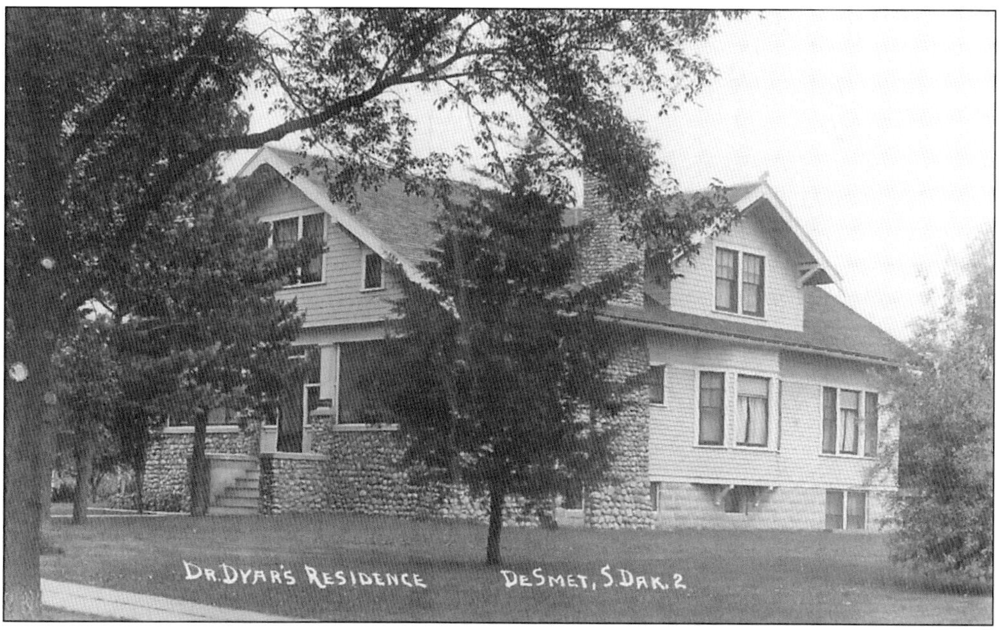

Practicing medicine in De Smet in 1909, Dr. B.A. Dyar had this stylish home built on Second Street. A.J. Ryland bought the house for his family and later sold it to Jake and Louise Kruse. It is currently the home of Shane, a grandson of Jake and Louise, and Monica Roth.

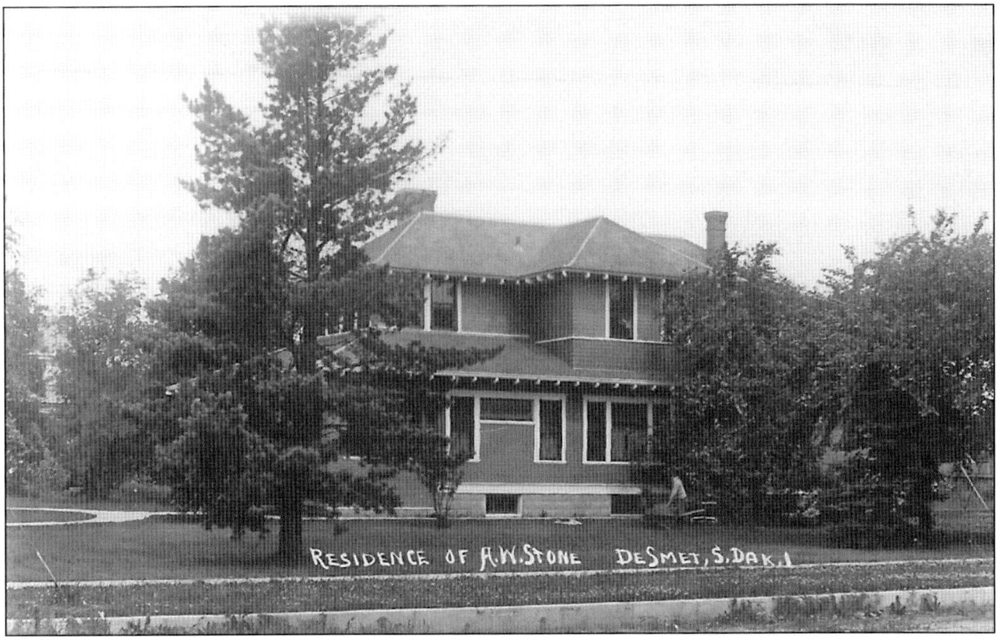

The A.W. Stone residence has long been on the corner of Second Street and Sherwood Avenue. A truly magnificent structure, this home housed the family of George William and Patricia Coughlin and is owned by their son Anthony and Julie (Smith) Coughlin and their family.

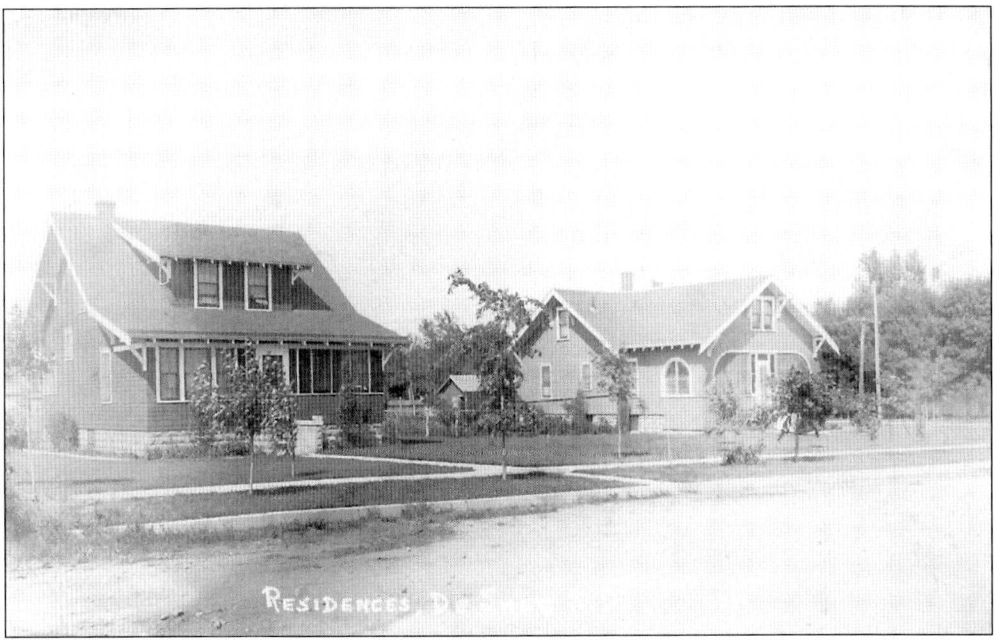

The striking home on the right was built by K. and Jenny Knudsen in 1922; it faces Second Street and Washington Park. It has been tastefully remodeled over the years, and the owners have included August Gehm, Harry Eggen, and, presently, Dollie (Eggen) Purintun. A modern touch has been given to the house on the left and bears some resemblance to its forerunner. Built in 1922, its owners have included F.L. Brewer, Dr. Robert Bell, and Charles Johnson.

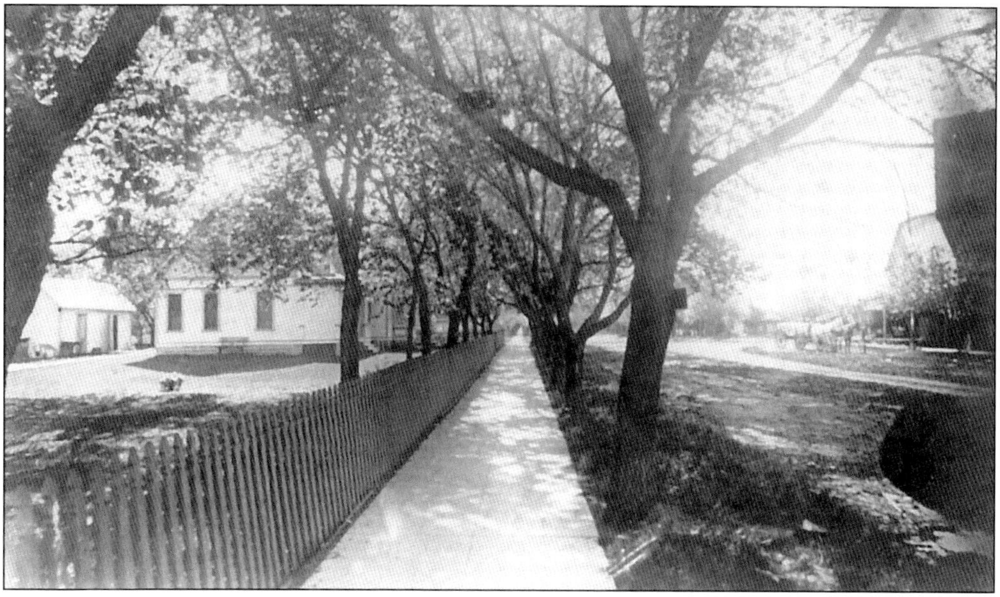

A cement walk and picket fence run in front of E.H. Couse's residence on Fourth Street, to the west of the schoolhouse. It was remodeled for use as two apartments, but today it has returned to use as a one-family private residence. Around 1900, the Couse house was moved from the corner of South Dakota Highway 25 and Second Street to Fourth Street.

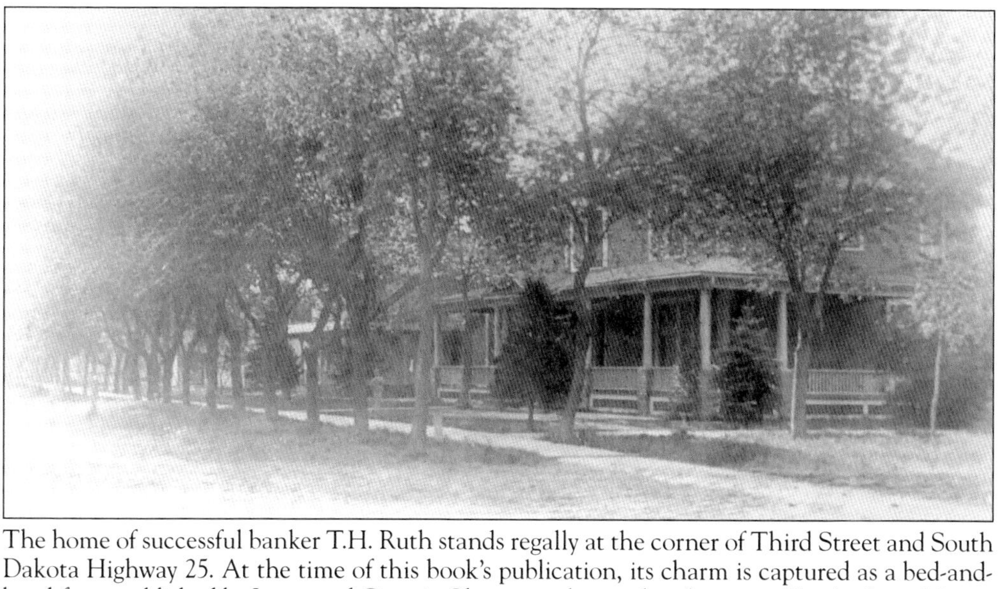

The home of successful banker T.H. Ruth stands regally at the corner of Third Street and South Dakota Highway 25. At the time of this book's publication, its charm is captured as a bed-and-breakfast established by Larry and Connie Cheney and owned and operated by Andy and Jenny Todd. It has an irresistible appeal to folks traveling in the De Smet area. Many may recall this house as the O'Keefe apartment building.

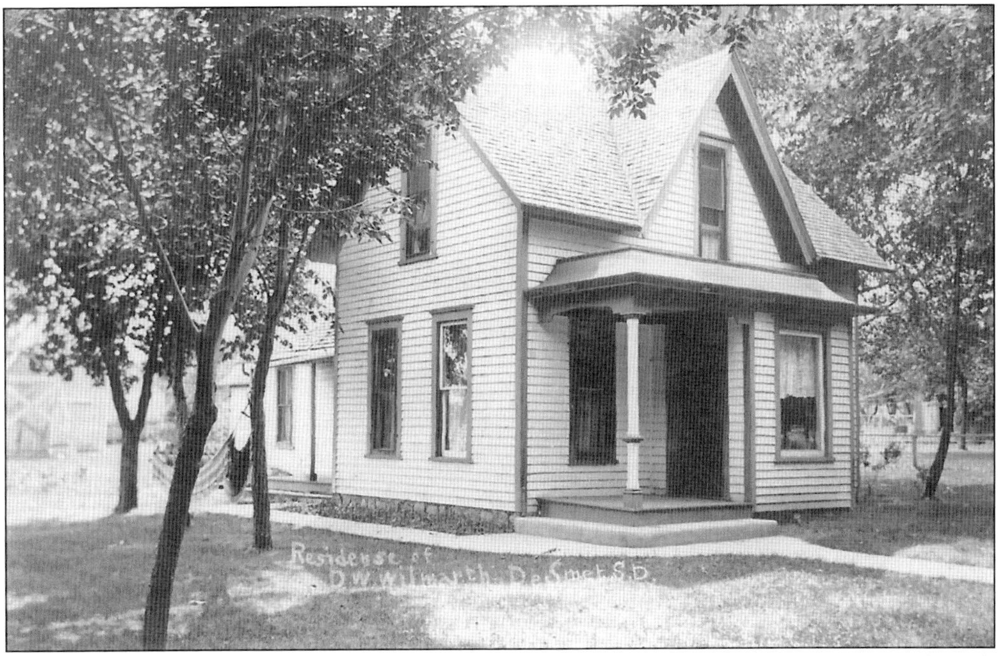

Everyday life could be viewed from the hammock stretched between two trees at the D.W. Wilmarth house. Wilmarth was a local grocer in De Smet's early days.

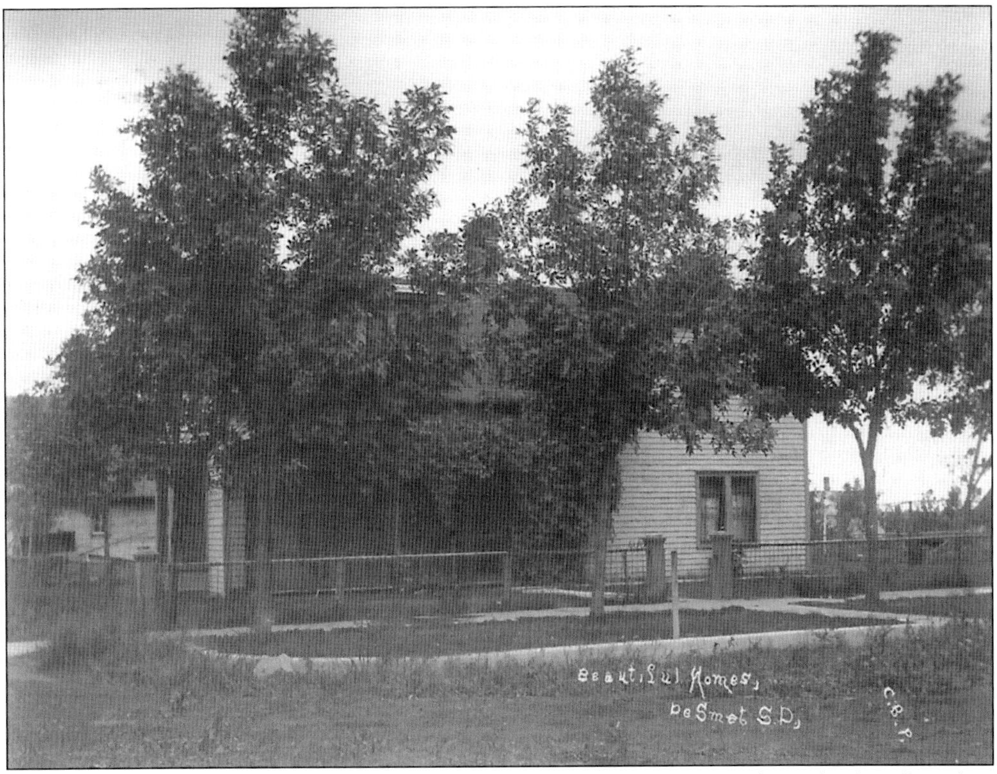

This unidentified home in De Smet sports a hitching post, cement curb, and sidewalk. It has plenty of shade trees in the front yard.

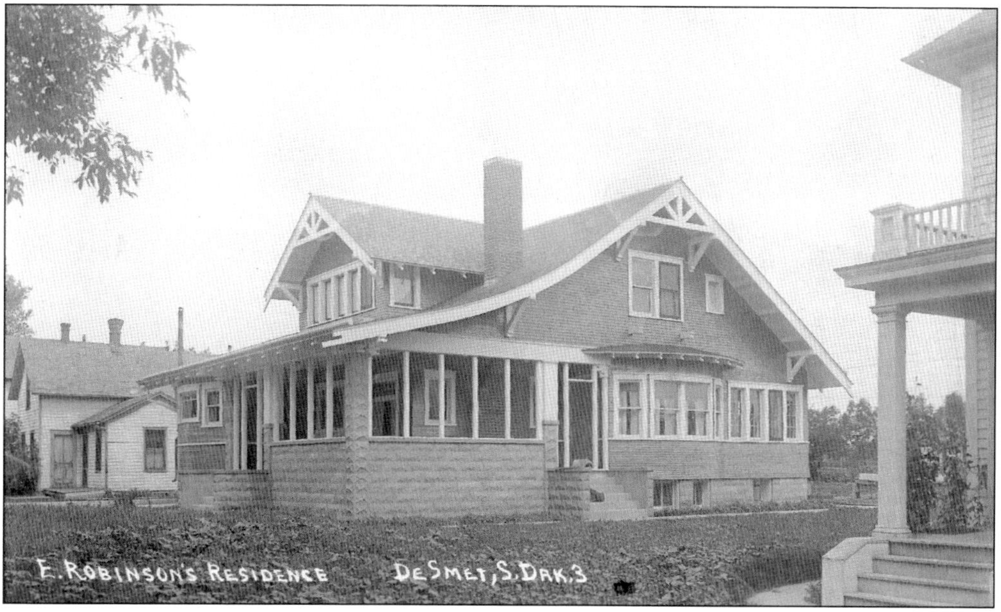

Elmer Robinson had many materials available for building his home, as he owned and operated one of the lumberyards in De Smet. Owning this house later became a multigenerational affair involving Roy Hansen, his grandson Lowell Hansen, and Lowell's daughter Christy (Hansen) Hubbard.

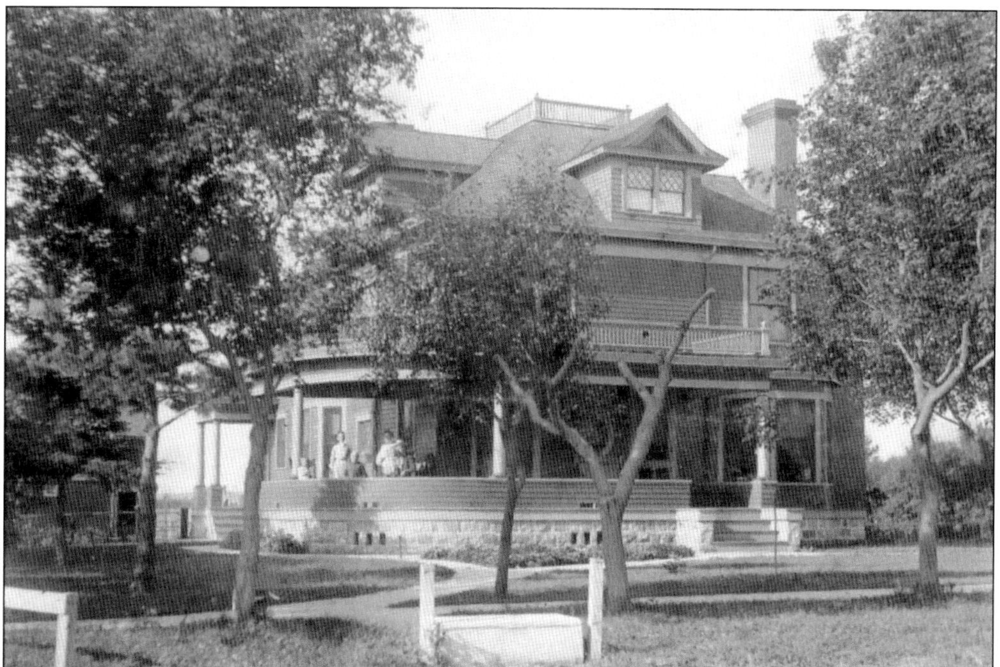

Shown here is Dr. Vernon Beasecker's home as it stood on the corner of Third Street and Ingalls Avenue (now the site of a school parking lot). The Beaseckers lived upstairs, and Dr. Beasecker operated his chiropractic business from the first floor. In 1989, the house was moved to William and Roxana Poppen's farm, northeast of De Smet, and was remodeled as a family home.

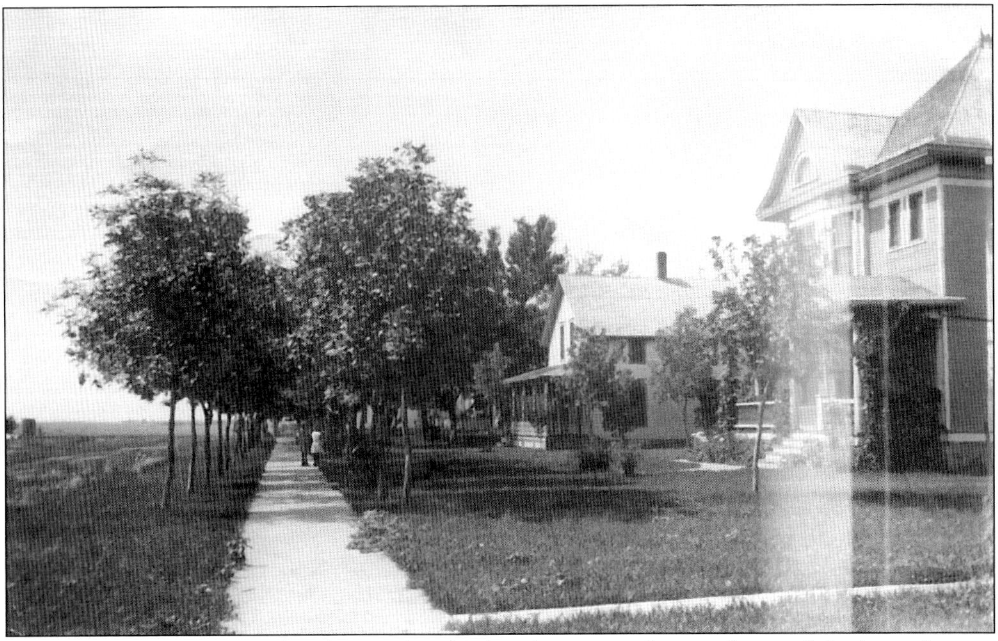

Down in the old neighborhood, trees lined Joliet Avenue and gave plenty of shade to the two young girls standing on the sidewalk.

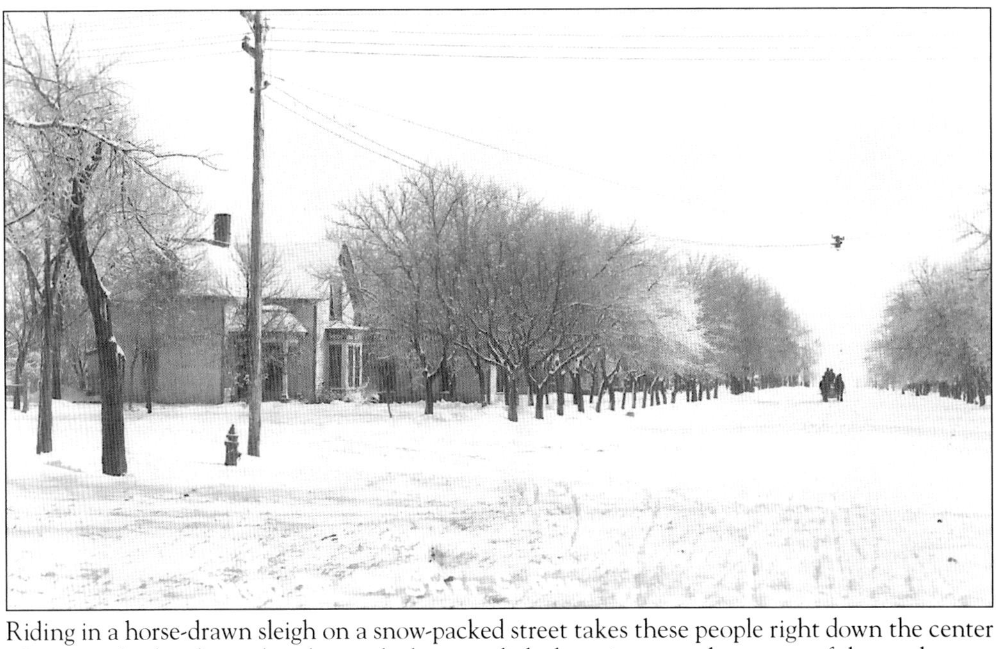

Riding in a horse-drawn sleigh on a snow-packed street takes these people right down the center of trees on both sides and underneath the streetlight hanging over the center of the roadway.

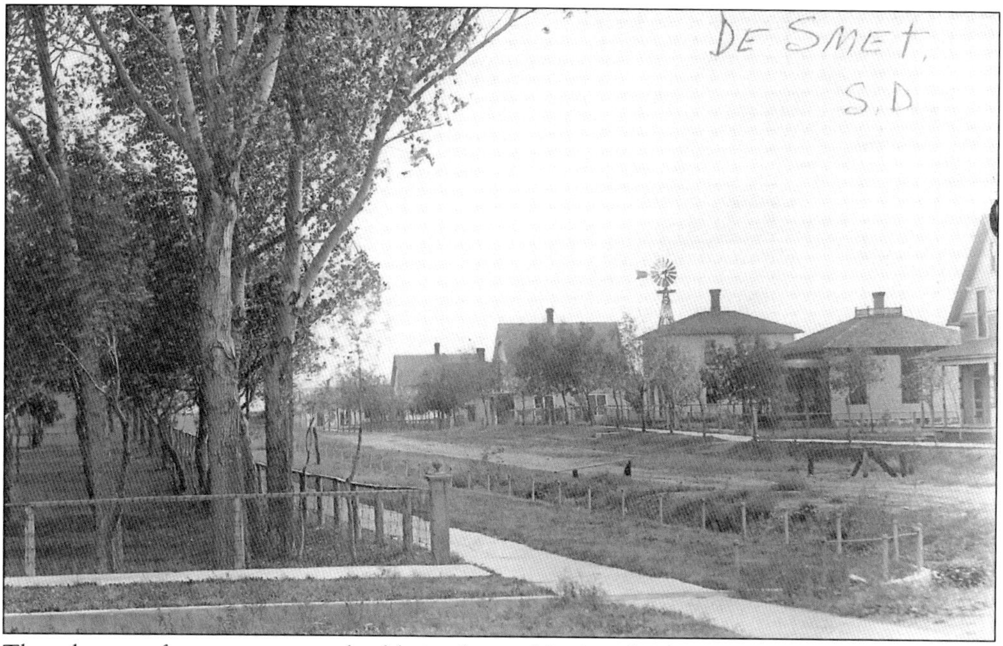

These homes of yesteryear were the fabric of a neighborhood. The view in this image looks east and was taken on Second Street across from the courthouse. Seen from this perspective are, from left to right, the homes of Martin Larson, J.O. Purintun (currently Rollo Peterson), Cliff McKibben (currently Cody Sivers), and Nate Tackaberry (currently Marty Weiskus), and then the corner of the Ely house. The Ely and Larson houses have been razed, but the others are maintained as private residences; the current owners are indicated in the parentheses.

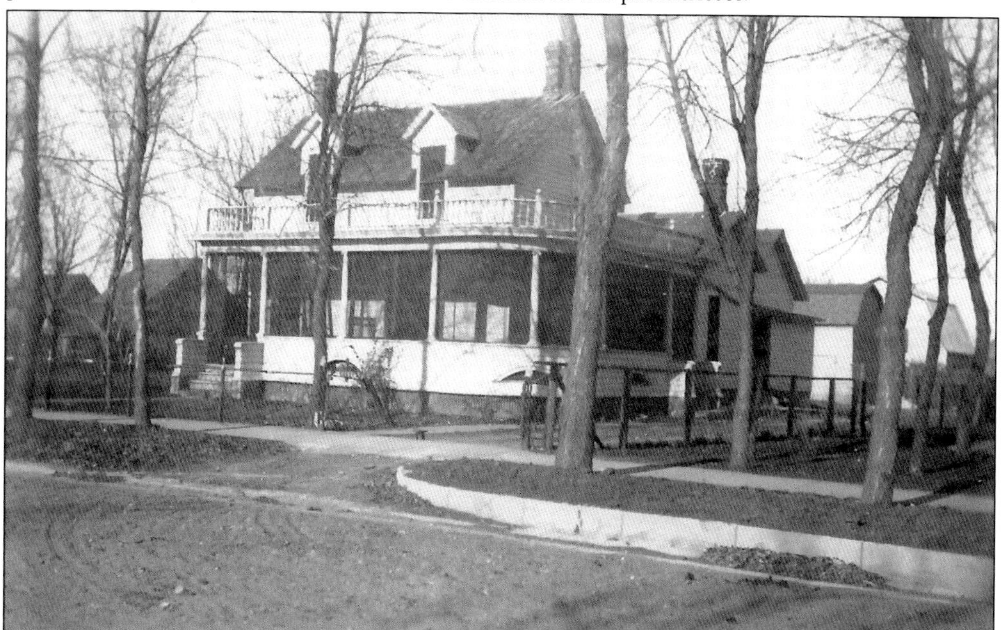

With distinct features of dormer windows and a wraparound porch that provided a perfect view of neighborhood activities, the house of Dr. L.H. Straight is no longer standing. It stood on Second Street and was owned at one time by Wiley Glessner.

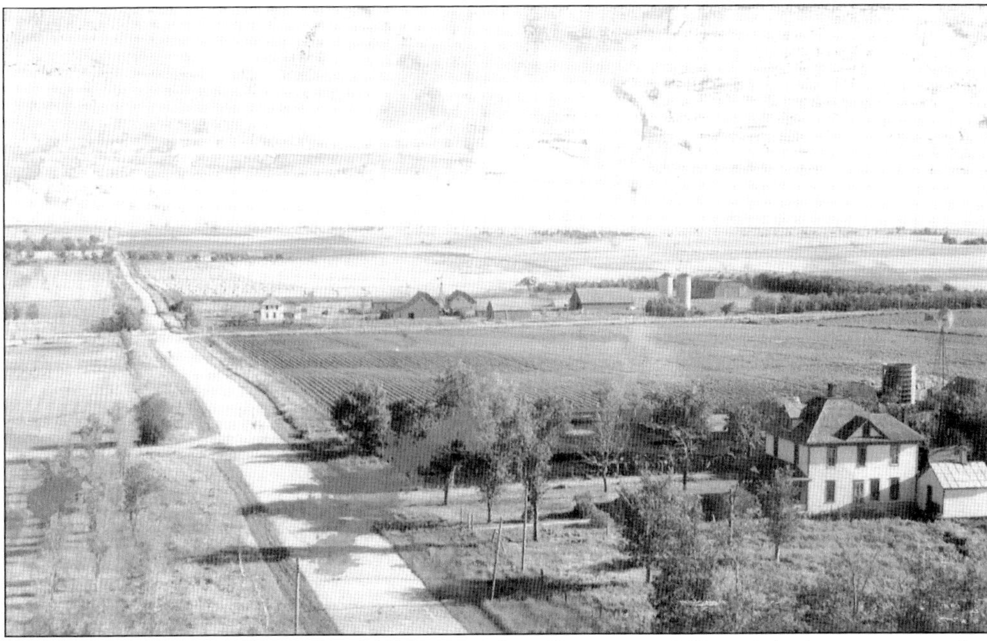

F.P. and Jane (Baxandall) Hardy sold this site to Roy Hansen in 1933, and the home remained in the Hansen family until it was sold to Mark and Brittani Wilkinson. In 2013, it was purchased by Briann (Spader) Halversen. C.C. Fritzel's home, seen in the top of the photograph, is situated on US Highway 14; the site is now owned by Arthur Geyer.

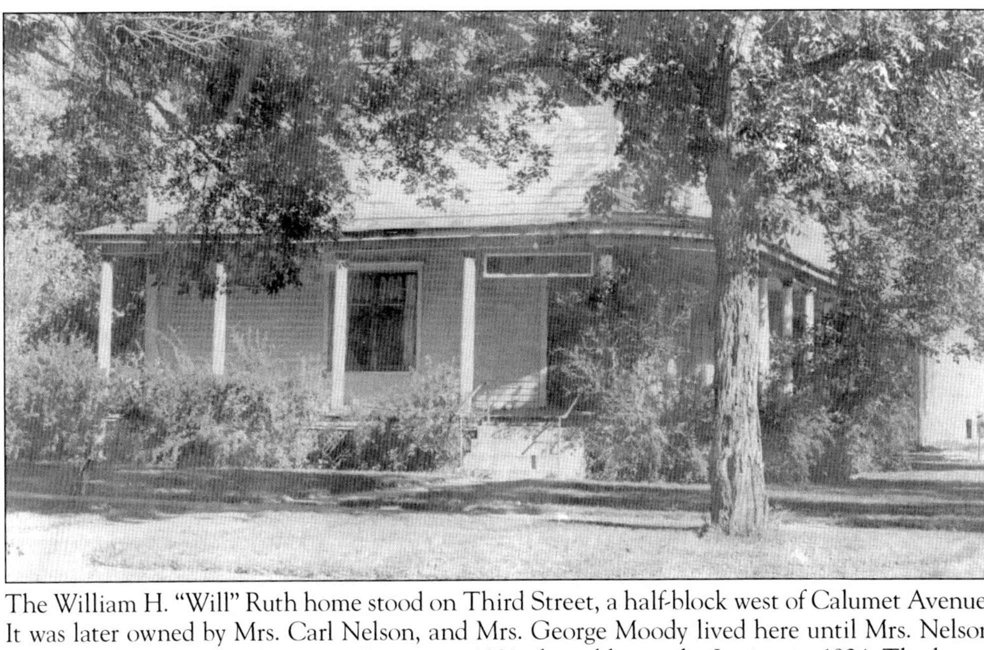

The William H. "Will" Ruth home stood on Third Street, a half-block west of Calumet Avenue. It was later owned by Mrs. Carl Nelson, and Mrs. George Moody lived here until Mrs. Nelson leased the house to the American Legion in 1921; she sold it to the Legion in 1924. The house was razed to make room for the present American Legion building.

Eight

Postcards from the Past

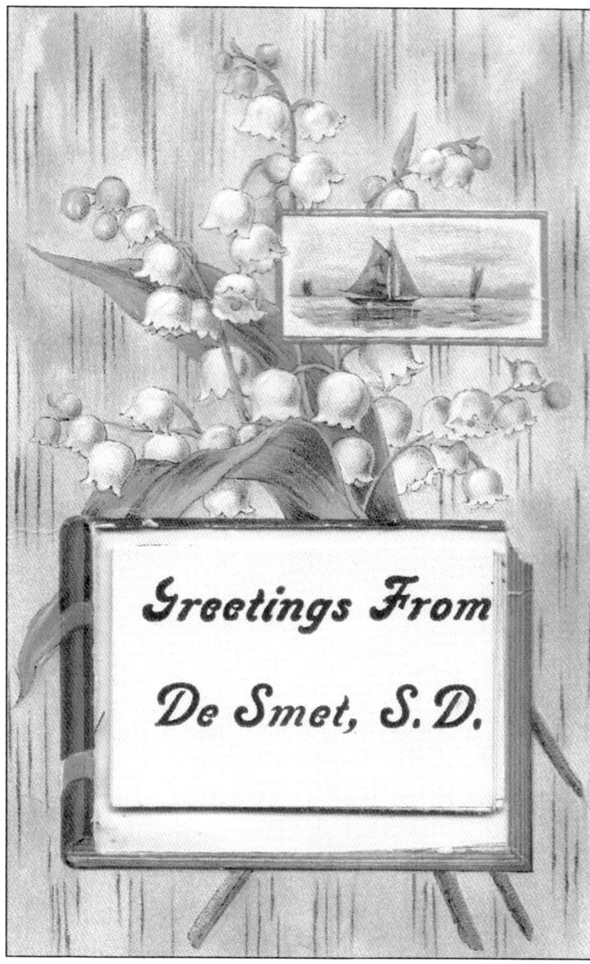

After its appearance in America in 1893, the postcard had its golden age heralded in 1905. Few homes were immune to its advent. Towns showed a love for their community by featuring their main street or other important sites on a promotional card. Middle or upper classes had bulging albums of these on their parlor tables, and today these same cards help people to recall the past.

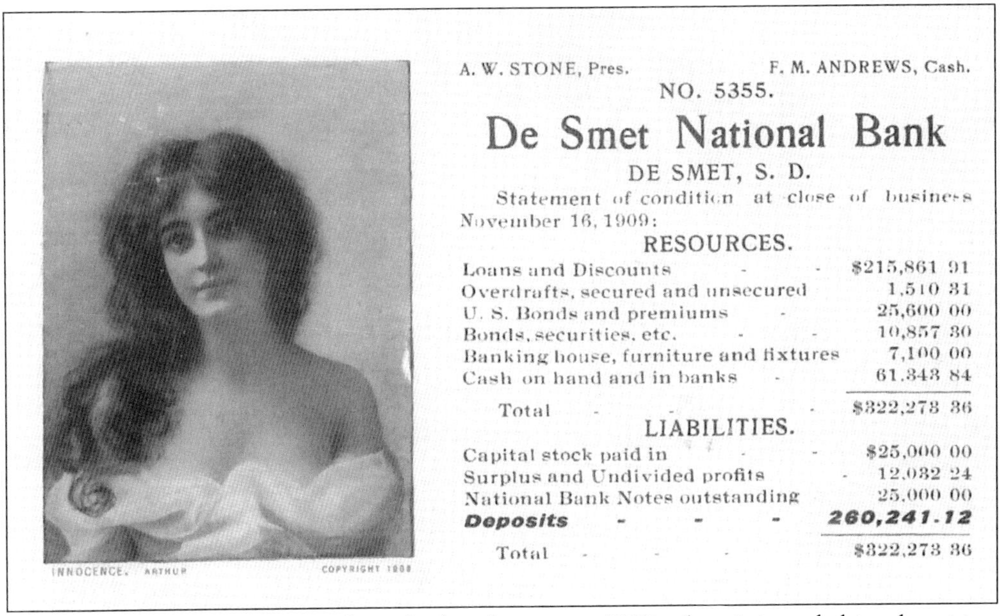

A. W. STONE, Pres. F. M. ANDREWS, Cash.

NO. 5355.

De Smet National Bank

DE SMET, S. D.

Statement of condition at close of business November 16, 1909:

RESOURCES.	
Loans and Discounts - -	$215,861 91
Overdrafts, secured and unsecured	1,510 31
U. S. Bonds and premiums -	25,600 00
Bonds, securities, etc. - -	10,857 30
Banking house, furniture and fixtures	7,100 00
Cash on hand and in banks -	61,343 84
Total - - -	$322,273 36
LIABILITIES.	
Capital stock paid in - -	$25,000 00
Surplus and Undivided profits -	12,032 24
National Bank Notes outstanding	25,000 00
Deposits - - - -	**260,241.12**
Total - - -	$822,273 36

De Smet National Bank jumped on the bandwagon in 1909, when it issued this advertising postcard. Beginning in 1912, local postmasters could confiscate risqué cards, including those displaying feminine attributes (as here) or lovers in romantic poses.

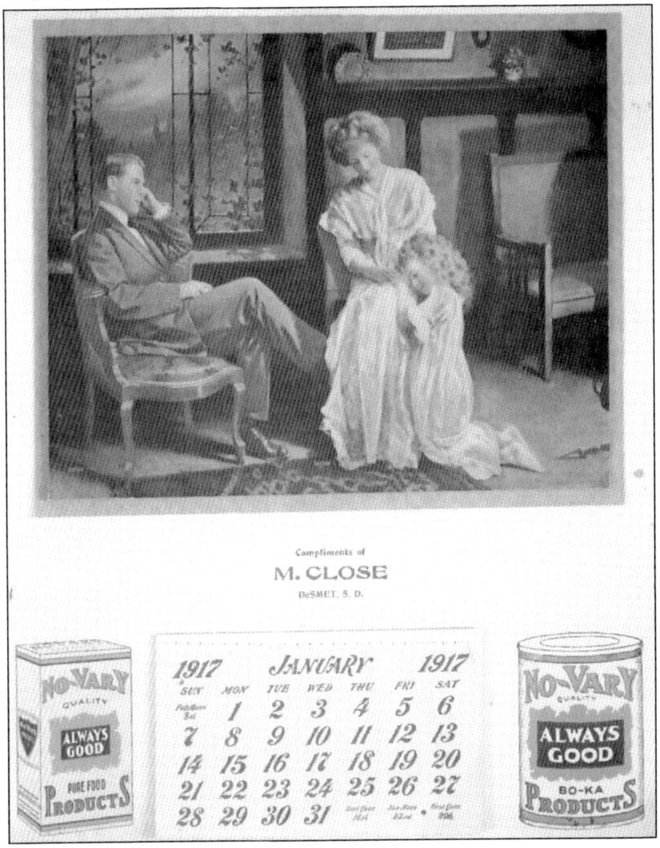

Warm and cozy cards, such as M. Close produced in 1917, were a welcome sight in most homes. These also got the word to customers, both present and future. It is estimated that this card was sent around Christmastime in 1916.

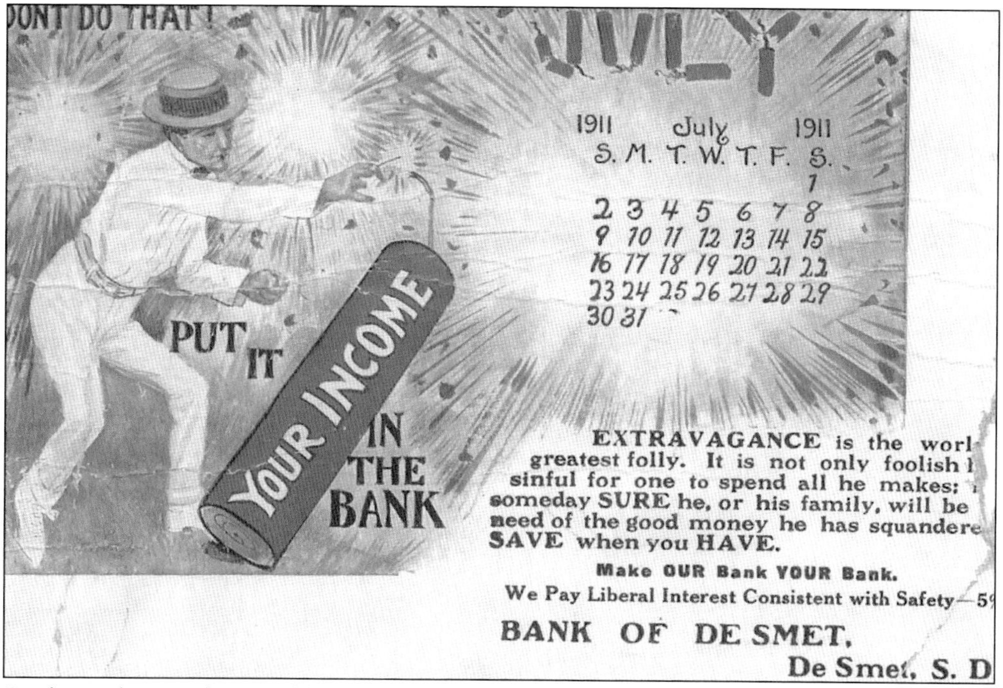

Cards in vibrant colors would catch the eyes of customers as well as extend bits of advice. Note that the Bank of De Smet advertises paying five percent interest in 1911.

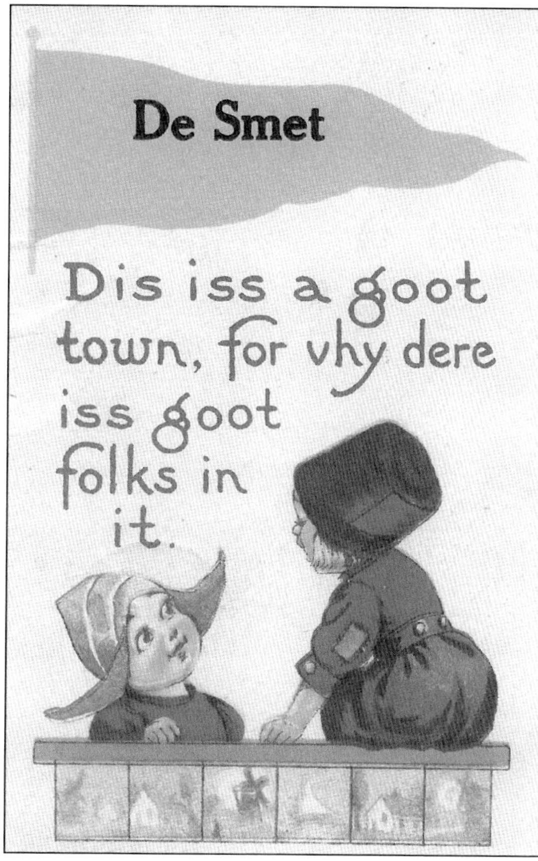

There was often some magic in receiving a written note from family or friends, and these penny postcards could provide the perfect answer.

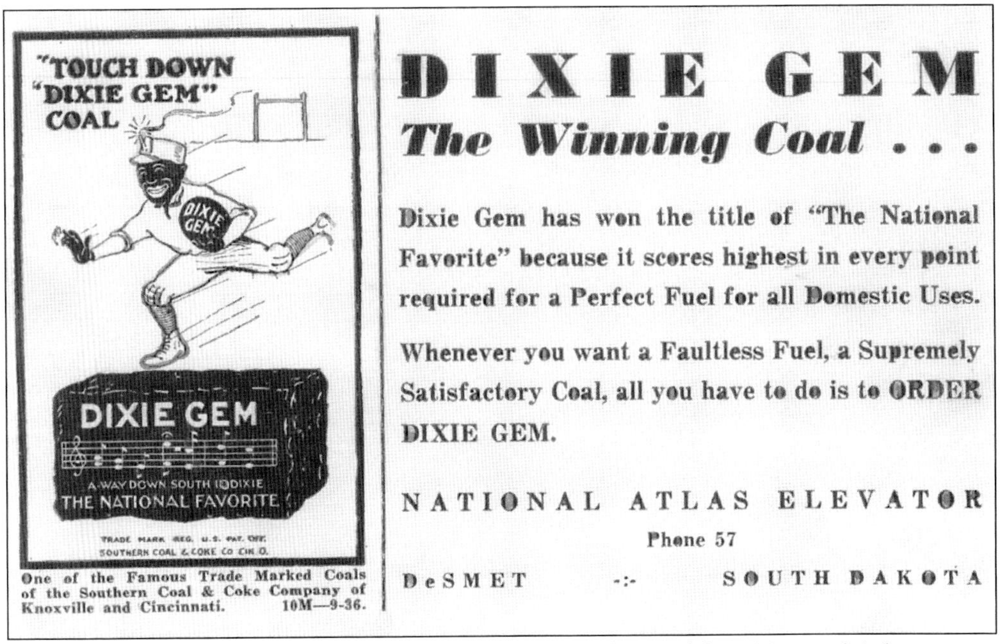

This card from National Atlas Elevator focuses on advertising coal as a perfect fuel for all domestic uses.

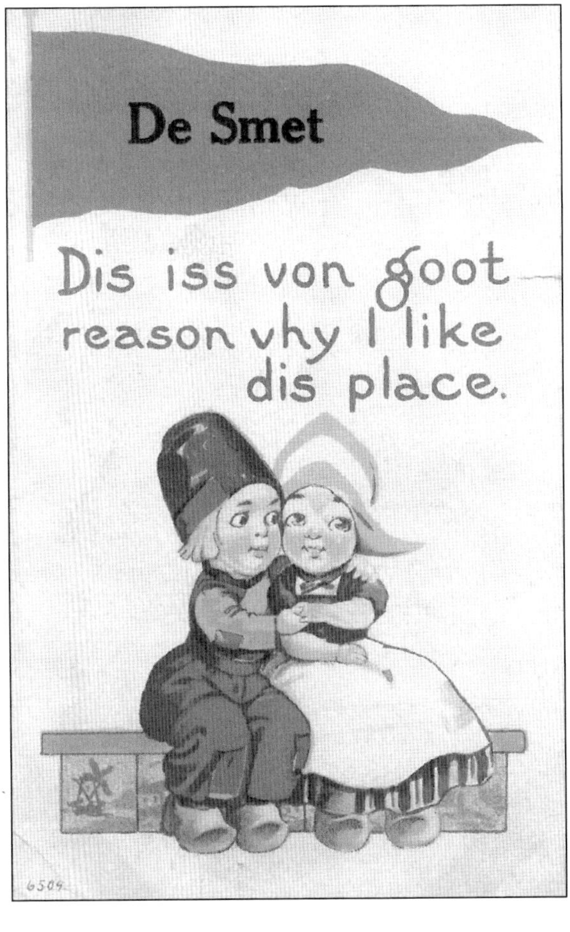

Embracing American humor, postcards were an inexpensive way to stay in touch and add a smile to someone's day.

The interesting fact about this card is the misspelling of De Smet. The figures and the wording appear to have been drawn by hand.

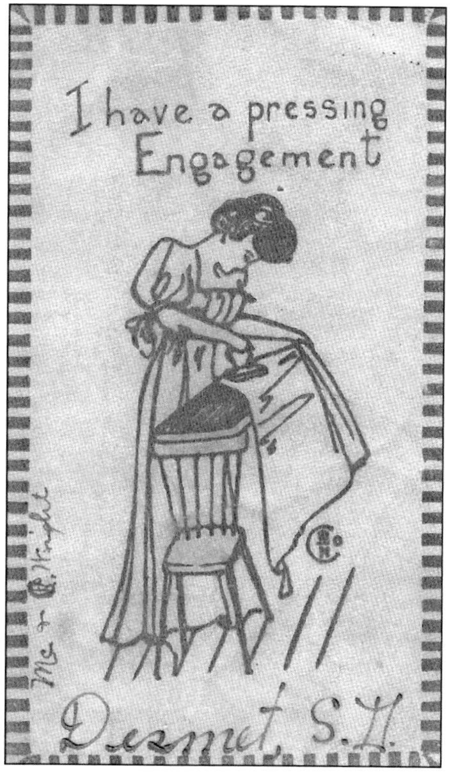

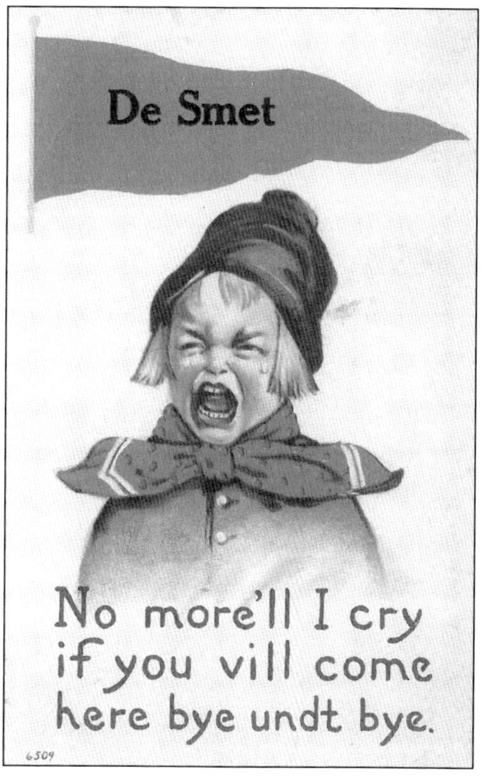

Picture postcards were printed for the benefit of advertising a locale, an event, or, as in this case, a feeling. The sender of the image of this young man is hopeful that his crying plea will bring visitors to him or her and to De Smet.